The 100 Most Pointless Things in the World

The 100 Most Pointless Things in the World

Alexander Armstrong and Richard Osman

CORONET

First published in Great Britain in 2012 by Coronet
An imprint of Hodder & Stoughton
An Hachette UK company

5

A CIP catalogue record for this title is available from the British Library

ISBN 978 1 444 76204 4

Set in Celeste Regular 11/16 pt
Typeset by Palimpsest Book Production Limited, Falkirk, Stirlingshire

Printed and bound by Clays Ltd, St Ives plc

Hodder & Stoughton policy is to use papers that are natural,
renewable and recyclable products and made from wood grown
in sustainable forests. The logging and manufacturing processes
are expected to conform to the environmental regulations of the
country of origin.

Hodder & Stoughton Ltd
338 Euston Road
London NW1 3BH

www.hodder.co.uk

For Ruby and Sonny
The two least pointless things in my world.

For Rex, Paddy and Edward

ACKNOWLEDGEMENTS

We would like to take a moment to thank the following people for their enormous help in writing this book.

The brilliant *Pointless* producers, John Ryan, Ed de Burgh, Michelle Woods, Jess Enderby, Tom Blakeson, David Flynn and Richard Hague.

The even more brilliant *Pointless* question team, given that they actually do most of the work while the producers are watching *Bargain Hunt* and drinking lattes. Bronagh Taggart, Sean Carey, Rose Dawson (not the one from *Titanic*), Angus McDonald, Ben Polya, Ed Egan, Helen Morris, James Ellis, Julia Hobbs (who was in the final of *Mastermind*. How about that?), Nick Shearing, Rebecca Milloy and Thom Poole. And special thanks to Chris 'Halestorm' Hale and Tom 'No

Nickname' Banks, for going above and beyond the call of obscure trivia duty.

Thanks for many inspirationally pointless conversations with Neil Webster, Shaun Parry, Cat Lynch, Nick Mather, Kellie Turner, Tim Hincks, Gemma Martin, Lisa Kirk, Peter Holmes, Ben Caudell, Lisa Callow, Kate Stannard, Ben Powell-Jones, Charlie Bennet, Simon Craig, Aaron Rosenthal, Dom Waugh, Kate McGlade, and the Three Musketeers, Matt Edmonds, Rocco Sulkin and Dave Tanner.

Thanks too to Juliet Mushens at PFD, Charlotte Hardman at Hodder & Stoughton and Lucas Church and Claire Heys at Endemol, for all willing this book into existence.

Special thanks and undying gratitude* (*not contractually binding) to the wonderful and very funny Aidan Hawkes, Matt Hulme, Simon 'Weekesy' Weekes (Crazy nickname, crazy guy!), and Marie Phillips.

And finally, gold medal thanks from us both to the unstoppable, incomparable Glenn Hugill.

CONTENTS

100
INTRODUCTIONS TO BOOKS

I'm never sure what the point of introductions to books is, so there will be no introduction to this one. Introductions are the hundredth most pointless thing in the world. Here's why I believe they serve no purpose.

I mean, I'm guessing you already know what this book *is*? Someone has probably bought it for you for Christmas – maybe a grandchild, your loving husband short of gift ideas, or perhaps that woman at work who clearly doesn't know you very well. (What is it with her anyway? Who buys books for people at work? I think maybe she has a thing for you.)

And you've read the *back* of the book, so you already know that what lies ahead is a list of the 100 most pointless things in the world. Irritating things, infuriating things, bizarre things, even pointlessly wonderful and magnificent things. You have recognised immediately that it would be a good book to leave in the guest bedroom, or maybe in the toilet. If the guest bedroom has its own toilet, then that would be *perfect.*

You've glanced at the front, too, so you'll already have worked out that these 100 things have been written by those two men from *Pointless*. One is Richard – that's me, the tall one with the glasses, hello – and the other is Xander, the handsome, urbane one, who would make such a wonderful son-in-law.

So there is absolutely no need for an introduction.

I mean, there are little things you won't know yet, like there will also be lots of pointless quiz questions and facts that you can annoy your family with. But you'll find that out for yourself soon enough. In fact, you'll find it out *right now*.

Let's start with the favourite fact I've learned in four hundred episodes of *Pointless*:

POINTLESS QUIZ QUESTION

What is Patrick Clifton's famous TV job?

The answers to all the questions you'll be vainly attempting will be found at the back of the book. That's *exactly* the sort of thing you might read in an introduction.

Now that I really think about introductions, it would also be nice to find space somewhere to say how much Xander and I enjoyed writing this book, and how much we hope you enjoy reading it. Even if it's mainly on the toilet. But without an introduction, I'm afraid, I won't be able to do that.

And maybe we *could* have used an introduction to reassure regular *Pointless* viewers that every question we've ever been asked about *Pointless* will be answered somewhere in this book. And rest assured, the *Pointless* favourite, Central African Republic, will be making an appearance.

But introductions are pointless, which is why you won't find one in this book. Please accept my heartfelt apologies and let's move straight on to number 99 . . .

99 CUSHIONS ON BEDS

I have a friend who works in a cushion factory. She doesn't earn much, but she's comfortable.

Cushions are like home-furnishing heroin. You buy one cushion for the sofa (because the sofa, which is essentially *made out of cushions*, needs a cushion). Before you know it, you've bought two more, for the corners of the sofa, then another two, one for each armchair.

No problem so far, right? You simply have five cushions. You're aware, of course, that the number of cushions you actually need is none, but you are only five over this limit, so no harm done.

But now you find yourself thinking about cushions at work. Perhaps browsing the odd cushion website in your lunch-hour, nothing serious. You decide that the chair in the dining room would look pretty good with a cushion. And, now you look again at the sofa with its three lonely cushions, you suddenly realise that it could probably take five (maybe seven?), and the armchairs were surely built for two cushions each.

This is the point at which your family (it's always the family who suffer most) start politely putting sofa cushions on the floor before sitting down. They don't mean to be rude, but there are so many cushions that they're forced to be on the edge of their seat, even when watching *Countryfile*.

All you want to do now is buy cushions. You start hanging around John Lewis at lunchtime with other addicts. You see a cushion you love – plump, velvety, soft – but you can think of nowhere to put it. The sofa now has fourteen cushions on it, and your family has long ago had to abandon the living room to cower, frightened, in their bedrooms. The armchairs each have th— Wait . . . rewind. Did somebody mention *bedrooms*?

What a fool you've been! Your bed! Thirty-six square feet of virgin uncushioned pasture! Your prayers are answered. You could fit an almost infinite number of cushions of different shapes and sizes on your bed!

Your addict brain ignores the fact that there is no earthly reason to put a cushion on a bed. I mean, you have *heard* of pillows. You also know that for the rest of your life you will have to take every single cushion off the bed before you go to sleep, then put every single one back on the bed after you've got up. You know you might as well be putting cushions on the kitchen worktop, clearing them away every time you prepare a meal, or piling them high inside the front door, brushing them aside every time you want to go out.

If you are reading this and you – or someone close to you – insists on putting cushions on beds, it is not too late to seek help. Sit them down, tell them you love them, but tell them it has to stop. Though, obviously, it's best to do this in a neighbour's house, as there is no longer anywhere to sit in yours.

98
27–30 DECEMBER

If the year were a human body, then that run of days from 27 to 30 December would be the little valley between the second-toe-in and the little toe. A functionless little pocket, tightly hemmed in between the last two bones of the foot. That's where the rot sets in.

Even Time overlooks those days. Theoretically, there's a whole week in there somewhere but you'd never know it. From Christmas lunchtime onwards, it goes something like this.

My husband and I . . .

Glug glug glug . . .

No, Mr Bond, I expect you to die . . .

Guzzle guzzle guzzle . . .

Happy Christmas, Lord Grantham, so it may please you milord . . .

Glug glug glug . . .

Waaah, waaah I . . . can't . . . find . . . any batteries . . . Dad-dy . . . waaaaaaah . . .

Guzzle glug guzzle . . .

Pe-ppa PIG (plink plinkety plonk), Pe-ppa PIG . . .

Gluzzle gug . . .

Broadsword calling Danny Boy . . .

Guggluz . . .

SHOULD AULD ACQUAINTANCE BE FORGOT . . .

So, I have two plans. Either (a) we all, as a nation, follow a strict regime for those days, maybe led by Mr Motivator – assuming all these 27–30 Decembers haven't worn him down to Mr Meh – where he gets us all up and exercising, perhaps something involving good deeds and lots of fresh air, so we don't lose track of ANY hour of those four days.

Or (b) we arrange to have those days removed from the calendar so we go straight from Boxing Day into New Year's Eve. I don't think anyone would notice. And then we've got four extra days in hand that we can just fold into the coming year when we need a breather.

Or (c) we could just eat loads, drink far too much and watch telly. Maybe sort something out for next year.

SOME POINTLESS FACTS TO GET YOU THROUGH 27TH–30TH DECEMBER

Richard has decided to cheer you up by coming up with a few facts about this pointless time of year.

DEC 27TH
On December 27th in 2002 an organisation called 'Clonaid' announced they had successfully cloned the first human being. We're still waiting for them to present any evidence to back up this claim. Though has anyone checked how old Jedward are?

DEC 28TH
A day for fans of the cinema as:

a) It is the birthday of cinema! The Lumière Brothers' first demonstration at the Grand Café in Paris was on this day in 1885. So it is probably also the birthday of over-priced popcorn.

b) Dame Maggie Smith and Denzel Washington were both born on this day.

c) Michael Winner wasn't born on this day.

DEC 29TH

If you think you're having a bad December 29th spare a thought for Thomas à Becket who was assassinated on this day in 1170. A sad day indeed, but it has a happy ending as on December 29th a mere 758 years later Bernard Cribbins was born.

DEC 30TH

The Samoans have got the right idea. In 2011 *they skipped December 30th altogether*, due to changes in international time zones. Very clever people the Samoans.

97
JUKEBOX MUSICALS

Throughout this book we'll be presenting you with a series of quizzes on pointless subjects.

They are designed to provide some healthy, family fun, bringing together the generations in a celebration of intellectual curiosity and academic competition.

Of course what they will actually provide is furious eggnog-fuelled arguments, tears from overwrought children and the sickening sight of your dad looking smug because he's just remembered who had a hit with 'Star Trekkin'.

Let's start as we mean to go on. 'Jukebox Musicals' is the name given to the extraordinary surge of West End shows based on the songs of one particular band or artist.

This is all well and good when that artist has, say, twenty or so huge, much-loved hits. But these acts are very few and far between, and as these shows continue to multiply, we are fast approaching the bottom of a very pointless barrel. I confidently predict that we will see all of the following in the next eighteen months:

SHED SEVEN THE MUSICAL!

AFTERWHAM!
THE SOLO HITS OF ANDREW RIDGELEY

SHADDUP YOU FACE!
THE JOE DOLCE STORY

Here are twelve genuine jukebox musicals. Can you name the band or artist on whose songs each is based? Then let's take a vote on which one we'd least like to see. I'm voting for number 6.

POINTLESS QUIZ

Here are those questions:

1. *Mamma Mia!*
2. *Good Vibrations*
3. *Jersey Boys*
4. *All Shook Up*
5. *Ring of Fire*
6. *All the Fun of the Fair*
7. *Tonight's the Night*
8. *Never Forget*
9. *We Will Rock You*
10. *Movin' Out*
11. *Our House*
12. *Saturday Night Fever*

96 PANDAS

Pandas are idiots. There, I've said it.

REASON ONE WHY PANDAS ARE IDIOTS

All they eat is bamboo. Bamboo is a construction material. Construction materials, as an extremely reliable rule, tend to be low in nutritional value. As a result, pandas are forced to eat the stuff continually in a desperate attempt not to keel over from malnutrition. Duh!

Now, perhaps this could be forgiven if it was an unfortunate quirk of Fate and bamboo was all that pandas were able to eat but, frankly, it isn't. They are carnivores. That's right, *carnivores*. They have a digestive system expressly designed for meat. So they could eat a nice, juicy steak that would keep them going for days but instead they choose to eat wood.

You know what the primary use for bamboo is in Asia? Scaffolding. Doesn't that sound delicious? Idiots.

REASON TWO WHY PANDAS ARE IDIOTS

Pandas have the worst camouflage ever. I mean, what exactly are pandas trying to blend in with? Nuns? Did all of the bamboo in ancient China grow in the garden of a local crossword club?

They are already slow and heavy, and now they stand out. Way to go, pandas. No wonder you're always getting killed by monkeys or horses, or whatever kills pandas.

'Save the Panda'? '*Shave* the Panda' would do more good.

REASON THREE WHY PANDAS ARE IDIOTS

They don't like mating. Even the hot ones. FACT: it is easier for a *fifteen-year-old boy* to have sex than a panda.

Never invest in a business running 'Speed Dating for Pandas' evenings.

REASON FOUR WHY PANDAS ARE IDIOTS

In the early sixties, at the height of panda-mania – or 'panda-monium' I think they called it – they failed to copyright their name, or sign an exclusivity deal on image rights. They have lost billions from the World Wildlife Fund alone.

If, after reading this, you're still in doubt as to whether pandas are idiots, maybe this *Pointless* question will change your mind.

POINTLESS QUIZ QUESTION

Pandas have a rudimentary opposable thumb. Humans used their own opposable thumbs to build tools, create art and found great civilisations. What is the only thing pandas use their opposable thumbs for?

95

4 A.M.

Four in the morning is far and away the most pointless time of the day. There are lots of hours to choose from (*Stat Corner*: there are twenty-four) but none comes close to the appalling, unbearable pointlessness of 4 a.m.

Here are the only things you will EVER do at 4 a.m.

1. Sullenly wander up and down a landing cradling a screaming baby, while silently cursing your appalling sleep-deprived life and vowing never to have sex again.
2. Fight the beginning of your inevitable hangover while you look in vain for a taxi, wonder where your right shoe has gone and try to work out if you can sleep in the doorway of Rymans and still be in tip-top shape for work in the morning.

3. Flick through the Freeview channels to see that there is literally nothing on – not even a repeat of *QI* – pausing only to register shock that they no longer show pages from Ceefax.

4. Test how good you are at counting seconds by predicting exactly when your bedside clock will change from 4.01 to 4.02. Then try to beat that record.

5. Repeatedly wail, 'Why did she leave me?' into your pillow in the hope that it might eventually send you back to sleep. (FYI, she left you because she was sleeping with Dave from work.)

6. Wrestle with that awful 'Should I go to the toilet?' dilemma.

So, is there anyone in the world who would miss 4 a.m.? If you are EVER awake at 4 a.m. you are either awake much too early, or you're awake far too late.

Here's what we should do. We have an absolute 'yesterday' cut-off of 3.30 a.m., and we start 'tomorrow' at 5 a.m. This will simply involve doubling (or possibly trebling) the length of the minutes between 3 a.m. and 3.30 a.m., and between 5 a.m. and 6 a.m. It will thenceforth be impossible to either wake up or still be awake at 4 a.m. Make it happen, David Cameron.

As you know, we like to ask you a few quiz questions in this book, so here's a little teaser for you:

94

ANSWERPHONE MESSAGES

Ring-ring . . . ring-ring . . . ring-ring . . . ring-ring . . . ring-ring . . . ring-ring . . . CLUNK . . . pause . . .

'You've come through [says a voice very carefully] to David and Yvonne Trimwell. We can't take your call right now but if you leave a message after the beep, stating your name and telephone number, and what it is you're calling about, we'll get back to you as soon as possible . . .'
Beeeep.

All of which could be cut down extremely effectively to this:

Beeeep.

Back in the 1970s it was a different story. Remember when an answering machine was the size of a modest Kentish apple orchard and merely owning a phone in a colour other than black or white meant you were HIP TO THE SHAKE (unless it was red, which meant you were Leonid Brezhnev or Gerald Ford)? Then, of course, it was not only polite but vital for a friend of the Trimwells to be talked through this crazy kit like they were a stewardess at the controls of a juddering DC10. But now? Now when we know stuff? Now when we've all recorded, deleted, re-recorded, deleted, and finally recorded and saved OGMs of our own? OMG, I think not. Now the answer-machine message is truly pointless. But as with no-smoking signs and ashtrays in aeroplane arm-rests, which will doubtless be with us long after we've all forgotten what cigarettes actually were, we've become addicted to the rigmarole.

93

EXTENDED WARRANTIES

There follows a conversation you will never hear. It takes place between you and your friend Steve from work:

INT. OFFICE. DAY

Steve walks into the office; he is whistling a happy tune. You have just had your hair done and you're looking awesome.

YOU

Hey, Steve, you're in a good mood!

STEVE

The most wonderful thing has happened.

YOU

You haven't won the lottery, Steve?

STEVE

Better than that.

YOU

Someone's given you an *Armstrong &
Miller* DVD?

STEVE

Equally as good as that. You know
my toaster?

YOU

The Russell-Hobbs T-170 Toastmaster?
Of course I know it. It was the talk
of the office when you bought that
little baby.

STEVE

Well, the bagel function stopped
working.

YOU

Steve! No!

STEVE

Yep, it just upped and quit. One
minute bagels, the next minute bagels
that only browned on one side.

YOU

Forgive me, Steve, but this sounds
like a horror story, every inch the
modern nightmare, and yet you're
happy. What gives?

Steve reaches into his man-bag (you're
still not sure about his man-bag, but
Steve's a nice guy so you haven't said
anything) and fishes out a piece of
paper. He passes it to you with a
flourish.

STEVE

Extended warranty!

YOU

Steve, you genius!

STEVE

Yep, just £8.99 a year for the last four
years. And all I have to do now is send
the toaster back to the manufacturers

with four pieces of documentary proof
that the bagel slot malfunction was
caused by machine error rather than
misuse by consumer, pay postage and
packing, sign up for a further extended
warranty period at an increased price,
then wait four or five months and my
repaired four-year-old toaster will be
back in action. Which all saves me going
to buy a new £29.99 toaster.

YOU

Hurrah! The lesson here is always
take out an extended warranty. They're
the bargain of the century, and not
just an overpriced, aggressively sold
con trick to increase the profit margins
of electrical retailers.

STEVE

Can I just say how attractive you're
looking today? Have you done something
with your hair?

YOU

Steve, I'm not going to go out with
you. How many times have we been
through this?

STEVE
OK, sorry.

Scene ends.

Though it is worth noting that three years later you marry
Steve.

92

WIND CHIMES

Bells are alarms. Firebell? Engine coming. Church bell? Service coming. Cowbell? Cow coming.

Bells are alarms and alarms are meant to cause alarm. They always carry a message like 'Look out! Something's happening! Someone's phoning! You have to get up! Smoke detected! You've broken the terms of your curfew!'

The alarm message that wind chimes carry is this one: 'Look out! The air is moving!'

Now, I don't know about you, but I don't need to be notified when the air is moving. Especially when just the faintest breath is enough for the wind-chimes alarm to sound. I like information as much as the next man; nevertheless I simply don't need to be notified of a small, normal amount of wind. And not just notified, constantly updated.

No. Bells are alarms. And proving it is fun. See if you can add to this list of alarms . . .

BLUEBELL? SPRING COMING.

PACKARD BELL? LAPTOP COMING.

TACO BELL? NACHOS COMING.

MINI BABYBEL? INDIGESTION COMING.

DOOR BELL? GOOD NEWS ABOUT JEHOVAH COMING

ANDY BELL? ERASURE COMING.

ALEXANDER GRAHAM BELL? TELEPHONE COMING.

Well done if you got any of those at home.

91
TV SHOW SPIN-OFFS

When a successful show ends, usually due to the financial demands, or painkiller addiction of its stars, the temptation for a TV channel is to create a spin-off show. This allows the channel to keep the fans of the previous show happy, while only having to employ the one actor from the previous show who is not currently in rehab or awaiting charges in a Thai prison.

And if you're wondering just how pointless a spin-off show can be, I recommend you get a box-set of *Joey*. Except I doubt that they ever released a box-set of *Joey*.

When *Pointless* finally ends (due to a tabloid investigation of my complicated tax affairs, and the discovery of my secret, illegal zoo) the BBC already have the spin-off lined up.

It will be called *Everything's Pointless* and will consist of Xander asking questions of the contestants, before turning towards a lonely laptop on an empty desk, then bursting into tears, sobbing, 'Where's Richard? Where's Richard?' I smell a hit.

 POINTLESS QUIZ

Can you name the TV shows from which the following came?

1. *The Green, Green Grass*
2. *George and Mildred*
3. *The Colbys*
4. *Lewis*
5. *Tucker's Luck*
6. *Rhoda*
7. *Torchwood*
8. *Mork and Mindy*
9. *A Different World*
10. *Frasier*
11. *Benson*
12. *Knots Landing*

90

INAPPROPRIATE CARAVAN NAMES

Quite regardless of what you may think about caravans, and for what it's worth I can genuinely see the appeal of them (apart from having to tow the blessed thing behind you, or stay in a caravan site, or live with your entire family in a tiny space while it rains for fourteen days running – they're perfect!). But caravans are curious things. Obviously they can double journey times during the summer but you've got to admire the adventurous spirit of any family prepared to take on this kind of ordeal.

But that's not what I'm here to talk about. No. I'm here to draw your attention to something else entirely. We spend so much of our lives with the rears of caravans just a few feet in front of us that we probably never stop to think about the frankly bizarre names that the manufacturers give to their creations. Below I have listed some caravan names. I would like you to read each one and contemplate the actual meaning of the word. For fun I have put one made-up name in there, but the rest are absolutely genuine. See if you can spot the incorrect one.

FIRESTORM

MARAUDER

REGAL CONNOISSEUR

CRUSADER

CONQUEROR

HUNTER

CHALLENGER

89

ONE PENNY COIN

I think we can all agree that the 1p coin is on the way out?

They sit in our drawers, in our pots, on our hall tables, looking at us, all tiny and coppery. Their utter, remorseless lack of use led, of course, to the famous rhyme:

See a penny
Pick it up
And all day
You'll have to carry a penny around with you, serving
no earthly purpose whatsoever.
So leave it exactly where you found it
And all day you'll have good luck.

The central problem, I think, is this.

When we get home and take things out of our pocket – perhaps a gum wrapper, a Greggs receipt we had mistakenly thought was £10 (see number 41 Receipts), or a used bus ticket – we immediately throw them in the bin. However, when we take a 1p piece out of our pocket, we don't throw it in the bin because something deep in our genetic code knows that it's wrong to throw away money. We physically can't do it, so the pile of 1ps grows and grows, until we have hundreds. Which take up drawer space, smell all coppery and are still worth practically nothing.

You can't even buy anything *with* them. They are, unbelievably, only legal tender up to 20p! If you pay for something with twenty-one 1p pieces, you are contravening the Coinage Act 1971, and I know that's an Act you wouldn't dream of contravening. Just ask Robert Fitzpatrick who, last year, was prosecuted for trying to pay an accountant's bill of £804 in pennies dumped in crates in the accountant's garden. They sure sound like a couple of pals.

Thus, up and down the country, we all have these pointless piles of 1ps, unwieldy copper mountains in every house. So what does the Royal Mint do? Admit defeat and take the 1p out of circulation? Offer to come round and collect them all, while proffering their apologies for burdening us with such a pointless and outdated coin?

Not a bit of it. In fact, in 2011, the Royal Mint produced 210 million *new 1p pieces*! *210 million*! I mean, admittedly that's only about four each, but surely we already have enough. What does the Royal Mint want us to do with them? Team up and send them to Greece to form the basis of a new currency?

There's only one penny that I'd be interested in finding in my change, and that's the 1933 penny. Only seven were ever minted, and were mainly used to place under cornerstones of buildings that went up in that year. There's one buried under the University of London in Bloomsbury, and two more under the Church of St Cross in Middleton, and St Mary's Church, Hawksworth. If you had one of these beauties, you could sell it for at least £50,000. Leading, of course, to the famous rhyme:

> See a 1933 penny,
> Pick it up,
> And all day
> You'll be buying a new Audi.

POINTLESS QUIZ QUESTION

Why is every 1p coin minted since 1992 more attractive than every 1p coin minted before 1992?

88

SHARING PACKS

You've seen sharing packs, right? Those big bars of chocolate, bulky bags of sweets or super-sized crisps clogging up the aisles of the supermarkets and the arteries of the shoppers. They're the perfect size for sharing with a loved one, while dreamily staring into each other's eyes, talking over your gentle hopes and schemes for the future.

Well, below you'll see the results of a scientific investigation I conducted into the actual consumption of sharing packs.

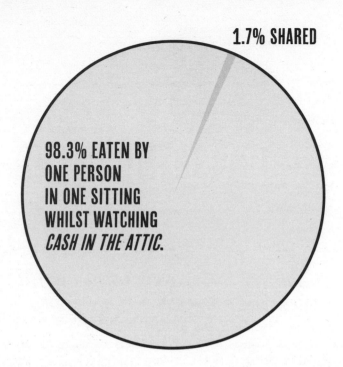

1.7% SHARED

98.3% EATEN BY ONE PERSON IN ONE SITTING WHILST WATCHING *CASH IN THE ATTIC*.

It is also worth pointing out to all supermarkets that any meal that says it 'serves two' never does.

Below are some anagrams of popular sweets, crisps and chocolate. Can you work them out?

EASY

1. So twist
2. Nut boy
3. Kilt sets
4. Ice churn

MEDIUM

5. Bloke reduced
6. Trust bars
7. Girls pen
8. Barn oil
9. Alter mess
10. Frailest tulips
11. Irk malady
12. Slim rents

HONESTLY, I WOULDN'T BOTHER WITH THESE ONES, UNLESS YOU HAVE SOME TIME ON YOUR HANDS

13. Thriftily shrug desk
14. Dole rewoken an achiness
15. Earthlings worries

87 NEWS MUSIC

You can tell news music from a mile off. The portentousness, the gravitas, the for-God's-sake-man-sit-up-and-listen-ness of it. Apart from those hilarious occasions when you discover that the same music is used on the other side of the world for a shaving-foam commercial, there is no mistaking it. It says, 'NEWS, now GROW UP!' For the most part the style of news music hasn't changed since telly first began broadcasting dinner-jacketed newsmen in heavily framed glasses into our front rooms many, many years ago.

At the heart of any news music, certainly in Western Europe, are French horns. These set a portentous Wagnerian tone that speaks of ancient Norse gods, of winds and tides lashing our shores, and the profound actions of Fate. 'Waaaah,' they seem to say, 'this is as it was ordained long, long ago. Every detail, right down to George Alagiah's hair.' In recent times this has been tempered by an overlay of echoing drums that conveys a sense of 'the wider world', sounding tribal, punchy, youth-y and just a teensy bit Hollywood. 'Yes,' say the drums, 'we recognise that Hot Chip are also a valid news story and part of what's going down. Clack-a-lack-a-lack-a-LACK (ack, ack, ack).' And then come the orchestral stabs that remind us that this is up-to-the-minute stuff we're watching that has just been beamed in from around the world. 'Tching! Tching! Tching-tching,' they say. 'Things happen suddenly in this world, my friend, and we bring it to you the minute it's out. If this news were any hotter, Martin Lewis' hair would be on FIRE.' And so it chunters on to its climax under complicated graphics of spheres spinning and coming together. Sometimes with a resonant DONG!

And then the news starts and here's where the problem lies. Most days the lead story, the very first thing to come out of the newsreader's mouth, is along the lines of 'Anger in town halls up and down the country as the communities minister attacks their wayward spending.'

I would suggest that we have a range of different news musics to cover all news days from 'Blue Rondo à la Turk' for a slow day, the normal news music for a middling kind of news day, but for a day when the news is harrowing or truly era-defining, maybe something a bit lighter to temper the impact. I'm thinking 'A Swingin' Safari' would fit the bill.

86 PALINDROMES

OK, it's quiz time again! I know – awesome, right? And, even more excitingly, this quiz is about palindromes!

Palindromes are words or phrases that read the same backwards as they do forwards. They should, strictly speaking, be called palindromesemordnilap, or maybe palinilap or semordromes. But they're not.

Here are a few well-known palindromes to get you into the mood. The awesome palindrome mood. All of these read the same backwards as they do forwards. Check if you don't believe me.

WAS IT A CAT I SAW?

DAMMIT, I'M MAD!

CIGAR? TOSS IT IN A CAN. IT IS SO TRAGIC.

LIVED ON DECAF. FACED NO DEVIL.

MY GYM TAXES SEX AT MY GYM

LAMINATE PET ANIMAL

A TOYOTA. RACE FAST, SAFE CAR. A TOYOTA.

And how about these two?

ON A CLOVER, IF ALIVE, ERUPTS A VAST PURE EVIL;
A FIRE VOLCANO

ARE WE NOT DRAWN ONWARD, WE FEW?
DRAWN ONWARD TO NEW ERA?

And if you think those are long palindromes, perhaps the
most pointless exercise in literary history was a novel written
by David Stephens. Its title was *Satire –Veritas* which is, of
course, a palindrome. And, in fact, the *entire novel* was a
palindrome, spanning an extraordinary 58,795 letters.

This has to go down as a gloriously pointless achievement,
one of those things that there was no need for anyone ever
to do, but which secretly I'm glad they did. I hope he won
the Bookerekoob prize.

POINTLESS QUIZ

Okay, twelve questions coming up. All of the answers read the same way backwards as forwards. Can you score lower than the rest of your family? Don't forget that Mum and Dad are both palindromes, so should be pretty confident. The same goes for your visiting Romanian uncle Elcnu.

1. Classic 1952 Western 'High . . .'
2. Martin Shaw's TV judge John . . .
3. Singer Shola . . .
4. Australian supermodel Macpherson
5. Miley Cyrus character Montana
6. Two crotchets
7. 1974 Eurovision Song Contest winners
8. Object-detection system
9. Bing Crosby's 'Road' partner, Hope . . .
10. Canoe used by Inuit
11. Surname of John Lennon's widow
12. Modern county town of Meath

85
DISPOSABLE RAZOR RESEARCH AND DEVELOPMENT

'You can't stop progress,' so the saying goes. Although another claims, 'Everything stops for tea.' So, to combine the received wisdom, 'Only tea can stop progress,' and anyone who has ever employed non-Polish builders will confirm this to be the case.

Over the years, the mighty hand of progress has seen Darwinian levels of adaptation and improvement in all areas of that most vital commercial sector: men's toiletries.

Deodorant is an excellent example of just this evolution. Invented in 1888, the first deodorant was a sticky zinc chloride and wax paste, which stopped underarm odour by killing bacteria and, essentially, gluing your arms to your sides. This formula was improved over the next two decades, using aluminium chloride to reduce acidity, actively inhibit sweating and reduce cases of zinc poisoning. This meant you could now raise your hands above your head without simultaneously losing the skin in your armpits. The product was still dabbed or smeared on, however, until, borrowing wholesale the design for the newly invented ballpoint pen, the product became a roll-on around 1940. Ten years later saw the advent of the first aerosol deodorant and then, shortly afterwards, the realisation that they could make a 'men-only' version by putting it in a black and silver can and giving it a name like 'Crankshaft'.

Deodorants' developments are far from pointless. Unlike those of the disposable razor.

When, in 1901, King Camp Gillette invented the disposable razor, he did humanity a great service. A safety razor with a wafer-thin disposable steel blade that could be replaced when worn out without junking the whole thing. Perfect. And that should have been that.

However, the advent of the electric razor got people twitchy in the R&D departments of disposable-razor companies worldwide. Despite having a fully evolved product, they now felt they needed a higher species.

'I know!' said someone with glasses on. 'Let's put a second blade on there!'

'What for?' asked someone who was fired the following week.

'Ssssh,' said Dave from Accounts, who was very good with money.

So, we were asked to believe that the single blade that had shaved us adequately for decades was now quite useless without a second blade to mop up behind, making up for the embarrassingly bad job the first blade had done. The marketing angle was that one blade would shave you closely, but the second one would shave you *even more closely*.

It was unclear how this might be true, unless the first blade was positioned marginally further away from the face, but we totally bought it.

So, after what I can only assume was the shortest period of time that they thought they could get away with, they stuck a third blade on there. Probably while giggling. Now the first blade shaved you closely, the second one even more closely, but the third *even, even more closely*.

To illustrate the point we were now treated to scientific cartoons that would show the second blade, which until recently we had believed was doing a sterling job, was in fact leaving a dirty great sprig of stubble that only the third blade finally whisked away. And don't even get me started on the first blade. It now barely seemed to do any cutting at all. Instead it seemed only to bend the hair over momentarily before allowing it to spring back into position, like the wind in a corn field.

Next came the strip of lubricant. Now, you'd think it unlikely that a thin streak of dried green jelly would in any way increase shaving effectiveness on a face already coated with wet foam but 'Ssssh,' said Dave from Accounts – by now hemmed in on all sides by cash – and on it went.

At this point you'd think they would struggle to add further blades or tiny lines of unguent as the razors were starting to resemble a venetian blind taped to a biro.

But, undaunted, we now have a razor with its entire head on a hinge, so it automatically follows the contours of your face in case you have suffered a climbing accident that has lost you the use of your wrists. And we have a vibrating razor you need to put a battery in. And, as inevitably as night follows day, and pee-break follows tea-break, the five-blade razor is now in the shops.

Enough now, surely. You can't put more than five blades on a razor?

'Ssssh,' says Dave from Accounts. Who, by the way, has a full beard.

84

CHARGES AT ATM MACHINES AT SERVICE STATIONS

£1.99? £1.75? £1.79? What's it to be?

Just come up with a plausible figure and stick to it. And at least make it look like these aren't numbers you plucked from thin air in a meeting room, while you were laughing so hard you could barely get the words out.

83
READY-SALTED CRISPS

I don't want anyone ever saying that this book is not controversial, and I know that this entry won't be popular with everyone.

Plenty of you *like* ready-salted crisps, and it gives me no pleasure to upset you. The only consolation I have is of knowing that you are all absurdly and utterly wrong.

And here's why.

Ready-salted crisps only exist because for more than a hundred years no one knew how to make *any other type of crisp*. They are a pioneer crisp, sure, an extraordinary breakthrough, but so were those huge brick-like mobile phones they had in the eighties, and no one's using them any more.

Eating ready-salted crisps is like driving a Model-T Ford. It's like, instead of writing this on a computer, I have sent it off to be transcribed and illuminated by thirteenth-century monks. These are things we *do not need to do any more.*

Crisps were invented, reputedly, by chef George Crum in Sarasota Springs on 24 August 1853, when he minutely sliced a potato for a fussy customer, before frying, then seasoning it with salt.

And so things stood for the next 100 years. Sure, in the 1920s, Frank Smith of Smiths Crisps introduced his famous little twist of salt in every bag, to much popular acclaim, but crisps never really caught on. Because – let's face it – they were ready-salted, and therefore boring.

So what happened? How did crisps go from low-selling, boring salted potato to become the extraordinary worldwide phenomenon we know today? For that we have to go back to the 1950s, and travel over to Ireland, the home of Tayto crisps.

Tayto head honcho Joe 'Spud' Murphy and his colleague Seamus Burke started experimenting with adding seasoning to crisps during manufacture and, after an exhaustive search, finally hit gold, producing the first two flavoured crisps in human history. And what were those first two flavours? Those first experimental attempts?

Salt and vinegar, and cheese and onion.

You have to hand it to Joe and Seamus. In a world where we, rightly, revere the great innovators and inventors – Edison, Watt, Bell, the guy behind the Spacehopper – the invention of salt and vinegar and cheese and onion crisps *at the same time* surely cements their place in history. They are the Isambard Kingdom Brunel of snacks.

The world beat a path to Tayto's door, making Murphy wildly rich in the process, and crisps became an overnight sensation. Before you knew it we had prawn cocktail, and Worcester sauce. We had roast chicken, and smoky bacon. The Europeans had their paprika and the Americans their sour cream. The Japanese had their teriyaki, takoyaki and yakitori.

All of which meant that no one had to eat ready-salted crisps any more. In the same way that no one has to use outside toilets any more, or heat their homes by rubbing two sticks together.

And yet people still eat them. In fact – and I can barely believe this – ready-salted is the biggest-selling crisp in the UK!

Well, shame on you all. Ready-salted being the biggest-selling crisp is like leeches being the biggest-selling over-the-counter cough medicine.

So, controversy be damned, I say that ready-salted crisps are pointless. In honour of the fine work of Spud Murphy and Seamus Burke (*Sir* Seamus Burke, Your Majesty?), here's a question for you.

POINTLESS QUIZ QUESTION

We know that ready-salted are undeservedly Britain's best-selling crisp. But can you predict the second, third, fourth and fifth best-selling in 2011 according to Walkers?

82
DICTATOR'S PETS

Now, let's say you're thinking of becoming an evil despot – and, seriously, there are hundreds of openings available as long as you're prepared to travel – what kind of pet would you have? Think about it. I don't just mean what kind of animal have you always wanted. This is important: it's the animal you'll be photographed with at, say, the executions of your enemies' families, or at the mass rallies that precede your weekly four-hour orations. What I suppose I'm saying is, this is your opportunity to make a big statement about the kind of dictator you are. And, as such, I think it requires a bit of thought.

To help you, here's a list of what some other evil geniuses have had as their animal consorts of choice.

Idi Amin	–	Crocodiles
Benito Mussolini	–	Lioness
Arkan Raznatovic	–	Tiger cubs
Saddam Hussein	–	Lioness
Kim Jong-il	–	Chinese dolphins
Muammar Gaddafi	–	Ostriches
Adolf Hitler	–	German Shepherd Dog
Nicolae Ceauşescu	–	Three dogs

As you can see, it's a sliding scale. We start with the outright-killer pets belonging to those dictators who presumably, had they been born under different circumstances, would have been happy driving around Bolton in souped-up Mitsubishis as long as they had spoilers, massive exhaust pipes and number plates with something like 7OSS3R written on them. (To be fair, Saddam wasn't entirely original, but he took 'Lioness' and really made it his own.) Next come the genuinely strange pets (Muammar and Kim, I think you know who I'm talking about); these – for my money – are the scariest of all.* And finally what I'm going to call the wasted-opportunity pets. Adolf, I'm guessing you were going for something emblematic and Aryan but I'm afraid it's just not coming over. And, Nicolae, that's just embarrassing.

....

* What would have happened if I had offended Kim Jong-il? I would have been bottle-nosed to death?

81 US STATES

I like to organise competitions on Twitter from time to time (@richardosman). Some are – how shall we put this? – *mind-blowingly inane.* For example, I recently thought of a number between 1 and 300 and invited my followers to guess what it was.* That particular competition trended worldwide, giving you some idea of the sort of competitions that set Twitter alight.

But I also occasionally organise much geekier and more obscure competitions, my Geeky Wordplay Quizzes. For those who like them – hello, Karen, hello, Mike! – they are far from pointless, but I have to accept that others – hi, everyone else! – may disagree.

....

* It was 184. Well done, if you got that at home.

See what you think as I present fifty cryptic clues, each one pointing to the identity of one of the fifty US states (if I were you I'd print out a list). As you look through them you will realise that either

(a) You will find them utterly, utterly pointless. In which case please move straight on to the 80th most pointless thing on the list.

Or

(b) You will want to answer all fifty. In which case they will ruin your family Christmas.

Either way, enjoy!

MY FIFTY GEEKY WORDPLAY CLUES TO THE FIFTY US STATES

Anyone who gets all fifty is officially awesome. Some are anagrams, some are cryptic, but most are just weak puns. Hooray!

1. Heavy laundry
2. Something's missing from my shed
3. A feelm weeth James Caan
4. A Chiming Mess

5. Specialist Subject – 'Only Fools and Horses'
6. Honour among thieves
7. Horsehair
8. Sick badger
9. Sick badgers
10. Derby County
11. Heaven with a heavy cold
12. Cole and Solskjaer both did
13. Two things you might need for a PhD
14. Exploding Osmannite!
15. Tweed proprietor
16. Nothing greeting nothing
17. Tiny snake in German/French mountain
18. Get prisoners to their cells quickly
19. Motorway Man
20. . . . And I'll fetch the gravel
21. Smilie's cruise ship
22. Vorderman's cruise ship
23. I can't understand why you can't be more merciful
24. Breaks an' breaks
25. Mum lent me £20
26. I wonder if Mum will lend me another £20
27. Smash a frail icon
28. Switch off saw
29. Boo! your mandible is rubbish!
30. Walsh date Ford
31. Nicolas Sarkozy's sunbed
32. Hbneswlug

33. Virgin theme park
34. Oxicemo
35. Noah's Christmas list
36. Revisit Wigan in disguise
37. Bring back Bergerac!
38. Carreras
39. What posh people don't like paying
40. Jack eats a pavlova
41. The bottom of a tin
42. Arrest our spending
43. T
   A
44. D
   A
45. Fine French writer
46. Andover and over
47. Never heard a thing
48. More ruddy
49. Pines for Neil Pye
50. Aah! wii broken!

Later in this book I'll set you another challenge. This time a Christmassy one! You literally can't wait, right?

80
WEARABLE BLANKETS

You know wearable blankets. Those warm and toasty blankets, available via late-night TV infomercials, that you can stick your arms through, making you look like a velour monk or perhaps a koala mermaid. They are made for those people who simply cannot lie underneath a normal blanket without becoming hopelessly trapped.

They are in many ways the zenith of infomercial excellence. Infomercials are an industry whose business plan involves sitting around all day, thinking of a minor inconvenience, then creating a product that solves this minor inconvenience – usually using steam, titanium chopping blades or magnets.

It must be quite the moment at these companies when they hit upon a minor inconvenience that *no one has thought of before.* So one can only imagine the joy the day they hit upon the unignorable problem that *blankets don't have armholes.*

I don't know about you but I literally cannot count the number of times I have woken up in the night shaking with horror that my blankets don't have armholes. I cannot count for the simple reason that I cannot use my fingers. Why? *Because my blankets don't have armholes.* If only they did have armholes I could have poked my hands through and manually recorded how many times I had woken up in the night shaking with horror that my blankets don't have armholes. In fact, such breathless freedom of movement might even have allowed the use of my bedside abacus. Although, irony or ironies, this, of course, would not have been necessary as, given in this scenario my blankets did indeed have armholes, I would have nothing to wake up in the night shaking with horror about. I would sleep soundly on, safe in the knowledge that I might have my problems in life, such as a profound inability to exercise rational judgement with regard to late-night purchases, but at least, damn it, I wasn't some trapped idiot whose blankets didn't have armholes.

79
DUTY FREE SHOPS

Duty Free shops actually stopped being duty free years ago but a pleasing whiff of duty still hangs about them, even if it's just the 'duty' that we feel to flock there in our millions as soon as we set foot 'airside' so we can mop up some of the most marginal discounts since the Mr Pound Winter Sale. Oh, sure, they make it feel special with their per-person allowances and their 'Please may I see your boarding pass?'

Q: What do they actually do with your boarding pass when they take it?
A: NOTHING – that's what!

A bottle of gin is fully 1p cheaper at the Heathrow Duty Free shop than it is in a high-street supermarket so we pounce on it and lug it all the way to Spain and back in a bag whose handles won't even make it onto the flight.

Why do we suddenly imagine that, just because we're going abroad for a few days, we're suddenly going to become committed spirit drinkers? How much of that Advocaat actually gets drunk? Even the more plausible Stoli is barely a quarter gone by the time you're liverishly packing for the return. This is because when we're abroad we tend to drink beer in bars (much like at home) and possibly wine with food (again, very much like we do at home) rather than sitting around in our room trying to find something other than milk to mix with our Gordon's. And when it comes to the morning of the return flight, we've usually forsworn alcohol for the next year anyway on account of massive over-indulgence despite having touched NONE of the stuff we bought in Duty Free.

I also throw in here that booze is generally a heap cheaper on the Continent than it is in Britain. Why? BECAUSE THEY'VE GOT LAKES OF THE STUFF BEING LEFT IN THEIR HOLIDAY RESORTS EVERY CHANGEOVER DAY.

78

RESTAURANTS ADVERTISING THEMSELVES WHEN YOU ARE ALREADY EATING THERE

Dear Pizza Hut,

I'm in your restaurant in Cambridge. You know, the one by the cinema. A couple of things:

1. One of the Gents' toilets is blocked.
2. We ordered some garlic bread. Do you know if it's on its way?

But more to the point of this book, I would like to talk to you about how much advertising you have in your restaurant. I don't know how much all these posters for Cheese-filled Stuffed Crusts, leaflets about Gourmet Italian Pastas and little laminated booklets about doughnuts in wooden stands are costing you, but I think I can save you some money.

You see, I'm actually already *in* your restaurant. You've got me! I have already made an intelligent, informed choice to visit Pizza Hut.*

I would argue that *inside your own restaurant* is the only place in Britain you *don't* need to advertise. Because, surely . . .

Inside your restaurant everyone is eating at Pizza Hut.

Outside your restaurant everyone is *not* eating at Pizza Hut.

So, why not take the money you're spending on trying to encourage people who are already eating your food to eat your food, and spend it instead on encouraging the people who aren't eating your food to eat your food?

* The queue at Nando's was too long.

I know it's not just you. McDonald's tell me to eat in McDonald's when I'm already in McDonald's. KFC like to tell me how much I might enjoy a KFC while I'm halfway through a KFC, and even Pizza Express politely ask whether I've ever considered trying Pizza Express even as they're handing me my dough balls.

If I'm enjoying my food, I'll come back. If I'm not enjoying it, I won't come back, no matter how many posters you put up encouraging me to. Unless, as ever, the queue at Nando's is too long.

And, if you decide that it might be too expensive to advertise to people you haven't already persuaded, then could I suggest you spend the savings on:

1. Fixing the Gents toilet
2. Bringing me my garlic bread

Yours hungrily,
Richard off *Pointless*

In a genuinely impressive piece of marketing, what extraordinary place did Pizza Hut deliver a pizza to in 2001?

NOVELTY SONGS

Novelty songs are so obviously, ear-bleedingly pointless that we've featured them twice on the show. Hence a bumper quiz for you below.

For this quiz the scoring will be as follows. Every player gets the score for their individual answer (scores at the back of the book), plus

10 POINTS FOR OWNING *ANY* OF THE RECORDS BELOW

20 POINTS FOR OWNING 'THE BIRDIE SONG'

30 POINTS FOR OWNING 'SNOOKER LOOPY'

50 POINTS FOR 'AGADOO'

There is also a series of five-point penalties for anybody caught singing any of the songs during this round.

So, who originally had a hit with the following songs? May the Lord have mercy on their souls.

 POINTLESS QUIZ

Here are your questions:

1. 'The Chicken Song'
2. 'Combine Harvester'
3. 'The Elements'
4. 'The Birdie Song'
5. 'Barbie Girl'
6. 'Ullo John, Got A New Motor?'
7. 'Do The Bartman'
8. 'Star Trekkin''
9. 'Can We Fix It?'
10. 'Doctorin' The Tardis'
11. 'Snooker Loopy'
12. 'Ernie (The Fastest Milkman In The West)'
13. 'The Laughing Gnome'
14. 'Who Let The Dogs Out?'
15. 'My Old Man's A Dustman'
16. 'The Winner's Song'
17. 'Funky Gibbon'

18. 'Achy Breaky Heart'
19. 'I Am A Cider Drinker'
20. 'Agadoo'
21. 'Tie Me Kangaroo Down Sport'
22. 'Whispering Grass'
23. 'Right Said Fred'
24. 'What Are We Gonna Get 'Er Indoors?'

76

A POINTLESS RANT ABOUT GRAMMAR

During my time as a host on top teatime brain-teaser-type programme *Pointless*, I have received numerous complaints about my English usage. Why, people ask contemptuously, do I murder our mother tongue daily by insisting on saying 'less' when I SHOULD be saying 'fewer'?

Well, the answer is, I think we should all just calm down a bit about this fewer/less business. Linguistically it's a comparatively recent obsession although I recognise it's a very strongly held one. I have friends whose everyday conversation is otherwise strewn with howling solecisms yet who suddenly feel driven to take up the cudgel over this one issue. I don't necessarily blame them – in fact, I think it's great that people (a) listen, (b) care, and (c) will be my friends.

The fact is, to our modern ear we feel it sounds more elegant to say 'fewer' when talking about a quantifiable plural ('*fewer* chaffinches') and to keep the blunter-sounding 'less' for more abstract nouns ('*less* atmosphere') and nouns that don't pluralise ('*less* miaow-miaow'). But there are still areas where we exercise a bit of judgement when choosing which we go for. For example, we say '*less* than three miles from where Shakin' Stevens was born' because if you said '*fewer* than three miles' you'd sound like a mentalist.

But here's the truth: you can use 'less' across the board and it's *not incorrect usage*. This obsession with strict differentiation started some time in the 1950s or 1960s. Read any good writing from the early- to mid-twentieth century (Evelyn Waugh, Graham Greene, Dorothy L. Sayers, as a random sample) and you'll find they rarely say 'fewer' unless it's for particular quantitative emphasis. ('You only sent over twelve girls, that's fully three fewer than the fifteen I was promised') ('for my female RUGBY TEAM. What kind of novel do you think this is?')

So, on *Pointless* I say 'less'. 'Forty-two people or *less*' equates to a score of forty-two or less, and 'less' works in both contexts whereas 'a score of forty-two or *fewer*' would be the babbling of a madman.

It's not murdering the mother tongue. It's not even roughing her up a bit. It's fine.

75
DOUBLE CHECKING

Right at this very moment, someone is walking back up a driveway to tug on the door to make sure they definitely shut it when they left, and discovering that, as always, they did.

In at least twelve locations across the globe, people are rummaging through rucksacks for the tickets they can't remember if they put in there or not, then sighing with relief upon finding the envelope in the pocket they always put their tickets in.

And now someone is getting out of bed and going downstairs to check they turned the oven off after removing the casserole. Of course they did. Though while they're down there they might as well quickly hold their bare palm up against the iron to check it's not on.

It does make sense to double-check *some* things . . .

AN IMPORTANT CONTRACT

A LIFE-ALTERING DIAGNOSIS

THE EXACT WORDING OF YOUR WEDDING VOWS, AND ANY LEGAL RESPONSIBILITIES ENSHRINED WITHIN THEM

WHETHER YOU'RE SUPPOSED TO CUT THE RED WIRE OR THE BLUE WIRE

. . . but time spent checking that you shut the front door when you came in, or whether you left the light on in the downstairs loo, has always been wasted and you know it.

On average, people will spend ninety hours of their entire lives going back to check that they've done something they already secretly know *for a fact* that they've done.* That's all time that could be spent with loved ones or on self-improving activities or going to Nando's. Mmm, Nando's.

. . . .

* I've just double-checked this. It is actually ninety-one hours.

74
CUSTOMER FEEDBACK

Nothing comes close to the enveloping sense of impotence I feel on reading the words

We Value Your Opinion.

This is what's written on that shiny bit of paper that blows off the desk in your hotel room when you finally give up trying to sleep at a temperature that would pasteurise milk, and fling open the window overlooking the bottling factory on the other side of the street.

Customer feedback is right up there with weekly fire-alarm tests (always Tuesdays, always 10.30 – your better class of arsonist must surely be aware of this) in the league of box-ticking gestures. Imagine for a moment that there exists in the world a pen that would actually write on that kind of glossy paper (and that biro by your bed, incidentally hasn't been the full shilling anyway since that Dutch salesman used it to prize open the trouser-press three weeks ago) and you dutifully fill it in (How was your welcome? Outstanding? Average? Poor?) and then hand it in at the front desk. What happens next? Either it goes to the hotel manager so he can keep a stack of them by the loo for when the next Bowater delivery's late or it goes to the company headquarters in some part of Sweden where gimlet-eyed men in rimless glasses check the quarterly profits to see if they need to care.

If I owned a hotel I'd care desperately. If I owned nine hotels I'd care but in an altogether *richer* kind of a way. I would guess the point after which I'd stop giving so much of a toss would be around the owning-twenty-hotels mark. Then I'd hand over 'Caring' to my low-paid individual hotel managers and I'd hand over 'Making It Look Like I Care' to the people who print up the 'We Value Your Opinion' papers.

73
BODY HAIR

A Poem

Body hair, oh, body hair,
One wonders, frankly, why you're there.
I do not mean to seem obtuse,
Or blandly throw about abuse,
But, really, have you *any use*?

You crop up in all sorts of places,
Most commonly of all on faces.
You sit there blithely misbehaving,
Needy and forever craving
Waxing, bleaching, plucking, shaving.

And if a man just won't address it

He'll soon resemble Brian Blessed.
Or, even worse, I beg your pardon,
Be taken for the late Bin Laden,
His face an unattended garden.
And women face still greater trouble
(As they can't get away with stubble).
They're forced to part with pots of cash,
And risk the most unsightly rash.
Just to lose their nascent 'tache.

Moving on to other charms,
I spy our friends, the underarms.
This dewy moss, this messy tangle,
Hard to shave at any angle.
Then let's address – I think it's time,
The hairy back! The greatest crime!
Now time to take a trip 'down there',
The contents of our underwear,
The home of *much* unwanted hair
(Just ask the guy who made his millions
Persuading us to have Brazilians).

Then women's legs, their toughest task
(I don't shave *my* legs, since you ask)
This daily, weekly, monthly feat,
Sponsored by Immac and Veet.
And now, let's finish with our feet.

The reason why no girl can handle
A full-grown man in open sandal
Is, as everybody knows,
The dreadful sight of hairy toes.
Body hair both sucks and blows.

So, body hair, oh, body hair,
We dearly wish you were not there.
Shaved or waxed or ripped or hacked,
Electrolysed, or left intact,
You're simply pointless, that's a fact.

72 ANIMAL HYBRIDS

We all like animals, right? Cute, furry, always getting their heads stuck in plant pots, and falling off televisions on *You've Been Framed*?

But we mustn't forget some of their more unsavoury characteristics. Chief among them is the fact that they will literally sleep with *anything*.

Here is a quick quiz for you, taking in some of the more unusual outposts of the animal kingdom. Below you will see twelve pointless 'animal hybrids', the result of two different species mating. Can you tell us the two different species in each case? You can be fairly sure that at least one of the species woke up the next morning remembering very little about it, and the other species is now wondering why he's not returning her texts.

POINTLESS QUIZ

So, which two species created the following? You should be able to work a few of them out, but there are a couple of very low scorers on the list.

1. Pumapard
2. Huarizo
3. Hinny
4. Grolar
5. Dogote
6. Beefalo (this one is not, as someone suggested on the show, the offspring of a bee and a buffalo)
7. Zedonk
8. Liger
9. Cama
10. Dzo
11. Leopon
12. Yakalo

71
THINGS HANGING FROM PUB CEILINGS

I appreciate that furnishing a pub can present a challenge but, let's face it, there's no shortage of paraphernalia. For publicans lacking imagination, the brewery itself will provide any number of lively notices advertising beers and alcopops. Otherwise, there's the usual drinking ephemera. Tankards, bottle-openers, old beer bottles, corkscrews, old whisky bottles, beer mats, vintage beer mats, signs, vintage signs, barrel ends, hops, plastic grapes, toby jugs, and small metal plates with 'I'm not as think as you drunk I am' written on them. These are all fine first-base pub decorations. Also fitting are vintage photographs of the pub, its brewery, its brewery drays from the 1920s, postcards sent to the publican and his wife by locals on Portuguese holidays, and other associated alcoholia.

Appropriate at a second remove are sporting items: cricket bats signed by local teams, racing accessories, trophies, black-and-white photographs of local football or cricket teams, vintage photographs of boxers, old leather footballs, boxing gloves, fishing rods, hunting horns, tennis racquets, whips, saddles, or small metal plates with 'My wife says if I don't give up golf she'll leave me. Shame – I'm really going to miss her' written on them.

Just about appropriate but getting quite niche now, you can have farming tools: old ploughs, old tractor seats, vintage seed dibbers, photographs of old ploughing teams, walking sticks, animal traps, photographs of pigs, or small metal plates with 'Young farmers do it in their wellies' written on them.

Anything that doesn't belong to the above categories* is poor pub accessorising and must not be tolerated in any way.

....

* And, the Old Red Lion, I'm talking specifically about old baking trays, hats, leather-bound law reports, and any calendar that features local characters poorly photographed and naked but for a tractor wheel/cash register/prize turnip covering their privates.

70

ANSWERING QUESTIONS ON TWITTER

Twitter is wonderful in lots of ways, but it is a very bad place to answer questions. As soon as you answer a question, your answer gets shunted further and further back through time, until five minutes later it has disappeared and you have to answer the same question again. And again, and again.

So, let's take the opportunity of this book to answer the questions we are both most frequently asked. If you are not an ardent fan of the show, please skip this section and move on to number 69. For the purposes of this interview you can be Twitter, and I'll be Richard from *Pointless*.

Hello, Richard!

Hello!

Do the contestants get one trophy between them, or one each?

One each. So married couples can use them as bookends. Or sell one on eBay. They do occasionally turn up on eBay, but this makes both Xander and me cry, so shame on you.

Who are the 100 people you ask?

They are all surveyed anonymously, online, a cross-section of ages and geographical areas. That's boring, isn't it?

Can I be one of the 100?

Afraid not. If the 100 was full of Pointless *fans it would suddenly get much cleverer and there would be no more pointless answers. It has to be a representative sample. We can't have Central African Republic suddenly scoring 78 on every question.*

What is Xander like?

He's nice when sober, but I'm frightened of him when he starts drinking. Which is usually about 11 in the morning.

Are you really 6 foot 7?

Yes.

Wow.

I know.

Anyway, moving on. How can I apply to be on *Pointless*?

Whenever applications are open you'll find a link on bbc.co.uk/beonashow

How do I get tickets to see *Pointless*?

Usually through www.sroaudiences.com

How many shows do you film in a day?

Three a day. Two in the afternoon, one in the evening. It is actually quite a fun show to be in the audience for. We do muck about a lot. If you want to see how tall I am in person, or if you want to hear Xander swear, then this is the place for you.

Who has been your favourite contestant ever?

I have liked every single one of them equally.

Why does the BBC keep showing repeats?

For the last few years the show has been on about 250 times a year, and we simply can't film that many, so they fill in the gaps with 'classic episodes'. Interestingly the ratings stay much the same, so you can see why they do it. At least it means you can cheat.

Why don't you put all the pointless answers on a website?

Too expensive apparently. Creating and managing it (and the 50,000,000 viewer queries it would generate) would be a full-time job. Which neither the BBC nor I will pay for. If you know someone who will pay for it then let's talk, it would be great. I do try to read out as many of the answers as I can without boring everyone to tears.

So, it's the BBC's fault?

I didn't say that.

You did sort of imply it, though?

How dare you? I'm going to take no further questions on this issue.

Sorry.

No, I'm sorry, I shouldn't have overreacted.

Would you like a glass of water?

Thank you.

Why don't you bring out a *Pointless* board game?

We did! You can get it in the shops, next to, but not as good as, Hungry Hippos.

Why don't you bring out a *Pointless* book?

We did! You're totally reading it! On the toilet!

Why don't you bring out a *Pointless* app?

Again, according to people I know and trust, it is too expensive and not profitable enough. That's capitalism, I suppose.

What is on your computer during the show?

I'm afraid I can't answer that question, on the advice of my lawyers.

Is long-time *Pointless* producer Ed de Burgh related to Chris de Burgh?

No. Luckily for them both.

How do you get your hair so shiny?

I will never reveal my girlish secrets.

What is your favourite ever *Pointless* question?

See 100: INTRODUCTIONS TO BOOKS.

Will you marry me?

Yes, I will.

And finally, seriously this time,
what is Xander like?

I'm not kidding, he has a real problem.
It'll all come out one day.

69 WAR

I am *strongly* anti. Though if my neighbours play The Lighthouse Family at 2 a.m. ever again, I will personally sanction the use of ground troops.

68
TOASTER SETTINGS

We all like toast – sure we do. Mmm, crunch, yum: toast.

We know what toast is. We ask for it – most of us – without ever having to explain the cooking method to our waiter/ mother/man-behind-the-counter. And yet, AND YET, domestic toasters all come with carefully gauged settings for 'done ness' covering every toasty outcome from doughy bleurgh to charcoal. This most utterly, utterly needless gift of control is handed over to us with pious solemnity by the manufacturer in order to make us feel special. Thank God water boils at a uniform temperature or kettles would all come with carefully calibrated dials, and asking for tea would be like ordering a steak.

Now, there's another. Please abuse me roundly (but legally) on the social networks (@XanderArmstrong) if you disagree but, by and large, we all like our meat to be medium rare. Don't we? That's the default setting of all chefs, after all. Some people, for good reasons that I can understand, like their meat well done, and about a handful of pervy closet vampires like it rare (but only if they've got an audience – at home they have it medium rare just like the rest of us) and yet wherever you order steak – it might be a place where your sleeves stick to the table-top and where they certainly didn't ask if you *didn't* want lipstick and a dried lemon pip stuck to your glass – they will lean forwards diligently, fix you with their good eye, and ask, 'How do you want that done?' Why do they suddenly care? And why about the steak and not about the buggered Xpelair in the Gents? Or the vibrant insect community in the chiller cabinet?

Some consumer-adjustable settings (at the time of writing) for which I am grateful:

THE ACCELERATION IN A CAR

THE VOLUME ON A RADIO

THERMOSTATS ON HEATERS AND ON ANY FORM OF OVEN

Some consumer-adjustable settings that are beyond the needs of mankind:

GRAPHIC EQUALISERS

LAWNMOWER THROTTLES

FRIDGE SETTINGS (I JUST WANT IT COLD. COLD ENOUGH TO KEEP THE MILK CANNY, BUT NOT SO COLD IT CRYSTALLISES THE LETTUCE – IT'S NOT MY JOB TO KNOW WHAT TEMPERATURE THAT IS)

POINTLESS QUIZ QUESTION

What was invented first? The electric toaster or sliced bread?

67 BAD FILMS

Every day is precious. We must try to fill each one with happiness, kindness and friendship, with dreams met and memories made. Every day a blank, fresh canvas upon which we must paint with beauty, truth and compassion.

All of which got me to thinking about bad films. And the two hours of my life that each one of them steals.

Imagine if I hadn't – by *choice* – watched the following twenty-four hours' worth of films:

DIE HARD 4.0

THE BLAIR WITCH PROJECT

SPIDERMAN 3

STAR WARS – THE PHANTOM MENACE

SEX AND THE CITY 2 (this one was not
strictly *my* choice)

MATCH POINT (Woody Allen tennis film.
Possibly the worst film ever.)

BATMAN AND ROBIN

THE HANGOVER 2

WILD WILD WEST

CITIZEN KANE (not even *one* car chase)

AVATAR

Imagine I could have that precious day back: what things could I achieve? What cathedrals could I build? I could probably even have a lie-in watching *Saturday Kitchen*.

Each year, the antidote to the Oscars, the Golden Raspberries, is held to honour the very worst films and performances of the year. Below you will see fifteen universally terrible films. Can you name the actor or actress who won a Golden Raspberry for their work on each one?

There is one pointless answer, though in a very real sense they are all pointless answers.

POINTLESS QUIZ

Without further ado here are your bad film questions:

1. *Rambo 3*
2. *Battlefield Earth*
3. *G.I. Jane*
4. *Big Daddy*
5. *Showgirls*
6. *Catwoman*
7. *Basic Instinct 2*
8. *All About Steve*
9. *The Blair Witch Project*
10. *Armageddon*
11. *Stop or My Mom Will Shoot*
12. *Under the Cherry Moon*
13. *The Blue Lagoon*
14. *Robin Hood, Prince of Thieves*
15. *Glitter*

Please, on no account, attempt to watch any of these films at home. Instead, why not fly a kite, watch the sun rise on a deserted beach, or tell someone you love them?

66 TONER

Take a look in your bathroom. What do you see? Oh, God, *really*? Well, give that a flush and take another look. Yep, hidden among the thousands of bottles you'll see toner.

While men simply wash their faces, if that, women have a skincare *routine*. It is only slightly less complex than the one performed by Torvill and Dean to Ravel's 'Bolero', which won them a record of twelve perfect 6.0s at the Sarajevo Winter Olympics in 1984, leading every single person in Britain to marvel at their skills and to speculate on whether they were secretly sleeping with each other.

The average woman puts 515 chemicals on her face every day. As a point of comparison, there are only 118 elements in the Periodic Table (information correct at time of recording).

At the beginning of the skincare routine, women cleanse. This is not to be confused with *cleaning*, which is merely the process by which something dirty becomes not dirty. Cleansing is the ritual removal of impurities. At the end of the routine, they moisturise. This is the ritual addition of new, better impurities, which can be cleansed off again at the end of the day.

In between cleansing and moisturising there is a stage known as toning, and this is the completely pointless stage.

It is true that some people have insufficiently cleansed faces (a.k.a. 'greasy') and others insufficiently moisturised (a.k.a. 'sandpaper'). Nobody in the history of faces, though, has ever had an *insufficiently toned* face. Toner is marketed as stuff that finishes cleansing the face you have just cleansed and prepares it for the moisturiser you are about to put on it. It is a thin, nicely scented liquid, which stings slightly when you wipe it over your skin. That's it. It has no additional purpose, aside from helping sell the totally unnecessary cotton-wool pads you need to use to wipe it across your face.

In recent years, some women have got wise to the pointless ways of toner and have stopped using it. To those women a new product is now marketed, called serum. Serum is a moisturiser that you wear under your moisturiser. It is exactly the same as moisturiser except that it is sold in a smaller, pricier bottle. The most expensive serum retailed at Boots costs £125 for a tablespoonful and thus by weight costs more than diamonds.

The only substance in the world more expensive than serum is printer ink. It is probably only a matter of time before researchers at Laboratoires Cosmetiques decide that printer ink is entirely essential for the maintenance of healthy, young-looking skin.

And, no doubt, toner will be the only thing that can get it off again.

65
INTERNET PASSWORDS

The time has come for passwords to go. Good riddance, I say. We liked you when you were new, when we had to remember only one of you, when it still felt like belonging to a secret gang,* but be gone now, with your strange insistence on mixing letters and numbers and your edict that we should all be able to remember seventeen different passwords. Are you mad? Numbers AND letters? The ONLY way we'll

....

* I don't think my brother will mind as we haven't really 'used' our gang, as such, for about thirty-six years, but our password was the following: the first person said, 'Eggs and bacon', and the second person said, 'Bacon and eggs'. That way my brother knew it was *me* he was speaking to and I knew it was *him*. Clever, possibly too clever. But all the same I'd appreciate you keeping this to yourselves . . .

remember these is if we write them down. And Rule 1 of passwords is we don't write anything down. So now every conversation I have with my bank ends with them sending out yet another form so I can reset my password. However, passwords are themselves passing. They have realised they have been their own undoing. This pleases me, but . . .

The time has come for security questions to go. Good riddance, I say. Oh, I know why they came in: because nobody could remember their million different passwords for all their various accounts. But the only security question I know the answer to is the one *anyone* could find out by watching my episode of *Who Do You Think You Are?* My mother's maiden name. Everything else is a mystery. Your first car? Well, I don't know! Was it the first car I remember my parents having (Mini Clubman)? Or was it MY first car (Golf)? Your first house? Could be anywhere. And worse still: your favourite subject at school? Well, that all depends on which school. And when. I used to like music but only when Mrs Dakin taught it, and then I started to prefer English . . . Anyway, you get my gist.

I tell you what I long for and that's a return to the days when we used to speak to people who knew who we were. Can we have that back? It was ace.

POINTLESS FACT

Below is the top 10 most common (and therefore worst) passwords of 2011

1. Password
2. 123456
3. 12345678
4. Qwerty
5. abc123
6. monkey
7. 1234567 (alright, we get the idea)
8. letmein
9. trustno1 (oh the irony)
10. dragon

At number 13 on the list is 'iloveyou', an admirably long way ahead of 'football' at 25. Also very high on the list is the seemingly obscure 'qazwsx'. If you want to know why that's so common, just take a look at your computer keyboard.

64

POINTLESS SHOPPING LIST

I don't have time to go into why each and every item here is pointless, but if you want to indulge in the most pointless trip to the supermarket of all time, simply cut out and keep the list below.

Caffeine-free Diet Coke

Cheese Strings

Pre-peeled orange

Daily Express

Big bag of ice

Cereal Variety Pack

Pot pourri

Bottled water

Pre-chopped onion

Fun-sized choc

Skimmed milk

Justin Bieber album

Lettuce

Twix

While you're there, don't forget to ask for a Bag for Life: they can be incredibly useful. And on your way back could you pop into WH Smiths, and get me any of those items by the till for a pound?

63 UNADJUSTABLE SPANNERS

In the earliest stages of Levantine Neolithic culture, several thousand years before Christ, ancient man first shaped the wheel.

Following the most basic of instincts, this man – let's call him Richard – fashioned his creation from wood using his primitive tools. In so doing, he not only made the single greatest advance in the history of humankind but set in motion an inexorable chain of events that would one day lead to the industrial revolution. Well done, Richard.

Unfortunately, he couldn't attach the wheel to the cart until someone invented the nut and bolt.

Which seamlessly introduces number sixty-three on the *Pointless* miss parade, unadjustable spanners.

Nuts come in many different sizes, as any fan of muesli or regular traveller on a night bus will attest. Historically this meant having a leaden briefcase full of spanners so that modern-day Richards could be certain they had the correctly sized tool for the job. Annoying, right? But what was the alternative?

Well, luckily, some time in the mid-nineteenth century, the adjustable spanner was born and the unadjustable version, like phone booths, floppy disks and VCRs, should have become instantly pointless.

The invention of the adjustable spanner is widely attributed to one of two English engineers: Richard Clyburn of Gloucester, who registered his design in 1843, and Edwin Beard Budding of Stroud, who invented the screw adjustment, still used on modern examples, just before his death in 1846. Budding claimed to have invented the adjustable spanner in 1830, at the same time as he invented the lawn mower. Which must have been handy, if you think about it.

It is because of these two pioneering Englishmen that in almost every Western European country the adjustable spanner is called 'an English key'. Though Americans call their version a 'monkey wrench' – make of that what you will.

But definitively the work of these two clever chaps means that no one need ever carry round a heavy bag of spanners. Ever, ever, ever. And yet people still do. Mainly your dad. Proving that some nuts will never shift, however hard you try to make them.

POINTLESS QUIZ QUESTION

Which of these tools is named after its inventor?

(a) Monkey wrench
(b) Ratchet spanner
(c) Pipe wrench
(d) Ring spanner

62
CELEBRITY BIOGRAPHIES

'The young nurse, scarcely more than a child herself, gazed down at this miraculous baby with his blue, blue eyes and powerful voice. "You," she whispered to the infant, "will have the world at your feet." Francis Albert Sinatra wasn't five minutes old before he had stolen his first heart.'

Nothing pleases me more when studying the lives of the rich and famous than to read the fanciful typings of some paunchy journalist as he sits in his mum's spare room, spinning out three tiny fragments of original information across two thousand pages of sub-Barbara Cartland fairytale. My absolute favourite – and definitely the worst – kind of celebrity biography is the one that starts as early as possible in the childhood of its subject. I haven't looked into this exhaustively but I'm pretty sure there's a link between how bad a biography is and how soon post-partum it takes up the narra-tive. ('It's a boy, Mrs Barrymore!')

The practised chronicler of starry lives has many tricks at his disposal. Actually, hang on, no, he doesn't, he has three. The first – as we have seen – is the brazen Making Stuff Up thing. And what I particularly like about this is not that the author SIMPLY CANNOT KNOW the tone and nature of private conversations of nearly a hundred years ago, but the reverential drum-roll with which such fictions are revealed as if his readers are FOOLS, moo-ha-ha-ha.*

The second trick is the stagy focus pull from the story's shabby present to its earth-shattering apex when the subject is finally prime minister/sent down for multiple murder/lead singer of Matt Bianco. This invariably takes on that wearying kind of reverse bathos much loved by sentimentalist bores the world over ('It may only have been his mam calling him in for his tea, but one day the shout of "Peter Beardsley" would have the whole of St James's Park on its feet').

The third trick is the most cynical and it works something like this: links to any powerful group of (possibly shady) individuals are bestseller gold (this is what the revelation on page 1674 is going to be all about). So, our author can set

....

* He's probably right – we know we've got to trudge through this crap if we're to get to the racy new details on page 1674.

about teeing up any event in his subject's life, however inconsequential ('One man who remained on the fringes that evening was Willie Moretti', 'For Mandelson it was all about timing', or, more thrillingly, 'David Van Day was biding his time – the Dollar moment would come'), to give it planetary significance within the story. This allows for fantastic smudging of historical detail and association that almost verges on the paranoid. Consider how much more fun:

Also present that night was Lord Boothby, sometime member of London's infamous Clermont Club, another member of which was Lord Lucan.

is than the equally true:

Also present that night was Lord Boothby, chairman of the Royal Philharmonic Orchestra.

The first hangs with harmonic implications (LITERALLY so does the second, come to think of it . . .), which mean our journalist can raise an arch eyebrow (before yelling to his mum to bring up more pink milk and choccy biccies) without actually revealing anything at all, apart from fury at a world which is full of people who GO TO THINGS where OTHER PEOPLE MIGHT ALSO BE PRESENT. Anyone who has ever wondered despairingly why the words 'Old Etonian' attach themselves so perpetually to newspaper articles ('Old Etonian Charles Sandbrook said he was putting up a £500 reward for the return of the cat') will recognise this for the lazy, class-system-enhancing, curtain-twitching nonsense it is.

But maybe, deep down, that's why we love a really good, bad biography.

The following is a list of celebrity autobiographies. But who wrote each one? There are a couple of *very* low scoring answers out here.

1. *Dear Fatty*
2. *I Don't Mean to be Rude, But. . .*
3. *A Long Walk to Freedom*
4. *Ooh What a Lovely Pair!*
5. *Dreams from My Father*
6. *The Woman I was Born to Be*
7. *It's Not What you Think*
8. *My Booky Wook*
9. *Look Who It Is!*
10. *The Sound of Laughter*
11. *Humble Pie*
12. *Moonwalk*
13. *My Side*
14. *Learning to Fly*
15. *A Whole New World*

61
EXPLAINING RULES ON EPISODE 400 OF A QUIZ SHOW

'Now, we've put all of today's questions to a hundred people before the show, and you are looking for the answers that the fewest of our hundred people gave. What everybody is looking for, of course, is a pointless answer, an answer that none of our hundred knew. Find one of those and you'll add £250 to the jackpot.

'We're about to show you six clues on each pass and all you have to do is tell us which breed of bird/type of cheese/Eastern European serial killer they describe. The more obscure your answer the fewer points you'll score, but give us an incorrect answer and you'll score a hundred points. Twelve in all for you to have a go at at home.'

Every quiz show – and, as you see above, *Pointless* is no exception – feels the need to explain its rules every thirty seconds. The reason behind it is simple and valid. Broadcasters and producers don't want viewers to switch on their show, get confused, and switch off before giving the show a chance.

But this thinking ignores the fact that every single viewer falls into one of the following two categories:

A) **People Who Are Really Good at Understanding Rules to Quiz Shows**

These people don't need you to explain the rules. They have worked them out already.

B) **People Who Are Really Bad at Understanding Rules to Quiz Shows**

These people don't want you to explain the rules. They'll work them out in their own good time, and would much rather be answering quiz questions than listening to an explanation of the rules.

By all means explain the rules in your early episodes. But by the time you get to episode 400 of a show, as *Pointless* recently did, pretty much everyone watching has seen it before. No one is sitting at home saying 'I'm going to have to watch the first 401 episodes, but if they haven't explained the rules by then, I'm switching off.'

Poor Anne Robinson was still explaining how contestants could 'bank' their money on episode 1,500 of *The Weakest Link*. You will notice that if you're watching *Match of the Day* Gary Lineker doesn't feel the need to explain the rules of football to you. He's assuming you already know.

POINTLESS QUIZ QUESTION

On which TV shows would you find the following deliberately complicated show spoofs?

a) Numberwang
b) Quizzlesticks
c) Bamboozled

'OK, that was entry number sixty-one in our book The 100 Most Pointless Things in the World. *We're now about to reveal number sixty. We're going to ask all readers to now turn to the next page of the book. As always, to "turn a page", simply drag the top right-hand corner of your current page until it flips over to reveal its reverse side. Is everybody ready? Let's read.'*

SIGNS

Signs are important. We like a sign – since the days of the first recorded fingerpost in the seventeenth-century Cotswolds, we have enjoyed knowing where we're going. Think how much we owe to the yellow sign with a picture of a man being struck down by lightning – the international symbol for 'Danger of Death'– without whose warning we would be climbing up pylons and getting arm-deep in junction boxes every afternoon of our (short) lives. Signs telling us which river we are crossing are also good, as too are those that tell us which romantic novelist's locale we are approaching ('You Are Now Entering Catherine Cookson Country' – thank you). All splendid, and signs ('*signs*') of a civilised and humane society.

But we don't like too many signs. No, because then we start complaining about 'street furniture' and 'nanny state'.

So, clearly there's a balance to be struck here, somewhere between wartime signlessness (how many Blitz romances hit the buffers after hours of aimless driving around – 'Let's try down here' – as if they didn't have enough to contend with . . .) and unsightly forests of Urban Clearway signs, Tiredness Can Cause Accidents signs, and Our Staff Have a Right to Carry Out Their Job Without Being Sworn At or Punched signs. For now I'll leave aside Dry Riser Inlet signs and those baffling signs that permanently say Ice! or Flood!

The other day I drove through the beautiful Cotswold town of Charlbury, famous in that region chiefly for its mainline station, which can whisk the passenger the seventy-odd miles into the heart of London's Paddington Basin in eighty-seven minutes (a speed that would have caused our seventeenth-century Cotswoldsman to grab the cloth cap from his head and cross himself while whistling gently through his wooden teeth). The sign announcing Charlbury at the side of the road has been changed recently. Where once it said 'Charlbury', with the tag-line 'Please Drive Carefully Through Our Town', it now announces the town with a series of symbols beneath it. These are a P, a bed, a crossed knife and fork, and Ladies and Gents toilet figures (toilet figures? did I really just type that?) – the international symbols respectively for parking, accommodation, restaurants and loos. Some time in the recent past a committee of townsfolk thought it necessary to trumpet the provision of these facilities in their town. At no point on the new sign does it mention the excellent transport link with London's Paddington Basin. Or, indeed, the abundance of Pavements, Buildings and Dogs.

This is not a new tendency. One has only to look at the signage of old pubs where some happy artisan has been handsomely paid to inscribe such helpful pointers as 'Bottled Beers', 'Brandies', 'Cask Ales', 'Wines & Spirits', 'Whiskies' and 'Knock-off Satellite Football' (I think that's right) all over the frontage for anyone not entirely sure what a pub is.

So, sign-makers, let's lay down some ground rules. On the whole we like what you're doing, but imagine the paint you're using is liquid gold and on that basis work out what's worth bunging up in print and what's essentially pointless.

POINTLESS QUIZ QUESTION

What do these words mean, on signs in Wales?

a) Araf

b) Ildiwch

c) Nid wyf yn y swyddfa ar hyn o bryd. Anfonwch unrhyw waith i'w gyfieithu

59

INSTINCTIVELY CLUTCHING YOUR VALUABLES WHEN WALKING PAST SUSPICIOUS-LOOKING YOUTHS

Since the 2011 riots, suspicion about small groups of young people has never been higher. There is the assumption that they are lawless, aggressive and hell-bent on the destruction of the society that they have been made to feel they have no stake in. While, in reality, only about 75 per cent of them are.

As such, when one encounters a potential gang on the pavement while walking back from the newsagent, it is understandable, even if not justified, that one would become wary and plan defensive measures, just in case the *Daily Mail* happen to be proved correct *on this particular occasion.*

While sensible precautions can be taken, like avoiding eye contact, trying to look a bit taller, and slightly quickening one's step to give oneself a head start in case running away is in order, the most pointless reaction is the one we are all secretly prone to: putting one's hand in or on top of the pocket that contains the most valuable item in one's possession at that time.

It is an instinctive motion, the idea being to give a reassuring feeling of protection over the precious phone or wallet or MP3 player that is playing an inappropriately jaunty song during this moment of heightened tension. (*Really*, Bill Withers? I'm about to be mugged and it's still a 'Lovely Day', is it?)

But this reflex is not just pointless, it's highly detrimental in both of the possible scenarios you now face:

1. The group of youths is totally harmless and completely uninterested in you. In this, the most likely of cases, the act of putting your hand in your pocket as soon as you see them is only likely to cause offence and possibly even incite anger at your obvious suspicion of them, thereby causing the very thing you were afraid of happening.
2. The group of youths is not at all harmless and completely interested in you and your personal property. In this highly unlikely circumstance, there is little you can do but be polite, agree to what is asked of you and have a strong cup of sweet tea when you get home

afterwards. Clutching your phone in your pocket is only going to alert the youths to the fact that you're protecting something valuable and showing them exactly where it is.

POINTLESS QUIZ QUESTION

In what year was the first ever mobile phone call made?

a) 1946

b) 1956

c) 1966

58

OLD-SKOOL HAND-DRIERS

Put your hands under a REAL hand-drier and, man, it's amazing. A truly twenty-first century jet is unleashed that makes your skin ripple like Roger Moore's face in the *Moonraker* test-pilot facility. Water is vaporised in milliseconds. You leave dry of hand and proud to be a member of the species that created such a machine.

Occasionally, however, you find yourself confronted by some yellowing box lurking behind a door and fringed with cigarette burns. You wave your hands under it, and inside, a little elf swears, lowers his (tiny) copy of the *Racing Post* and slowly, slowly reaches for an 'on' button. A click. Silence. More silence. Then the tiniest whine as some sort of 'fan' arrangement begins slowly to stir some air. A clammy breeze dribbles out over your wet skin. This, you realise, will never,

ever get your hands dry. Not if you stand there for a week. So you wipe them on your trousers and leave.

Now we have seen the future, this will not wash. Or dry.

57
TRADITIONAL WEDDING ANNIVERSARIES

Below you'll see twelve wedding anniversaries. Can you tell us what gifts are traditionally given on each one?

For the men reading, it should be noted that there is no anniversary for which 'a bunch of flowers from the twenty-four-hour garage' or 'a new dishwasher' is the traditional gift. Though, due to recent changes in EU regulations, the traditional gift for your seventeenth anniversary is now 'a Sky Sports subscription'.*

So, what gifts do you traditionally give for the following anniversaries? See if you can get a lower score than the rest of your drunk/under-educated/overstaying-their-welcome family.

....

* Good Luck!

POINTLESS QUIZ

Take a look at these wedding anniversaries:

1. 3rd
2. 25th
3. 35th
4. 40th
5. 50th
6. 55th
7. 1st
8. 5th
9. 10th
10. 11th
11. 30th
12. 60th

56
BABY VEGETABLES

OK, let's talk about tiny things.

I can get on board with model villages. I don't mean the model villages built by eighteenth-century philanthropic industrialists determined to give their workers a better quality of life. I am also not talking about villages whose inhabitants are all models, some of which I believe you can find in the Cotswolds. No, I mean actual model villages. Scale models that you can stride around, pretending that you arrived by beanstalk. Which, to be honest, I can do pretty much anywhere.

Similarly, tiny dogs: no problems here. The idle daughters of modern-day philanthropic industrialists, and indeed models, need poodles that are handbag friendly. Standard poodles would simply be too large, leaving no bag room for mobile phones, tiaras, Boots loyalty cards, etc.

I hope it is therefore clear that I have no inherent problem with miniaturisation *per se* as I add one tiny waste of time to your pointless rundown: baby vegetables.

And why are they pointless?

Well, take, for example, an aeroplane. Space is minimal. A perfect example of where miniaturisation is a must; hence small toilets, small pillows, those small bottles of booze you need three of, etc. Hand baggage must be of an acceptable size and weight – roughly poodle-sized – and stored in the cramped overhead lockers or under the tiny seat in front of you. This is a place where small is beautiful.

But no plane has ever been prevented from taking off on account of the carrots being too big. (Notes to editors: I haven't actually checked this, but none is springing to mind.)

The main reason for this is that vegetables *can be cut in half*, or even quarters, if you recently had dental work. There is no need whatsoever to have a wholly complete tiny sweet-corn: a normal sweetcorn cut in half will do just fine. And will contribute towards your five a day, rather than just your two and a half a day.

Why bother to create a smaller version of something when the original version can be cut to size? This would be like genetically engineering fitted carpet.*

You can't cut a village in half, or a poodle. But a courgette? *Pas de problème.*

···

* Note to self; possible business idea? Mention to Theo Paphitis.

55
KNICK-KNACKS ON CHAT SHOW SETS

What is this for? I'm speaking to you, chat-show hosts. IT'S. NOT. YOUR. HOME! How do I know this? Because nobody, NOBODY, has a tight four-piece playing bursts of dinner jazz every time someone walks into their house (or if they do, why don't I?).

Richard tells me that he set you some anagrams earlier, and that you really enjoyed them? Is that right? I have to say it doesn't sound right. Anyway I shall choose to trust him. He has now written 10 anagrams of chat-show hosts for you to unscramble. How many of these 10 can you solve? Richard is not here right now, so if you just want to quietly turn to the next page, he will never know.

1. Angry tower
2. Lankier champions
3. Lane joy
4. Charlatan Smith
5. Drug payola
6. My jerky eel
7. Ash on Trojans
8. Croon nodes
9. Hangman rotor
10. Hard candid jury

54
NOUGHTS AND CROSSES

Here's a simple way to make some money. Approach the stupidest person you know (for reference, this is usually your younger brother, though may also be your quiz co-host) and make the following proposal: 'I bet we can play a hundred games of noughts and crosses without me losing a single one.'

Eventually you will find someone who will take on this bet. A rich person would be best (so your quiz co-host would be *perfect*).

And then begin. And don't worry, there is no con involved, no tricks or clever wordplay. There is just this fact. Noughts and Crosses is utterly pointless because: IT IS IMPOSSIBLE TO LOSE A GAME OF NOUGHTS AND CROSSES.

I don't just mean it's difficult to lose, or you'd have to be up against a genius to lose but, rather, it is mathematically impossible to lose if you follow a few simple rules.

1. If you are playing first, put your X in the middle square.

Whatever your opponent does next, simply block them. Nothing clever or fancy.

2. If you are playing second and your opponent puts his O in the middle, place your X in any corner square. And, from thereon, simply block.

3. If your opponent starts in a square that isn't the middle, then take the middle yourself and simply block.

Try it a few times, I guarantee you won't lose. So you can very safely play 100 games against anyone you choose without losing a single one. Don't forget to send 15 per cent of your winnings to me, as per the terms and conditions you didn't look at when purchasing this book.

If both people know this strategy you can, of course, play to the end of time with every single game ending in a draw. What fun!

This is actually a problem shared by Connect 4, but the maths explaining how it's impossible to lose a game of Connect 4 would fill a whole book. Which I'm not convinced would be a bestseller.

So, if you want a simple game that always delivers, I'd go with Battleships, and if you want a game of mind-boggling complexity, where the rules themselves can take a lifetime to master, I'd suggest chess. Or maybe the *Pointless* board game.

POINTLESS FACT

There are 255,168 possible outcomes to a game of Noughts and Crosses. All of them are boring.

THINGS THAT PRETEND THEY ARE GRAVY BUT AREN'T

Can I be frank with you? I'd like to think I can, as we're now approaching the middle of the book, and especially since you've probably read the greater part of it on the toilet.

So, you'll forgive me if I speak with absolute candour when I say this: I don't really understand posh food.

And I *particularly* don't understand things that pretend to be gravy but aren't. You know the kind of stuff I mean.

When I was a child we would eat out only once a year, at a carvery, for my nan's birthday. The carvery gravy boat was so enormous that Roman Abramovich once held a party on it.

Then, some time late in the last century, these sauces meta-morphosed from 'gravy' into 'jus' though the concept remained roughly the same. The only things that changed were the price and the number of people asking waiters if 'jus' meant 'gravy'. 'Jus', just as its ancestor gravy had before it, made food palatably wet. If things had stopped there, we would be just fine. But posh food doesn't stop, as anyone who watches *Celebrity Masterchef* will tell you.

Chefs started knocking on the door of this pointless list when 'jus' suddenly transmogrified once more, this time into 'foam'. No longer rich, thick gravy designed to complement your meat and potatoes. Instead an insubstantial wisp, hacked up and spat onto your plate from a highly pressurised metal canister, the like of which had not been seen since you put that SodaStream in the attic.

I'm certain that 'foam' is harder and more impressive to make than 'gravy'. But, without wishing to step on the toes of food critics, it is 'less good' and 'not as tasty'.

And now you get the 'smear', a crescent of brightly coloured goo flicked onto your plate with the back of a spoon. If my nan were alive today she would send it back. Sadly, though, she passed away in the early nineties from beef poisoning.

52 LINKEDIN

I've got a great idea. Seeing how successful Facebook and Twitter have been, why don't I start up a new social network? Y'know, make it all about people being connected to one another but in an overtly business-y kind of a way because, hey, it's not *what* you know, is it?* I'm thinking of calling it something like 'ConnectedToPeople'. All I would need to do is get a few key people involved at the start (I'm sure I know enough people of my kind of business-y mindset who can take an acumen-based view and SEE that this is just a hands-down WINNER) and get them to go through their address books – under duress, if necessary – so I can fire out links

....

* No, it's who you know.

to each and every one of their contacts.** It can't fail. Think about it, who would say no? It makes perfect sense for the business-minded man or woman on the web who hasn't already established their own set of friends or business contacts. And on ConnectedToPeople we've removed the stigma from shameless networking by making it our core principle. So, while they might come over a little bit desperate, constantly asking for validation and updating you daily on every single new ConnectedToPeople contact they've made, that's just the way we run the network. And don't forget: coming over a little bit desperate is a great way of attracting business.***

Not long from now the day will come when everyone in the world can log on to ConnectedToPeople via a series of uncomplicated security questions and find themselves just three or four clicks away from all the people in their mobile-phone contacts list they don't especially want to keep up with.

....

** IT'S ALL ABOUT CONTACTS – THAT'S JUST THE WAY BUSINESS WORKS!
*** And friends!

51

ASKING QUESTIONS ABOUT CLASSICAL MUSIC OR POETRY

Every now and again on *Pointless* we have a round that everybody is terrible at. Occasionally it's a surprising one – no one could name any U2 top-forty singles or Robert Redford films, for example. Often it's something more obscure, like the films of Ralph Fiennes, or the novels of Sebastian Faulks.

If Robert Redford ever directed Ralph Fiennes in the film of a Sebastian Faulks novel it would surely be the most pointless film of all time. But at least I know who could do the theme tune.

Here are two questions that appeared on *Pointless*, which we agreed never to speak of again. One is on classical music, and the other is on poetry.

If you know some of the answers – or maybe you have a clever guest around for lunch? – then very well done. And if you know *none* of them, simply look at the answers, learn them, and you can pretend to be clever for the rest of time. That's what I do.

POINTLESS QUIZ

CLASSICAL MUSIC

Which composers wrote the following pieces?

1. *The Four Seasons*
2. *The William Tell Overture*
3. *Eine Kleine Nachtmusik*
4. *4'33'*
5. *Samstag aus Licht*
6. *Ride of the Valkyries*
7. *Rhapsody in Blue*
8. *The Blue Danube*
9. *Peter and the Wolf*
10. *Variations on a Theme of Frank Bridge*
11. *The Planets*
12. *The Trout Quintet*

POINTLESS QUIZ

POEMS AND THEIR POETS

Which poets wrote the following pieces?

1. 'Jabberwocky' (1871)
2. *The Charge of the Light Brigade* (1854)
3. 'If . . .' (1910)
4. *Paradise Lost* (1667)
5. *The Rime of the Ancient Mariner* (1798)
6. 'The Raven' (1845)
7. *The Ballad of Reading Gaol* (1898)
8. 'The Owl and the Pussy Cat' (1871)
9. *The Wasteland* (1922)
10. 'To a Mouse' (1786)
11. 'Ode to a Nightingale' (1820)
12. 'I Wandered Lonely as a Cloud' (1807)
13. 'Anthem for Doomed Youth' (1920)
14. 'The Soldier' (1914)
15. *The Divine Comedy* (1300s)

50 LUXEMBOURG

Name a famous person from Luxembourg. Wait, scratch that: just name anyone, *ever*, from Luxembourg. I can tell you there are over 14 million pointless answers.

If you said, 'The King of Luxembourg,' then you get a big red cross. It's a Grand Duchy and as such, unsurprisingly, has a grand duke. His name is Henri. Sort of like the footballer you *have* heard of.

So what answer should you have given?

Well there was actually one famous person from Luxembourg. His name was William Kroll. William was a metallurgist who invented the 'Kroll process' in 1940, which is used commercially to extract metallic titanium from ore.

I bet you are kicking yourself now, aren't you?

It may be a harsh truth but, frankly, Luxembourg doesn't do anything. At least, it doesn't do anything that its neighbours, France, Belgium and Germany, don't do bigger and better. And if you're trailing behind Belgium, then you've got problems.

It did once produce an EU president called Jacques Poos, which we all thought was pretty funny at the time, but even he has retired now.

So come on Luxembourg, if you want to get off this list, either pull your socks up, win the Eurovision Song Contest, or tell us where you've hidden Jacques Poos. In fact, turn his childhood home into the Museum of Poos, and I promise we will all come and visit. Though we might not eat in the café.

49

RESTAURANT LOYALTY SCHEMES

So, you've set up a restaurant/take-away business that is showing all the signs of becoming successful: you've got long queues at the tills every lunchtime, a lot of returning customers, and the *Sunday Times* Style section has featured you towards the bottom of its 'Going Up' fashion barometer (you're quite near their office and you serve food that goes down a storm with anorexic girls and gay men). Let's say you're a hummus restaurant. You've got a great name (GSOH – Good Sense of Hummus) and top-notch branding

Hum.mus (also Houmous) 'hʊm ʊs
n. 1. A thick paste or spread made from ground chick-peas and sesame seeds, olive oil, garlic and lemon. Orig. from Middle East*

What else do you need to do?

Well, apparently the next step is to start up a loyalty scheme. There's no logical reason behind this, unless

(a) You are strangely and wrongly convinced that through having a person's contact details you will somehow own them.
(b) Your shareholders will strangely and wrongly think that your business is doing better if it can show lots of names and addresses on its database.
(c) You quite want to have the contact details of some of those hot fashion journalists who occasionally pop in to share a flatbread. I think they work round the corner. *Sunday Times* or something.
(d) Once you have amassed a decent volume of contact details, these can be sold on wholesale to other companies for muchos muchos houmous, or
(e) A beguiling mixture of all the above.

....

* You can have these. And given the name, Sense of Hummus, this is one of the few times that that wearisome dictionary definition thing *almost* works.

(146)

But what, at the end of the day, can you offer to people who become Friends of GSOH? Seriously. Other than hummus? Or a free drink with large orders of hummus? Or some more hummus if you order a spectacular quantity of hummus? Well, I'm afraid the answer is: nothing. Apart from a newsletter. GSOH being the kind of place it is, this will be a breezy, chummy piece of ho-hum marketing written as if by some slightly simple family friend who's under the impression that you think he's HILARIOUS. Engrossing tales of how Charlie's mum used to make hummus for him when he was a boy and how Ed (occasionally called 'Eduardo' or 'The Edster') drank a bit too much on his stag (this illustrated with woozy stick-drawings and a poem). And that's it.

You have all the ingredients for a restaurant. And you have customers who like your restaurant doing what it does. The minute you try to use those restaurant ingredients to magic up something that is more than a restaurant, you have overstretched your capabilities.

Honestly. I tend to go to restaurants/take-aways because I want some lunch. I don't really want them as friends. Now, obviously if they're Nando's and are handing out VIP cards that will allow me and my family to eat there for gratis for the rest of time, then, yes, they can be my friends. But otherwise I like them more if they stick to what they're good at.

48 PET GOLDFISH

Swim, swim, swim, swim, open mouth, close mouth, swim, swim, swim, do a long green poo, swim, swim, bump into glass, open mouth, close mouth, die, get replaced by Dad so kids never know, swim, swim, poo, swim.

POINTLESS FACT

The world's oldest goldfish was Tish, from Doncaster, who died at the extraordinary age of forty-three.

Tish put his longevity down to regular early-morning swims. His last wish was to be buried at land.

47

A POINTLESS WALK

Start at Marble Arch at the gift shop named London's Best Gifts. Have a browse. They sell dolls in plastic tubes playing bagpipes, key-rings with pre-Docklands Light Railway tube maps on the fob that are so small that only the Sherlock Holmes doll with the magnifying glass and deerstalker (also on sale here) could read them, and postcards featuring bosoms painted to look like small dogs. London's best gifts.

When you have browsed to your satisfaction, come out of the shop and head towards the north-east corner of Hyde Park. This is the celebrated Speakers' Corner, and if it's a Sunday you're in luck. It might be Chris from Hatfield talking about CHOLESTEROL! Or a lady in a quilted jacket shrieking, 'How many more polar bears have to die, Mr Blair?' or, indeed, anyone talking about anything. That's Speakers' Corner for you!

Take the path due south, turning left out of the park and crossing Park Lane when you come to a grand pedestrian crossing. Stop when you're halfway across. Here you will find a monument to Animals in War. This, it says, is dedicated to all animals who died fighting for the Allied forces throughout history. And then at the bottom, by way of foot-note, it says, 'THEY HAD NO CHOICE.' Wrestle momentarily with the conflicting logic and history here (is the dedication a brilliant approximation of the meaninglessness of war itself? Or simply an exhortation not to have committees design monuments in future?), acknowledge the affecting simplicity of the monument, then walk on. On the other side of Park Lane, Mayfair awaits.

Aaaaah, Mayfair, the heavy Bentley blue of Monopoly's most prized property, the heady mottled whiff of a magazine unearthed in a wood next to a rotting ten-pack of Rothmans. It never disappoints. Stride along Brook Street, idly contem-plating where the original recruitment 'Bureau' might have been sited, until you reach Grosvenor Square. Here you will find heavy bollarding and equally heavy policing. This comes as standard when your most famous resident is the United States of America! The US embassy in Grosvenor Square is the only US embassy in the world that is not owned by the US. In London it is the tenant of the Duke of Westminster. As you walk around the square (we're heading for the exit at roughly two o'clock, Carlos Place), imagine how many sets of jumpy cross-hairs are following your every move.

Carlos Place links Grosvenor and Berkeley Squares and we are going to walk down it, past Timothy Taylor's gallery on the right, and taking the right-hand turn into Mount Street after the Connaught Hotel. Along Mount Street, pause to look in the window of Knight Frank, the estate agent. A 1,400-square-foot flat in neighbouring Hill Street is £6 million because there are only twenty-eight years left on the lease. There is an art dealer on Mount Street called Rich. Don't, as they say, go there, girlfriend.

At the end of Mount Street we hit South Audley Street. The shop immediately opposite on the left is Purdey's the shotgun makers, where Michael Gambon was once an apprentice. On his first day he was told to make a perfect cubic inch of gun metal accurate to the nearest fraction of a millimetre. Somewhere, Gambon's cube is sitting in a drawer; one of his less well-known works but doubtless another masterpiece.

Turn left down South Audley Street. Shortly we come to Thomas Goode on the left-hand side. The entrance to this high-priced-china shop features a glorious piece of old-fashioned engineering: a prototype automatic door wrought in knotty oak and polished brass. Its ingenious mechanism is activated by using the body weight of the entrant stepping onto a footplate to open the door. For anyone who questions the scarcely credible levels of pain inflicted by walking at pace into a half-opened door this splendid piece of Victoriana serves as a short but memorable tutorial, to which the practised nonchalance of the shop-workers is the perfect balm.

We will finish our walk with a drop-in at the Ritz! This we will earn by limping briskly down South Audley Street until we reach Curzon Street where we head left along to the north of Shepherd Market, home to some of London's snazziest prostitutes. A right-hand turn down Half Moon Street takes us niftily to Piccadilly where, after a casual promenade up the hill beside Green Park, our final destination awaits: the bar of the Ritz Hotel. And it won't cost us a penny.

What's that? Won't cost a penny? How so? Well, that's because, as you will discover, the Ritz bar operates a pleasing, nostalgic, we-won't-serve-anyone-not-wearing-a-tie policy so you will be brusquely asked to leave before you've so much as reached for your wallet.

46
POINTLESS THINGS YOU CAN DO IN 100 SECONDS

Listen to the first minute and forty seconds of John Cage's 4'33'.

45
GAME SHOW HOSTS

Why do I think game-show hosts are pointless? Well, consider this.

When the doctors go on strike we're up in arms. When the train drivers go on strike, the country grinds to a halt.

So, what would happen if game-show hosts went on strike?

Is it . . .

(a) Widespread panic buying of petrol and basic provisions as the British public dig in for a long, tough winter?
(b) Total breakdown of civil order, leading an emergency session of cabinet to order the army to present all TV game-shows until the riots subside?

(c) Nothing. Maybe someone tuts in Huddersfield?

Game-show hosts are all, essentially, trained chimps. Some of us are not even trained.

Can you name the *original* hosts of all the following TV game-shows? Trained chimps one and all, albeit some of them rather lovely trained chimps.

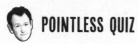 **POINTLESS QUIZ**

Your questions are:

1. *3–2–1*
2. *Only Connect*
3. *The Crystal Maze*
4. *Fifteen to One*
5. *The Weakest Link*
6. *Bullseye*
7. *Blockbusters*
8. *Turnabout*
9. *The Cube*
10. *Going for Gold*
11. *The Generation Game*
12. *Every Second Counts*

44
THINGS HANGING FROM REAR-VIEW MIRRORS

1914 was a year of profound retrospection. It was the year the Great War started, which, of course, caused the whole nation to look back wistfully. But it was also the year in which the rear-view mirror was introduced, which allowed everyone to look back in super-deluxe comfort.

In its first incarnation the rear-view mirror sat on the dashboard of the motor-car providing a first-class view of the stout Edwardian knees of whoever was sitting in the middle of the back seat. Some years later it was mounted on the windscreen, from which vantage-point the driver had full vision of what lay behind, albeit in a tight letterbox format.

I wonder, though, if the genius engineer who first elevated the mirror to its new windscreen home could possibly have known what it was he was creating. He was giving the car a personality that went way beyond the two headlamps and grille that simply 'looked a bit like a face': the motor-car now had soul. For only the third time since the iron age, humanity was being offered a whole new place from which to dangle things.*

Things hanging from rear-view mirrors fall into two categories: those with a function and those that have absolutely no purpose at all (other than to throw open a window into the psyche of a man who considered precisely WHICH pair of silver testicles to buy for his rear-view mirror).

The first category is short. In fact, it consists entirely of air fresheners. These come in all scents, from light pine forest to heavy vanilla ice-cream, which are often deeply impregnated into 'magic' trees. So potent is the magic that some drivers prefer to reveal a bit of tree at a time, pulling the cellophane gradually down, like the dress off some elaborate boiled-sweet-smelling burlesque. However, no tree has yet been magic enough to mask the sneezy smell of a minicab that is also its driver's bedroom.

In a strange grey area between the two categories we find religious insignia: rosary beads, pennants with Koranic script, Hindu deities, or crucifixes that swing wildly as they career

....

*1. The lady's (or pirate's) ear.   2. The Christmas Tree.

round one-way systems and get caught up in the driver's middle finger as it's flipped at other motorists.

And then there's the second category: wiggly-hipped Elvises, unsettling red plastic things that look like chilli peppers, mini boxing-gloves, CDs (who knows?), CDs in Jamaican colours, furry dice, skulls, teeth (i.e. an individual tooth of a shark, say, not dentures so much), CDs with Koranic script and, of course, the big silver testicles. These are occasionally ironic (furry dice), at best talismanic (unsettling red plastic things that look like chilli peppers), but ultimately, of course, pointless.

43

CVs

It's time we all admitted it: no one who has ever written a CV has ever told the truth. And no one who has ever read a CV has ever believed it. Why do we still bother? We know all the lies we're telling, and we know all the lies we're reading. Is it not time we were just more honest about things?

Below is how your CV looks now, and on page 161 is how it would look if you told the truth.

DEBBIE WILMOTT

A professional and highly focused IT professional seeking new challenges and opportunities in the computing, technology and service industries.

Professional Experience

2009–12 LimTex Consulting

Team leader implementing core IT goals and strategies in a constantly developing high-end environment. Responsible for key staff team, including appraisals, training and incentivisation. Reporting to David H. Edwards, Managing Director of LimTex Consulting.

2008–9 VimTech Solutions

Deputy team leader implementing core IT strategies and goals in a high-end, constantly developing environment. Working very closely with team leader Marcus Johnson, Deputy Managing Director of VimTech Solutions.

2003–6 Central African Republic Tourist Board

IT assistant.

2001–2 BurgerStar Inc

Technology consultant and operative, responsible for key end-user interface transactions, with responsibility for business to consumer satisfaction, and management of financial transactions.

Education

Our Lady the Redeemer School, Melton Mowbray, Leics
12 GCSEs, including A* in Maths, Further Maths, English, Information Technology, Physics, Chemistry and Mandarin

Hobbies

I enjoy hiking, visiting art galleries and museums, charity work, tap dancing, and amateur archaeology.

References (Available on request)

Work: Marcus Johnson – VimTech Solutions
Personal: Professor H. C. Carruthers, De Montfort University.

And now here's the same CV, but written honestly.

DEBBIE WILMOTT

Bored IT professional, unhappy that she's not allowed to access the *Daily Mail* website in her current employment. Also fairly sure that at some point they're going to work out she doesn't have a clue what she's doing, so keen to move on before that happens.

Professional Experience

2009–12 LimTex Consulting

Team leader implementing weekly biscuit-kitty collection and co-ordinating gossip about the new guy who's started in the post-room. Responsible for Carl and Sue. Reporting to the world's biggest tool, David H. Edwards, Managing Director of LimTex Consulting.

2008–9 VimTech Solutions

Deputy team leader implementing getting Elaine's leaving card signed. Left after refusing, repeatedly, to sleep with Marcus Johnson, Deputy Managing Director of VimTech Solutions.

2007

Please don't notice that I've left out 2007, when I sat on the sofa for most of the year eating Wotsits and watching *Jeremy Kyle*.

2003–6 Central African Republic Tourist Board

IT assistant.

2001–2 BurgerStar Inc

Worked the tills. Didn't ever quite manage to win a star, due to repeated late arrivals, and general 'not giving the first toss' about BurgerStar Inc.

Education

Our Lady the Redeemer School, Melton Mowbray, Leics
No one EVER checks this, right? How sad would you have to be to contact the school I left twelve years ago to discover I got two GCSEs, a D in Maths and an E in General Studies and that, perhaps most importantly of all, I failed IT?

Hobbies

I enjoy what everybody in Britain enjoys – watching telly, texting my friends, tutting at parents who shout at their kids in supermarkets, and sleeping. I once watched *Time Team*, and I donated to Comic Relief last year.

References (Available on request)

Work: Marcus Johnson – VimTech Solutions
(A wonderful reference, due to my eternal threat of telling his wife about that telemarketing conference in Loughborough.)

Personal: Professor H. C. Carruthers, De Montfort University

(My dad putting on a voice.)

So, CVs are utterly pointless. Even I – as a former astronaut and winner of the Wimbledon Ladies Singles Final in 1987 – know that.

One of the first CVs in history was sent to the Duke of Milan in 1482. It started 'I can carry out sculpture in marble, bronze, or clay, and also I can do in painting whatever may be done, as well as any other, be he who he may.' Whose CV was it?

TIES

There's an item of clothing, worn around the neck, which consists of a single piece of fabric, available in different colours, patterns and textiles, which is both jaunty and extremely useful. It's called a scarf.

Ties, on the other hand, are utterly pointless. Justification for the wearing of ties falls into two categories which instantly cancel each other out.

1. Tie-wearing as an expression of conformity: showing membership of the Rotary Club, the RAF, or your soul-destroying Saturday job at Curry's. This 'benefit' of tie-wearing is completely illusory as everybody already *knows* you're a conformist, due to your right-wing

politics, military bearing, or your complete lack of knowledge about any of the electrical goods you are trying to sell me.

2. Tie-wearing as an expression of individuality: if you are expressing your individuality through a piece of coloured fabric tied around your neck you really should not be expressing it at all. If you own, say, a wacky kipper tie, a hilarious musical tie, or a tie with any sort of cartoon character emblazoned on it, you need to understand that this is the reason that everyone at work has been avoiding you. Quite aside from anything else, just the idea that wearing a tie could be an expression of individuality has been responsible for some of the most disappointing Christmas presents in history. (Yes, I'm looking at *you*, Auntie Eileen.)

The apex of pointless tie-wearing lies in the school uniform tie: prescribed to be worn to express conformity to the school, then tied by every new generation of schoolkids in a distinctive fashion (e.g. short fat bit in front, long thin bit tucked into shirt) to express individuality in the face of enforced conformity, only to come full circle to conformity again because everybody is wearing it in the same individualistic way, and looking like a tit while they're at it.

Ultimately, aside from keeping you warm, the only reason to wear clothes *at all* is to attract members of the opposite sex who might want to sleep with you. But women who think, That's a great tie, I must shag that man immediately, are about as rare as men who think, She's interested in star signs? I must shag that woman immediately.

(Looking back across this entry I think anyone who uses the word 'emblazoned' is also pointless. Sorry about that.)

POINTLESS QUIZ QUESTION

According to James Bond, which of these is the mark of a cad?

a) A bow tie
b) A Windsor knot
c) A cravat
d) No tie

41 RECEIPTS

OK, I think I've got number 41

Go on . . .

Reciepts

Do you mean 'receipts'?

Yes.

And why are they pointless?

difficult to spell

Clearly

If I'm buying chewing gum I DON'T NEED A RECEIPT! I'm not going to bring it back because it doesn't work.

Even if it's poisoned? You wouldn't take it back if it was poisoned?

Depends how far away I was from the shop. But, anyway, I'm also not buying it as a gift . . .

Not after last Valentine's Day

Quite, she was NOT happy. And I'm not claiming it back on my tax.

Unless you're an MP

So what do I want receipts for? All that happens is that I leave them in my pocket, forget about them, and then later put my hand into my pocket and think, Ooh, lovely, I've got a tenner, only to take it out and discover that it's a receipt for a Greggs' sausage roll. Receipts are pointless.

Not all receipts though?

OK, if I buy a house I want a receipt, if I buy a Twix I don't.

Good rule. Let's write that in big letters at the bottom of the page and move on

IF I BUY A HOUSE I WANT A RECEIPT, IF I BUY A TWIX I DON'T.

POINTLESS FACT

Receipts have been around longer than writing. Split tally sticks and even bones were used to record transactions, debts and taxes right back to the Palaeolithic era.

40 COBBLERS

I'm not a man afraid of controversy. You don't get to be co-host of a weekday teatime BBC quiz show without being a crazy, usually drunk, maverick.

In general terms, I believe there is very little difference between the genders. I believe that if women are from Venus, then men are also from Venus, and the only reason they're currently on Mars is that they're lost and they're refusing to ask for directions.

But in the course of research for this book I may have uncovered one single fundamental schism between men and women. And that schism, appropriately, is 'cobblers'. Here's what happened.

My workplace is roughly 50:50 men:women, and the only fundamental difference between the men and the women is that they use separate toilets. And I only learned *that* after HR were forced to send me on an 'Inappropriate Behaviour in the Workplace' course. I tried out lots of the 'pointless' ideas for this book on my lovely colleagues, and it was generally a useful system (except in the case of my PA, Kellie, who blankly refused to join in any discussion unless I agreed that 'secret socks' should be in the book).

So when I witnessed what happened when I suggested that 'cobblers' were pointless, I was surprised by the results.

I am going to boil down every single conversation about cobblers to one discussion, purely because every single discussion was identical.

ME
(Businesslike, commanding the respect of the room)
No one ever goes to cobblers any more. Surely they're pointless?

EVERY MAN IN THE ROOM
(Practically high-fiving)
Yep, totally pointless, good one, Richard! He's done it again!

EVERY WOMAN IN THE ROOM
(Wide-eyed, incredulous)
What?

ME
(Pen in hand, still businesslike, etc.)
It's perfect for the book. Why would anyone ever go to the cobbler's?

EVERY WOMAN IN THE ROOM
(As if speaking to a newly discovered race of morons)
To get your shoes mended!

EVERY MAN IN THE ROOM
(As if speaking to a previously undiscovered tribe of utter halfwits)
You get your shoes *mended*?!

I tried this conversation over and over again, and I didn't stumble across a single solitary man who would *dream* of having a pair of shoes mended. Or a single solitary woman who would throw away a pair of shoes that just needed a simple repair.

So, have we accidentally discovered the true genetic difference between men and women?

Please try this conversation in your office/staffroom/tribunal, and report back your findings. Or if you work in a cobbler's, let me know what it's like. I'm guessing it's an awesome place to pick up women.

And, apropos of nothing, what is it with secret socks? I mean, why wear a bright colour if no one's going to see them? Totes ridic.

WEIRD HOBBIES

It's quiz time again!

NOTE FOR CHILDREN
I hope you realise that you can just cheat by looking at the answers at the end of the book. Astound your family as you answer all fifteen of these questions correctly. If you can play for money, all the better.

NOTE FOR PARENTS
Don't forget to dust the 'answer' pages of this book for fingerprints before accepting any quiz challenges from your children. Especially if it's for money.

NOTE FOR CHILDREN
Wear gloves.

The following are all names for people who collect, study or make different things. They have long names to make them seem more respectable and interesting, rather than just a pointless reason to spend all evening in the loft.

 POINTLESS QUIZ

What hobby do each of these enjoy:

1. Vexillologist
2. Philatelist
3. Arctophile
4. Horologist
5. Lepidopterist
6. Oologist
7. Numismatist
8. Conchologist
9. Deltiologist
10. Discophile
11. Bibliophile
12. Oenophile
13. Philographist
14. Porcelainist
15. Notaphilist

I think I'm probably a number 12 and a number 15.

38
FAKE SOUNDTRACKS ON NATURE PROGRAMS

OK, time for a bombshell.

Actually, first I should say that I don't *know* that this is true, but I reckon I know enough about how television works to be 100 per cent certain of it. And here it comes:

Soundtracks on natural history programmes are faked.

By which I don't mean the ambient sound, the chirps and buzzings of a rainforest, or indeed the erudite chattings of the presenter – those, I have no doubt, are all genuine. It's the pings and sticky clickings on the close-up shots, the footsteps of baby chameleons as they stalk along a leaf. They're all phoney. I mean, of *course* they are. They have to be. You only need to watch the underwater bits where foetal tadpoles are hatching from frog spawn to the accompaniment of teeny-tiny chewing noises, as if some hairy-arsed man in headphones with a big woolly boom-mike was wedged into the pond alongside the camera.

Of course, technology allows for some quite sophisticated directional microphone work but there is simply NO WAY that things happening at microbe level would (a) emit an audible noise or (b) make noises anything like the fanciful nonsense that some sound engineer has cooked up using a cabbage, a bicycle pump, and the rest of his smoothie.

Given the choice between watching nature programmes with completely made-up audio tracks or watching them to a deathly silence (that is, more faithful to how they were filmed), then of course I'll take the made-up audio every time. All I'm saying is: DON'T THINK I'M FOOLED. Y'hear?

POINTLESS FACT

The sound of polar bears crunching through snow is allegedly made by filling a stocking with custard powder and crunching it up.

37 CHIP FORKS

OK, we've talked about a lot of pointless things in this book, so I'm guessing that your pointless radar is now very well developed. Let's find out.

I had written a very simple first sentence for this entry, but I quickly realised that this one simple sentence contained an incredible *ten* pointless things.

Can you spot all ten pointless items in the sentence?

> *I was walking past a kebab shop this afternoon when I saw a bunch of schoolkids eating chips out of polystyrene trays, all using chip forks.*

Did you get all ten?

1. Me. Lovely though my mum thinks I am, and useful as I occasionally am when my children need money for sweets or video games, I have to accept that I've never invented a cure for anything, or ever saved a dog from a lake or some such. I'm pointless.
2. Walking. Who needs a cheap, environmentally friendly, super-healthy way to get around? Not me. I go pretty much everywhere in my helicopter.
3. Kebab shops in the afternoon. They might have the glimmer of a point late in the evening when you're drunk and in need of somewhere to conduct research into food poisoning while watching other drunk people argue, but in the afternoon they are pointless.
4. Polystyrene trays – We have long since lost the battle on wrapping chips in newspaper, due to the potentially toxic combination of newspaper ink and food, a combination responsible for killing entire zeroes of people. But polystyrene trays. Really?
5. Chip forks.
6–10. A bunch of schoolkids – there were 5 of them.

The only item in the whole sentence that wasn't pointless was 'chips'. Mmm, 'chips'. But you'll have noticed immediately that the most pointless of all the items is the chip fork.

Chip forks are not only pointless, they are antithetical to the very nature of the chip. I know that nobody asks you to eat roast potatoes with your hands, or to shove your face straight into a plate of mashed potato (though, Lord knows, go ahead if you want to), but the whole point of chips, aside from compressing the maximum amount of fat into the minimum amount of vegetable, is that they are the hot potato snack you can eat with your fingers. That is what they are designed for. They were literally invented so that you can pick them up. If you're going to eat chips with a chip fork, you may as well start eating crisps with a spoon.

Elvis Presley famously never ate any food that needed cutlery, and he ate so many chips that he died. Picture Elvis Presley with a chip fork. It's simply absurd. So next time you pick up a chip fork, just know that you're insulting the memory of the King.

36
CASHIER NUMBER 3 PLEASE

Thanks to *Dragon's Den* and some films, I like to think I have a pretty good idea of how inventors work. They potter about in their garages at home wearing faded boiler suits with red spotty kerchiefs tied around their necks, and then one Sunday in the spring they throw open the garage doors, call the family in, and pull off the tarpaulins to reveal their master-work. This quite often involves a few explanatory tippety-taps with the stem of their pipe on some of the salient features of the machine they have built.

Then, some time later, they go to an old warehouse in a cobbled back-street out in the east end of their nearest town. And there they present their invention to a panel of million-aires, on old study chairs, who get cross with them about their finances before eventually conceding that their rocket/

toy/desert irrigation system is in fact quite a good idea. The inventor then takes himself off to a dark corner of the bare-brick room for a couple of minutes on his own before shaking hands with a very tall man and a Greek.

Sometimes the meetings end with the inventor having to lug his *magnum opus* back down the stairs and all the way home to his garage, dejected, outcast and thoroughly put in his place about his finances. But at others the outcome induces unbridled euphoria, and there has been one instance when I would love to have been present to witness the joy. On this occasion the inventor, popping champagne corks and giggling like a fool, was the man responsible for the machine at the front of queues that tells everyone, a few moments after one of the cashiers has become available, that one of the cashiers has become available. 'Cashier number three, please,' it chirrups brightly, with a flashing red digital '3' on its panel (corresponding with the flashing red digital '3' over the relevant cashier's window).

Hell, we all have good days and I am not going to start begrudging our hard-working inventor community their day in the sun, but if this current recession results in the removal of utterly pointless detritus such as 'cashier number three' machines from our lives, we will not have lived through it in vain.

POINTLESS FACT

Terry Green, known as 'The Voice of Cashier Number 3 Please' has written a book called 'You're Next!' and is available for after-dinner speeches. His 'Queue-O-Meter' tells us that we must have wasted almost 2.5 million pounds through queuing this year alone. Which might not be entirely accurate.

35

OVER-COMPLICATED HOTEL SHOWERS

By and large hotels are awesome, so long as you are a fan of tiny soap and not really having to tidy up after yourself.

But we need to have a short word about the showers.

A hotel or B&B shower should be a fairly simple thing. I need to be able to:

a) Turn it on
b) Make it hotter or colder, according to my whim

I was in a hotel recently and the shower had four different dials. Four? A Challenger tank only has three! Looking at the gleaming chrome and the tiny numbers, the colours and symbols, and the terrifying levers and buttons, I felt like one of the intrepid scientists bravely entering the stricken Fukushima nuclear plant.

If, in the quiet and safety of your own home, you want to have a shower with four dials then go right ahead. You can have a massage function, a multi-jet function, or an 'intimacy' function (I've looked at a couple of brochures). But in your own home you have the luxury of time, and of an insanely long instruction manual (see 10: 98 Per Cent of Everything in an Instruction Manual).

Because the problem in a hotel is that you're only staying for one night and you really don't have time to crack the Enigma code when all you want is to look nice and smell nice for whatever meeting/wedding/disciplinary procedure that brought you there in the first place.

And it's not like you can even experiment with what the dials do, because hotel showers are almost always designed in such a way that to speculatively turn a dial you have to stand directly under the shower head, thereby freezing or scalding yourself at every turn. And even if you've cleverly slid in around the side of the shower head, you know the dial you turn will be the one that sends a jet of water directly into your unprepared face. Or, worse still, you'll activate the 'intimacy' function when you were least suspecting.

So Mr Hilton, Monsieur Ibis, Professor Travelodge and Dave

Novotel, save your money, over-complicated showers are pointless.

Though, to end on a positive note, is there anyone who doesn't like a self-service hotel breakfast? I might set up a chain of restaurants called Hotel Breakfasts. That's a billion dollar idea right there.

POINTLESS QUIZ QUESTION

What bathroom innovation did Sir Winston Churchill first use in the US in 1942, excitedly writing about it in his diary on the same day?

34 MICKEY MOUSE

He has never been funny. And he doesn't look anything like a mouse.

PERSUADING BRITISH PEOPLE TO SPEAK FOREIGN LANGUAGES

We are notoriously terrible at learning foreign languages. This is essentially due to two factors:

Speaking foreign languages is *really* difficult.

Most foreigners speak English. High five!

So, we Brits are the worst linguists in the world.

For example, could *you* say, 'I'm sorry about the imminent collapse of your society,' in Greek? Or 'When you've finished the grouting, could you take a look at the overflow pipe?' in Polish? Have you ever tried speaking Mandarin? It might as well be in Chinese.

So, as a little encouragement to discover what the rest of the world is talking about during the brief moments when they're not patiently explaining something to us in English, here is a quiz.

 POINTLESS QUIZ

The following expressions are all friendly greetings. But can you name which language each is in?

1. *Buon giorno*
2. *Kalimera*
3. *Selamat siang*
4. *Dzien dobry*
5. *Guten Tag*
6. *Dia duit*
7. *Bore da*
8. *Xin chao*
9. *Hyvaa huomenta*
10. *Shalom*
11. *Bonjour*
12. *Hola*

32
READING OUT VIEWERS' TWEETS ON TV AND RADIO

There are two things guaranteed to make any British viewer switch off their TV or radio but due to my fear of Piers Morgan's libel lawyers, I'm only allowed to write about one of them in this book.

I have decided to email 'The News' about the endless, and *surely* pointless, use of viewers' and listeners' tweets on supposedly intelligent shows.

To: The News
cc: All radio programmes ever
Subject: Viewers' tweets

Dear The News

I like you. I like watching and listening to you. I particularly like it when you get Paxman to shout at people. But I am now bored of hearing viewers' tweets on every subject under the sun.

So, for example, let's say David Cameron has an argument with Ed Miliband about taxing jacket potatoes. The following is a list of people I want to hear from:

1. David Cameron
2. Ed Miliband
3. The chief executive of Spud-u-Like (I wonder if that is actually someone's job? Wow! I would absolutely love to hear from him or her)
4. Krishnan Guru-Murthy with a tax expert, or a representative of the British Potato Growers' Association
5. Possibly Wayne Rooney (head like a potato. Interesting celeb angle)

The following is a list of people I do not want to hear from:

1. Gary from Woking

Trust me, if I want to hear Gary's opinion on something, I will travel to Woking and ask him personally. I'm guessing there won't be a big queue.

This goes for every story on every news programme ever. I was listening to a religious debate on a Radio 5 discussion programme last week. One listener tweeted to say the discussion was moot because God doesn't exist. This prompted another listener to tweet that, contrary to the previous tweet, God does exist. Unfortunately I had to nip out to the shops so I never found out who was right.

Anyway, enough from me. I've – genuinely – just asked my Twitter followers whether they like tweets being read out on the news. Let's take a look at some of the comments:

Jo dB says it makes me furious
Charley says waste of time that could be spent on actual news

Kate tweets It is a nutters' charter.
And Alasdair has got in touch to say
A fatuous replacement for proper journalism

How's that for balance? I'm afraid it's hard to find any in favour, though I haven't yet heard from Gary in Woking.

So, please keep doing what you do brilliantly: telling extraordinary stories, speaking truth to power, and giving a voice to people who genuinely need it. But enough of the tweets already. Don't forget that reading out viewers' tweets even managed to dumb down *Big Brother*. And you're supposed to be The News.

Your faithful servant,

Richard from *Pointless* (you know, with the glasses?)

POINTLESS FACT

The first ever tweet was sent by Twitter founder Jack Dorsey on March 21st 2006. It read 'Just setting up my twttr.'

The most retweeted tweet of all time is reportedly Justin Bieber's 'I'M SEXY AND I KNOW IT.' Good old Twitter.

31
SUPPORT BANDS AT GIGS

The days when support bands had a proper function are now so long ago that I don't think anyone alive can remember what it was. It used to be the same at cinemas: you'd show up promptly for your film (usually having eaten a scalding hot pasty in a mouth-searing thirty seconds or having run all the way because YOU HAD TO BE THERE ON TIME) only to sit through a twenty-minute B-film of John Betjeman reading about Miss Joan Hunter Dunn.

It's not hard to see why this was phased out. But, as with the B-side on an old 45 r.p.m. single, the music industry clearly can't resist finding a space to put something, even in the certain knowledge that it will never be listened to. They seem not to have noticed that times have moved on and we've changed in our habits. If we go to a restaurant, for example, we don't generally want to be force-fed weird experimental food for an hour before we sit down at our table. We've become choosier and we don't really like wasting things, least of all our time.

And yet the live gig experience remains unchanged.

Support bands shamble on an hour and a half before the main act and play mean songs that nobody knows on a stage that's mostly full of another band's equipment. It's not as if they're saving the main act any stage time and, anyway, presumably they have to be paid, transported, accommodated and looked after every night when they come off stage crying because nobody listens to them.

So, let us do away with pointless support bands. Gigs would be much quicker and cheaper without them and, best of all, everyone would know exactly what time they needed to pitch up.

30
BANK CARD SECURITY CODES

Ah, our new friend the three-digit security code on the back of bank cards. How ever did we live without you?

You are the most secret code of all. The CVC2. That's the Card Verification Code, the most fiendish unbreakable code in the history of cryptography. Created by super-computers so powerful they are currently being employed to work out the plot of *Inception* and the rules to Jasper Carrott's *Golden Balls*.

When the thieves and the fraudsters have unearthed our account number and expiry date, this security code keeps us safe. These cunning criminals can try to crack the code all day and all night, but they will never succeed. Unless they think of turning the card over and looking on the back.

Though, to be absolutely honest, they don't even need to go to *that* much trouble.

I've just ordered a pizza from Domino's and, without any thought, given my CVC2 code to a nice man called Lee. Now, for all I know, Lee might be the Mr Big of Chiswick credit-card fraud. Though he probably wouldn't be working in Domino's if he was. But maybe his brother is the Mr Big of Chiswick credit-card fraud, or his mum the Mrs Big. Either way, he knows my code and although it is *illegal* for him to write it down or keep a record of it, sometimes criminals do illegal things. Just the few bad apples, ruining it for all the other law-abiding criminals.

So what *is* the point of a security code that is clearly visible to anyone who has nicked our card, and easily available to any Tom, Dick or Lee who simply asks for it?

Were we always so lax with our security? This extract from 1955 spy thriller *The Last Three Numbers on the Back* would suggest not . . .

As the gun-grey skies above Leipzig pressed down upon him, Agent Hunt coolly considered his two options. To the east, the advancing East German staff car. To the west, the lip of the ravine, the Graz River roaring 100 feet below.

The three numbers pounded in his head '496'. These numbers had to be protected at all costs. The Stasi – even now he could hear their hunters' cries over the roar of the Graz – would torture him; this much he knew. But could he withstand the torture? That was the question for which Hunt had no answer. His bravado said that he would, but Hunt knew that the CVC2 code was too important to be risked on one damn fool's assessment of himself.

The engine noise drew closer, led now by the hungry barking of the dogs. Hunt opened the locket he kept in his breast pocket. He prised out the photograph of Helen and the children and scrawled his final words on the back: 'I WILL LOVE YOU ALWAYS – PAPA'. Hunt prayed the locket would survive his fall; though knew in his heart it would not.

He saw the staff car now. Goetze – he might have known – sitting impassively in the back, that damned cigar clamped between his thin lips. Dreaming, no doubt, of the riches that awaited him in Berlin and Moscow when he brought them back Hunt's CVC2 number.

Not today, General Goetze, thought Hunt. He stood, the dogs just seconds from him now, and saluted the General. He had time to register the cigar falling from

Goetze's lips before he turned, and ran headlong into the abyss; taking his CVC2 number down, down and down into the icy Graz.

So, I think CVC2 codes are pointless. We might as well have an additional security number painted on the front of our house, or tattooed on our foreheads.

I must end this here as Lee has just turned up to deliver my pizza. In an E-class Mercedes.

29

TWIX

I love chocolate, I love sweets, I love crisps. If anyone wants to set up a restaurant where you could have a bar of Dairy Milk as a starter, a packet of Salt & Vinegar McCoys as a main and a packet of Sour Skittles for pudding, I will gladly invest. That place would *rake it in*. You wouldn't even need a ktichen. Remember the golden rules though, 'red wine with Monster Munch.' 'White wine with a Crunchie.' Anyway, I digress.*

I recently organised a 'World Cup of Chocolate' on Twitter, where we decided, once and for all, what Britain's greatest chocolate snack was. And, before you ask, yes I do occasionally have too much time on my hands.

....

* Seriously though, who's in? Whoever runs Nandos, call me.

Chocolate bars and sweets were drawn into groups and we all voted on our favourites. After a series of knockout games we were left with a World Cup of Chocolate Final between Twirl and Maltesers. The closely fought match went to extra time and a penalty shoot-out (or, as a couple of my Twitter followers suggested, 'extra Dime and a peanutty shoot-out') before Twirl was declared the winner.

So Twirl is the greatest chocolate but what's the worst? I decided to repeat the experiment to find the nation's most pointless chocolate bar, the one that simply hasn't earned its place on the newsagent's shelves.

The definitive results are in the pie-chart on the next page. And they confirm what I've always suspected. Enjoy!*

---

* Or, rather, 'don't enjoy', buy a Twirl instead.

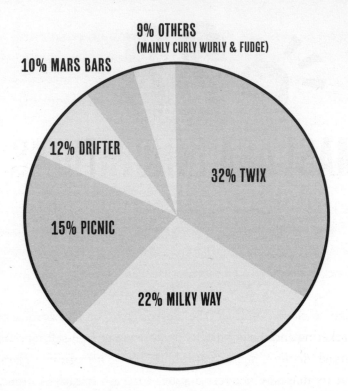

9% OTHERS
(MAINLY CURLY WURLY & FUDGE)

10% MARS BARS

12% DRIFTER

32% TWIX

15% PICNIC

22% MILKY WAY

And thus we scientifically prove the identity of the most pointless chocolate bar in Britain. The public have stuck both fingers up to Twix, mainly due to its paltry chocolate to biscuit rating. Come on Twix, take a look at the Chunky Kit Kat and mend your ways. I don't want you winning this poll again next year.

POINTLESS QUIZ QUESTION

We're agreed that the Twix is largely unacceptable, but what special achievement can Twix boast, that Snickers and Starburst can't?

28
MASCARA INNOVATIONS

Take a closer look at the dark, dark world of mascara marketing and the possibility of launching a best-selling range named '*Really*?!' seems entirely feasible. One product claims that its mascara 'delivers a 406% increase in lash volume'.

Anyway, for fun, I have listed below some mascara brands. One of them is made up: see if you can spot which one.

TARTE GIFTED AMAZONIAN CLAY SMART MASCARA

COVER GIRL NATURE LUXE MOUSSE MASCARA

BATON NOIR CRYPROOF NASA-TEC LASH TREACLE

BUXOM AMPLIFIED LASH MASCARA

27
CHRISTMAS NUMBER ONE SINGLES

Do you remember entry 81 in the 100 Most Pointless Things in the World? The one with the clues to the fifty US states? The one you either flipped over immediately, or that still has you screaming, 'Uncle Dean, you idiot! How could that possibly be *Wisconsin*?'

Well, here's a gentler one from my Geeky Wordplay Twitter Christmas Quiz. Below are ten cryptic clues to Christmas number-one singles (there have been about sixty of them, so, again, I'd print out a list). I say it's *gentler*, but it's still *fiercely* geeky, so feel free to turn the page and forget this ever happened.

1. Dr Owl
2. 'Mind the gap!'
3. Are thongs twisted?
4. 'I've watched it back, and it's taken a deflection off the defender, but it was going in anyway so I'm claiming it'
5. Cheryl Cole is
6. Consideration of family sleepiness
7. Lonely sheep
8. When do you go to the Early Learning Centre?
9. Hydrophobia means disaster
10. Mrs Isla Yingstrom

Of course, as I'm writing this I have no idea what *this* year's Christmas number-one single will be. It's vanishingly unlikely, but still technically possible, that I myself might have recorded and released a single that is currently atop the charts. In which case:

(a) I wonder how *that* happened?

and

(b) Thank you for buying my single.

26
WOODEN TOYS

Ask any parent: having children is, broadly speaking, a mistake. You go from a life filled with variety, fun and freedom to one in which you are essentially placed under house arrest and everything you own smells mildly of urine.

Luckily the boffins at toy companies, probably themselves driven by desperation to rediscover the life they once had before Junior arrived, invented electronic toys.

Now exhausted mums and dads can grab forty winks while their bundles of joy happily press multi-coloured flashing buttons. You can make yourself a daiquiri while the little one chats with BUNNI, a talking plush rabbit designed to encourage social skills and cognitive development. Toddlers taught to walk by interactive musical super trolleys are so deeply enthralled that, if you're really, really quick, you can make it to the off-licence and back before they even know you've gone.

Small and portable, these plastic marvels even suppress the 'are we there yet?' tendencies kids otherwise display on long car journeys. True, your little precious pressing the same button repeatedly does mean that by the seventieth rendition of 'Here We Go Looby Loo' you feel ready to turn calmly into oncoming traffic, but at least BUNNI's huggably soft animatronics will cushion any impact.

The problem is that well-meaning friends and relatives will always insist on buying your child *wooden toys*.

These wooden toys have now sprung up everywhere, as we pretend that we can wind the clock back to some idyllic Victorian age of childish imagination and wonder.

Your friends and relatives are trying to say, 'Childhood is that most magical of times, an age of purity and beauty, where wide-eyed children explore their own interior universe and appreciate the elegant beauty found in the simplest things.'

But never forget they are buying these things for *your* child: they are buying their own kid a piece of moulded Taiwanese plastic that makes farmyard noises and shuts them up when *EastEnders* is on.

And in practice, of course, lovely though they are as a present, your child will only play with wooden toys when there is absolutely *nothing else* in the room whatsoever, including pets, mud, insects, power tools, junk mail, carpets, electrical sockets or, indeed, the boxes the pointless things came in.

25
UNNECESSARY BLOODY MARY INGREDIENTS

Can we be clear on one point? The ingredients for a Bloody Mary are:

VODKA

TOMATO JUICE

There! That's it. That's a Bloody Mary. You mix those two together, then hand it over. Of course, the drinker is then free to add Worcestershire sauce and Tabasco, *if that's what they want*, but your job as the creator, the mixologist if you must, is a relatively simple one.

The trouble is, the Bloody Mary is the favoured drink of the hung-over, and the hung-over are the worst people in the world at making their ruddy minds up. From the minute they get up with a whamming headache they're led through a whole crystal maze of urgent cravings, none of which will actually make them feel any better. But the Bloody Mary is their bitch and they will make it DANCE for them. And there begins the hyper-evolution of a much-loved classic as it starts to acquire more and more unnecessary embellishment.

First came freshly squeezed lemon juice, black pepper and celery salt, doubtless brought in to add edge, tang and fresh-ness where the tomato juice was possibly a little too flabby. But that didn't feel like enough of a mouthful so horseradish sauce was added.* But that lacked a certain oomph so a nip of fino sherry arrived, but that started to come over all alcoholic so more vegetable juices went in to broaden the palate (celery and carrot juice) and a tiny spill of beef consommé. Oooh, now that's starting to taste a little bit naughty, mngum mngum, but it still needs something. And that something is . . . tequila!**

So, now I say, let this madness stop. Stop before egg yolks, bone marrow and Rice Krispies have been dragooned into service. Enough! Soon this eminent pre-lunch crowd-pleaser

....

* Let's just think about that for a moment. Only someone still drunk from the night before could have come up with it. And, if we're honest, it's never been entirely satisfactory – it doesn't really mix in, just floats around like something in Jordan's hot tub.

** I have honestly seen this added to a Bloody Mary. That was when I knew it was time to step in.

will have been phased out altogether because it will take most of Sunday to make it.

POINTLESS ANAGRAMS

Richard has been on the phone again, telling me about the amazing feedback he's been getting for his anagrams. Although at the time I'm writing this the book hasn't actually come out, so I think he may be lying to me. Either way, just to keep him quiet, here are his 10 anagrams of popular cocktails. He apologises that he couldn't think of a good anagram for Bloody Mary.

1. Co-pilot Osman!
2. Rank vomit aid
3. Molls tonic
4. Nostalgic deadline
5. Inhaled foods
6. Why kiss Euro?
7. Ailing spongers
8. Queasier insult
9. Backs urinals
10. Cheese 'n' hatbox

24

DRAMATIC PAUSES ON TV TALENT SHOWS AND REALITY SHOWS

There are all sorts of statistics about how much of our lives are taken up by mundane tasks. Did you know, for example, the following facts about the average human being?

> 1. We spend twenty-four years asleep
> (longer for cricket fans).

> 2. We spend more than thirteen months
> on the toilet.

> 3. We spend 169 hours queueing.*

But scientists have failed to investigate one modern activity, which is taking up more and more of our time. And that

....

* Great time-saving tip: try to get some sleep while queueing for the toilet.

activity is the hugely over-dramatic pauses before results are revealed on talent shows and reality shows.

You know the score. Our host – Dermot O'Leary, Tess Daly, Brian Thingy, that guy who took over from Davina on *Big Brother* – holds aloft an envelope. The expectant crowd hushes. The bright lights dim, leaving just a spotlight on Dermot, Tess or Brian (or is it Barry?). We hear the amplified sound of heartbeats. We are excited: this is it. We have been voting all evening and the results have been counted and verified. We are about to find out who's staying and who's going.

We gaze at Dermot and his *X Factor* envelope. Who's leaving? Maria, the recently bereaved office manager from Oswestry, or Greg, that guy in the hat you liked at the auditions but who, now you come to think of it, reminds you a bit of that weird guy who went out with your friend Sarah?

We gaze at Tess and her 'Strictly Come Dancing' envelope. Who's leaving? Martin, the former world-ranked number-eight snooker player, or Emma-Kate, who, in the absence of more information, you're assuming was once in *Hollyoaks*?

We gaze at Brian (Ryan? No, hold on – Steve?) and his 'Big Brother' envelope. Who's leaving? Christobel, the transgender unicycling hair-stylist, or Maxine, the other transgender unicycling hair-stylist?

'And the person leaving us tonight is . . .'

And you know EXACTLY what happens next.

Heartbeats grow louder, the camera pans to each contestant in turn, biting their lip in nervous frustration, staring at the floor to contain the cauldron of emotions within. The heartbeats continue, the camera pans across again. Isolated voices in the crowd start shouting out, 'Maria!' or 'Emma-Kate!' or 'Hat guy!' The heartbeats continue, the camera goes tight on the faces of the contestants, you nip out to make a cup of tea, the ice-caps continue their inexorable, slow decline, West Brom are relegated, then promoted again, your daughter takes her GCSEs . . .

How LONG is this pause? Well, in the interests of science, I have watched, and timed, the pause between 'the tease' and 'the reveal' of every single reality and talent show of the last ten years. From *Pop Idol* to *Popstars – The Rivals* to *X Factor*. From *Big Brother* to *Celebrity Masterchef* to *Strictly Come Dancing*. From *The Bachelor* to *Dancing On Ice* to Channel 5's *Celebrity Colonic Irrigation*. And the results are terrifying.

The average pause between 'tease' and reveal' has risen from just 2.9 seconds in the 1970s (*Opportunity Knocks, Tony Hart's Gallery*, etc.) to a mammoth 23.8 seconds today. I have calculated that every man, woman and child in Britain now spends two years and seven months of their lives watching the pauses before results are revealed.

And it's getting longer and longer and longer. We must, as a nation, as a people, rise up and demand a maximum interval between 'the tease' and 'the reveal' of 3.6 seconds (I have worked this out using science, maths, and the stopwatch function on my phone). This would give each and every British person an extra 114 hours and 17 minutes of free time per year, increasing productivity and consumer confidence, and adding an extra £6.4 billion to Treasury coffers.* It's a no-brainer – these increasingly long pauses are pointless.

....

* As a final note, this figure would be boosted still further by outlawing quiz shows from giving answers 'after the break'. And telling Noel just to hurry it up and open the boxes himself.

23 HOME GYMS

According to recent statistics, 17 per cent of the UK adult population has a gym membership. This is some 8.7 million people. Of this 8.7 million, precisely twenty-eight people actually go.

Twenty-nine, if you include that guy Greg who likes to steal towels.

The rest of us, an army of well-intentioned, flabby humans, watch helplessly as £39.99 is debited from our bank account on a monthly basis. We have been exactly three times (2 January, 3 January, 29 January) and the only machine we used was the one we bought a KitKat and a packet of Frazzles from.

It is now, when we are at our most vulnerable, that the info-mercials strike.

> *'Hey, you! Are you needlessly forking out £39.99 every single month for a dusty old gym that's so darn far away you don't even go there any more?'*

Well, yes. Yes, I am, thinks the viewer, who was just about to switch the TV off and go to bed for another sleepless night calculating how much they have paid so far per biceps curl and how they could do the same for free with a big pot of paint.

> *'Want an exercise routine that's quick and easy? That gets guaranteed results? One that fits into your busy lifestyle without breaking the bank?'*

I want all those things! thinks the viewer, who now sits back down on the sofa excitedly, turns up the volume and opens a bag of crisps.

> *'Well, get ready! Introducing . . . the Flababulator 9000 GTX Pro! In just twenty easy minutes per day, you can give yourself the body you've always dreamed of!'*

The viewer now watches people just like themselves, strug-gling in black-and-white to fit exercise into their hectic schedule, to use complicated and expensive gym equipment and, in many cases, to perform even the most basic human functions. *BUT THEN!* All their problems are solved as they burst into full colour once they get their eager hands on the Flababulator's fabulously sleek aircraft-grade aluminium chassis.

The viewer is now helpless to resist, particularly when they discover that if they order in the next fifteen minutes they'll get a second one for free.

So it is that the garages and attics of the UK now groan with pointless home gym equipment. Items that have raised a sweat just once, when your dad spent four hours trying to bolt together his MaxPro UltraThigh GluteBlaster 4000, before furiously dumping it behind the MaxPro LawnStrim WeedMaster 4000 in the downstairs cupboard.

22
PILOTS' BRIEFINGS

So, you've finally made it onto your flight. Quite tipsy from necking that half-bottle of white (by the time your drink finally arrived at the seafood bar they'd already been saying, 'Last call for Passenger Armstrong,' for five minutes). And if that wasn't bad enough, the Duty Free bag handles only went and broke (*op.cit.*) on the long walk to gate B127. So you've arrived on the plane cradling bottles of spirits and sun-cream with your boarding pass wedged between your teeth and a carton of Silk Cut under your chin.

But you're there now, your baggage is stowed and the tuts of your fellow passengers have long subsided. It's now time for the pilot's announcement.

These vary so little from flight to flight that I'm tempted to suggest they might be pre-recorded. A man (ALWAYS a man), in a deep voice with reassuring Classic FM inflections, introduces himself and his crew. He then proceeds to share with the full manifest a stream of technical data that is of limited interest to other pilots but is just words and clicks to the rest of us. (It's like when the in-cabin sat-navs show a TINY scale map of the world with just the key conurbations marked: 'Oslo', 'Addis Ababa', 'Haywards Heath'.)

The point of these little talks is their reassurance. For deep-seated paternalistic reasons, airlines want us to know that we have a man in charge. Not just a man but a man of such intense suavity that he can sound all calm, measured and 'Our Tune' even when he's in charge of a ruddy great aeroplane. Of course, none of this is relevant. All we actually need to know is this:

'This is your captain. I am sober. We are flying to Madrid. Shortly after take-off I shall be pressing a button that will fly us all the way there and land us, allowing me to finish this word-search puzzle then have a little kip. In charge of cabin service is Angela and, yes, I shall be giving her the full Outward and Return on our overnight at the Sheraton.'

21
THOSE LONG WORDS THAT DOCTORS USE

Here are fifteen questions about those impressive-sounding names that doctors trot out for one of the following reasons:

(a) If they tell you you've got something that you can't *spell*, you won't be able to go straight home, Google it, and prove them wrong.

(b) They know your boss will be more likely to let you have a day off due to diaphragmic myoclonus, rather than hiccups.

POINTLESS QUIZ

Can you identify the common ailments below from their more impressive-sounding medical names?

1. Daltonism
2. Hypertension
3. Varicella
4. Tinea pedis
5. Myocardial infarction
6. Myopia
7. Infectious mononucleosis
8. Rubella
9. Allergic rhinitis
10. Otaglia
11. Halitosis
12. Lateral epicondylitis
13. Dentalgia
14. Tetanus
15. Epistaxis (interestingly, also the name of my local cab company)

If you don't complete the quiz, may I advise you never to phone work saying you're having a day off due to either a case of halitosis or 'a touch of myocardial infarction'?

20
BABY ON BOARD STICKERS

The first 'Baby On Board' signs were yellow triangles. The intention was probably to warn other drivers to be patient in case of baby-related erratic driving. I sort of get that. Ish. I mean, it's a halfway sensible thing to let the guy behind know that you might have to stop at a moment's notice to wipe up sick.

But people got the wrong idea. And then they kept getting wrong ideas. First they thought it was an opportunity to say, 'Hey – we've got kids,' which is not a fact other road-users need to know. And then they started being sold signs that let people know what *kind* of kids they had ('Little Princess On Board', etc.), information that leaves the average road-user perplexed and troubled.

I'm happy with a 'Hazchem' sticker. I see it as an official hallmark of civic responsibility. When I start to see 'I'm a zany hydrobromic-acid driver' stuck on the back of a van, I'll begin to think it's time to put a call in to the authorities.

So let's have no more of this Baby On Board nonsense unless you're prepared to put up the triangle ONLY on those occasions when you genuinely have an in-car infant or, in the case of the above example, ONLY when you have an actual daughter of a royal house strapped into the back. These things have to be tightly governed.

19
ONLINE REVIEWS

The invention of the Internet has done some wonderful things. It has the capacity to educate (pandas can sneeze!), inform ('So *that's* what a Justin Bieber is') and surprise (I don't wish to be smug, but I *have* just won the Nigerian lottery).

But perhaps most importantly, the Internet can tell you what a disgruntled man from Truro thought about his cordless power drill.

Yes, online reviews.

The anonymity of the Internet means that everyone now has a voice and many use this voice to pour all of their joy, confusion and valuable time into reviewing everything under the sun for our reading pleasure.

Garden sheds, restaurants, industrial wood sealant, holidays, hats for dogs, Christmas books – think of literally anything and someone will be reviewing it online. Just take ten seconds to consider the sort of person who spends some of their actual time on this earth writing reviews of *plain white paper* on Amazon. Sixty-seven at the time of writing. Treat yourself to a quick read.

But where online reviews really come into their own is with hotels. There are millions upon millions upon millions of them. When booking a hotel it's easy to get caught in a hopeless spiral of reading these reviews and before you know it you're suddenly basing a genuine financial decision on the fact a Danish couple once had a below par breakfast and a creepy bellboy.

And you can also never be sure that, especially with hotels, these reviews aren't simply made up by the competition and perhaps the hotel isn't actually haunted and the reception staff didn't cast a spell on the guest's entire family when they asked for an extra pillow.

In short, online reviews are only useful to any of us who need advice when buying our next ironing-board cover. Which is none of us.

Did you find this article helpful? We welcome your opinion. Let us know exactly what you think by walking down to your local canal and shouting it into an abandoned skip.

18
MIME

Some 200,000 years ago, man began evolving separately from monkeys. Or not separately, in the case of the drunk Mancunian minicab driver I had last night.

Scientists believe this historic schism was due to the emergence of a new gene, which was nattily christened 'Forkhead box protein P2', widely referred to as FOXP2.

FOXP2 is also known as the 'God' gene, the 'Human' gene and most commonly the 'Speech' gene.

FOXP2 is, it seems, the reason we alone on the planet can talk.*

....

* Other than badgers. It is their secret. Ironically they don't like to talk about it.

I like to imagine early man just at the point where the FOXP2 gene has advanced enough to grant him a new power: the ability to form words. This is the very dawn of speech. I imagine him, much as toddlers do today, pointing at a rock and trying to make a sound that identifies it.

'RO-K!'

Then a second man repeats this sound . . .

'RO-K!'

. . . and the word is born. A species-defining moment. The stone-age equivalent of inventing salt and vinegar crisps (see 83: Ready-salted Crisps).

Then in the background, a third, silent, man, uninterested in these meteoric developments, paints his face white and pretends to be trapped in a glass box. He is history's first ever mime artist. The first two men watch him for a moment before moving calmly towards him and clubbing him repeatedly with the blunt objects they just named. And no one is able to say a few words at his funeral because they still only have one.

Mimes either don't have FOXP2, or they don't want it. They

are not interested in the one thing that sets our species apart from all others.**

Mimes, it seems, want to devolve. If you ask a mime where the bus station is, he won't say, 'End of the road on the left, mate.' Instead, he will perform an elaborate three-minute hokey-cokey that involves moonwalking, rope-climbing and his nearly being carried away on the wind by an invisible umbrella whilst you watch, all the while quietly missing your bus.

Get this, mime artists: nobody has been carried off by an umbrella since Mary Poppins, who herself may have been fictional (my mum won't tell me). And other than tourists confused by British phone-box doors, no one ever got trapped in a glass box except David Blaine.

Frankly, if the man who invented mime hadn't already been killed by two rock-wielding cavemen, I would shoot him.

With a silencer, of course.

....

** Again, except badgers. Spend a day in a hedge. Eventually you will hear them discussing stoats or wind farms.

17 MILK LABELLING

I don't trust it. It says 'fresh'. If I keep the milk carton out of the fridge for seven weeks, will that word 'fresh' disappear? Of course it won't.

Slippery milk types, don't think we haven't rumbled your game.

PHONE BOXES

Do I really need to explain this one? Even homeless people have mobile phones, these days.

It may be bad news for vandals, Superman and fans of Estonian massage services, but phone boxes are not long for this world. They join a list of once vital inventions rendered pointless by the wireless, digital age. See also . . .

FAX MACHINES

RECORD SHOPS

FILOFAXES

YELLOW PAGES

CHRIS DE BURGH

FLOPPY DISKS

ENCYCLOPEDIA SALESMEN

PAPER MAPS

CHEMISTS WHO DEVELOP PHOTOGRAPHS

NEWSPAPER CLASSIFIEDS

DIAL-UP MODEMS

CATALOGUES

PORNOGRAPHY FOUND IN HEDGES

PENS

ACTUAL FRIENDS

Sir Giles Gilbert Scott, who designed Battersea Power Station, also designed Britain's famous red telephone boxes. He was chosen as the winner of a 1924 architectural competition to find the perfect design for the new booths. That's right: those iconic red phone boxes were designed by a competition winner.* So we'll never know if his design was chosen for its timeless aesthetic, or because the guy who came second designed the boxes horizontally, forcing the occupant to make calls lying down. Or forgot to include a door. Or included interior spikes, like an iron maiden. Or made it out of fabric.

....

* Perhaps it was *Pip Idol*?

Or made it at $^3/_8$ scale, so that you had to persuade passing children to make your calls for you.

As the number of public payphones has dwindled over the last decade, it is interesting to note that, briefly, they were given hope when it was thought they could be used as public places to connect to the Internet – a forerunner to an Internet 'hot spot'. However, with the development of wireless technology, this idea, too, became obsolete, as clearly people would prefer to use their laptops while sipping coffee at a table rather than standing up in the street.

If you come across one of the few remaining red telephone boxes, do what I do. Convince your children that they are actually Britain's Tiniest Museum, a perfect re-creation of the inconvenience, the pungent odours and the remorseless vandalism of 1970s Britain.

POINTLESS QUIZ QUESTION

What is the only building in Washington D.C. to have a red telephone box outside?

15
TERRIBLE MOVIE TAGLINES

Here are twelve *great* movie tag-lines for you. Can you, or perhaps your drunk Uncle Ken, name the films that they're from? The answers, and the points they all scored, are at the back of the book.

But before you take the quiz, I just have to give you the five most pointless movie tag-lines in history.

5. *Crank* – 'He Was Dead . . . But He Got Better' – Even for a Jason Statham film this doesn't make sense.

4. *The Flesh Eaters* – 'Those of You Who Will Not Be STERILISED With FEAR Are Those Among You Who Are Already DEAD.'
   'Sterilised with fear' you say? Great date movie.

3. *Rocky 2* – 'Rocky Shows He's a Champ, and Wins!'
   Possible plot spoiler?
2. *Yogi Bear* – 'Great Things Come In Bears'.
   Words fail me.
1. *The Day of the Dolphin* – 'Unwittingly He Trained a
   Dolphin to Kill the President of the United States!'
   Admittedly I do now actually want to watch this.

I had to disqualify *Clash of the Titans* – 'Titans Will Clash'
because a little bit of me thought it might actually be the
best movie tag-line of all time.

We have already decided on the tag-line for 'Pointless – The
Movie' (starring Kevin Spacey as Xander and Denzel
Washington as me).

POINTLESS!

'IT WAS A COUNTRY. . . BUT IT WASN'T A SOVEREIGN STATE THAT WAS A MEMBER OF THE UN IN ITS OWN RIGHT!'

Good luck with the twelve questions below, a few obvious
ones, but also two pointless answers in there. Time to hide
the mint Baileys and show Uncle Ken who's boss.

POINTLESS QUIZ

The terrible taglines are:

1. 'Choose Life'
2. 'Enter the World'
3. 'Who Ya Gonna Call?'
4. 'I See Dead People'
5. 'Be Afraid, Be Very Afraid'
6. 'His Scars Run Deep'
7. 'The Mission Is a Man'
8. 'Don't Go in the Water'
9. 'On the Air, Unaware'
10. 'A Romantic Comedy, with Zombies'
11. 'Houston, We Have a Problem'
12. 'Collide with Destiny'

14 BEING FOURTEEN

It is a harsh truth, but true, that fourteen years old is the most pointless age of all. If you need proof, then take a look at this definitive analysis.

AGE	DIET	PASTIMES	GOALS
0-1	Milk	Vomiting	Look at colourful things
1-3	Rusks	Tantrums	Speech
4-8	Frubes	Yelling	Catch all the Pokemon
9-11	Happy Meals	Hamsters	Keep hamster alive
12-13	Nandos (extra mild)	Tutting	Avoid standing out in any way whatsoever

14	Unknown	Nothing	Reach age 15
15-16	Nandos (extra hot)	Texting	Everything immediately

Further explanation ought not to be necessary. Simply put, before the age of fourteen there's so much to experience and discover: starting to walk, to talk, learning to share, starting school, having a strange crush on Princess Peach from the Mario games, exploring your identity and becoming a teenager . . . Then, from the age of fifteen, so much more! Beginning exams, mopeds, learning to drive, university, love, alcohol, disappointing your parents and beyond.

But at fourteen? Nothing. Being fourteen is rubbish.

Now, maybe you have a fourteen-year-old child and you don't agree. But come on. Be really honest with yourself. Your fourteen-year-old is too old to be cute but too young to be profitable. Perhaps they were your favourite once; you know, at one of the good ages. And maybe they will be again, when they make you proud at a piano recital or if they get parole. But not for at least twelve months.

Maybe you're a fourteen-year-old yourself. It's possible. Perhaps this is an e-book.

If so, feel free to prove me wrong. Or, failing that, at least pull your pants up.

A COUPLE OF POINTLESS FACTS ABOUT BEING FOURTEEN

Richard II was fourteen when he put down the Peasants' Revolt.

Shakespeare's Juliet did not live to be fourteen. Which is a shame as fourteen is the minimum age you must be to drive a 50cc motorbike in Italy.

13

POEMS THAT ARE JUST THINGS WRITTEN DOWN THAT DON'T RHYME

Step
Into a railway station and at once
You are the tiniest moving
Part of a nation-sized
Clockwork device.
A device you are childishly powerless to affect.

Timetables, tracks, signals, whistles
Won't change for you.
Trains don't stop for humans.
You miss your train, it's gone, forget about it.
Get onto the next one.
Get tied to the tracks by bandits, forget about it.
Move on.

That's the thing about trains: they just don't stop.

No concern of yours are the
Tracks beneath you;
The farmsteads and station signs whistling past. No,
Just sit back and dream of that platform at
Waverley: you'll be
On it in precisely
Two and a half hours.

Except . . .

Arses,
It's Sunday.

So the train stops
Brusquely at a station
Whose name is just
Letters chivvied onto a board.
Its platform can't even handle a real train
But here, it seems,
You are to pick up your
Luggage, get out,
And onto
A bus.

It's Sunday.

Up steep hilly roads
You chug, on to
Another station you've never so much as heard
  whispered before,
Smashing through high-hanging boughs of beeches,
Through local rainstorms
That are no business of yours,
Into cagey mining towns with strange traffic systems
And pedestrian crossings
Tweaked to give
The motionless time to reach the other side.
And now in a suburb the engine is panting
As twilight
Spools across children's gardens.

When you go off the rails
It happens at speed
If they told you, you'd know
To bring something to read.

12
SHOUTING AT FOOTBALL ON THE TV

Football has its fair share of pointless peccadilloes: diving, Robbie Savage, managers wearing shorts, and big match build-ups so bombastic they make it look like Stoke City v. Wigan Athletic will be played with lightsabers on the moon.

But put that to one side for now because we're tackling that oddly cathartic yet utterly pointless pursuit of screaming abuse from a huge distance at a pampered millionaire after he slightly misplaces a pass.

Yes, shouting at football on the TV.

Who among us hasn't experienced the utterly pointless thrill of screaming at Frank Lampard, Howard Webb, or that new

Estonian defender that Hibs have just bought, in a mixture of tension, anger, poorly concealed homoerotic yearning and barefaced xenophobia?

You wouldn't go to the ballet and verbally abuse a dancer over her *plié* or pirouette, would you? Actually, bad example, you wouldn't go to the ballet at all. But still, why do it with footballers?

Here's something simple to remember:

> Cristiano Ronaldo *can't hear you.* If he could hear you, he *wouldn't understand what you were saying.* And if he understood what you were saying, he *wouldn't give a toss.*

Instead of screaming aloud at the TV during the match, it would *actually* be less pointless to drive to your nearest airport, spend £500 on the next flight to Lithuania, arrive, check into a hotel, have a wash and a shave, get some currency out, catch a taxi to the national stadium, break in and then spend half an hour berating the actual spot on the pitch where Stewart Downing over-hit a cross eight hours earlier.

If nothing else, shouting at the TV is simply disrespectful to the thousands of fans who have bravely travelled to the ground to shout their profanities at the players in person.

But in case you're still confused, here's a rule of thumb: just do everything you can to avoid that moment where you realise you're a grown adult, wearing cracked face paint, standing on your own in the living room, half cut, sweating through your replica shirt, shouting at a Dutch referee while your four-year-old daughter asks your wife what's wrong with Daddy. Not that I've ever done that.

TIMES WHEN IT'S OK TO SCREAM AT FOOTBALL ON THE TV:

YOU'VE JUST LOST THE WORLD CUP FINAL ON PENALTIES

YOUR TV IS SCREAM-OPERATED

YOU JUST DROPPED THE REMOTE ON YOUR FOOT

YOU'VE JUST SPOTTED THAT JOHN TERRY HAS A TATTOO OF YOUR WIFE'S NAME ON HIS ARM

ANY CLOSE-UP OF WAYNE ROONEY

11

CHARITY STROLLS

Now this is a tricky one – obviously – because these are splendid charitable affairs that raise millions of pounds for vital causes that affect us all. It's just . . . Actually, you know what? It's fine.

No. It's fine. Turn the page.

It's just . . .

Well . . .

When did this thing for not-actually-that-taxing charity-events start? A five-kilometre walk round a park? Hang on. I'm not quibbling about the fundraising – that's utterly brilliant – it's just that that is *literally* a walk in the park. What happened to cycling to Paris? What happened to doing twenty-eight marathons in twenty-eight days?

What I suppose I'm saying is that I would like to see a bead of sweat, perhaps, in exchange for my generous backing. That's all. And if no one says anything, I can see where this will end up. And I for one will have no part in sponsoring 'Watching All of *Homeland* in One Sitting'.

10

98% OF EVERYTHING IN AN INSTRUCTION MANUAL

I'm looking at the instruction manual for my boiler. My boiler is important to me because if it goes wrong I get very cold and I have to go to my local swimming-pool to use the shower.

The good news is that the manufacturers of my boiler have given me an instruction manual in case anything *does* go wrong. The bad news is that this instruction manual is *forty pages long*.

It covers everything from the fundamental differences between sealed heating systems and open-vented heating systems, the finer points of 'the ventilation of balanced flue (BF) and room sealed fanned flue (RSF) appliances', and the relative positioning of the gas to water heat exchanger and the water to water heat exchanger.

I don't *need* all this. I have now gone through the entire instruction manual and edited it down to information I actually need. The instruction manual now reads like this:

THANK YOU FOR PURCHASING THIS BOILER!

THE TEMPERATURE DIAL NEXT TO THE PICTURE OF THE RADIATOR CONTROLS HOW HOT YOUR RADIATORS ARE.

THE TEMPERATURE DIAL NEXT TO THE PICTURE OF THE TAP CONTROLS HOW HOT YOUR WATER IS.

IF THE LIGHT ABOVE EITHER OF THESE TEMPERATURE DIALS STARTS FLASHING RED, PRESS THE RESET BUTTON FOR FIVE SECONDS. THEN IT WILL START WORKING AGAIN.

Job done. That is actually so short that they could print it on the front of the boiler.

All instruction manuals include an insane amount of detail (as do video-game instructions – I just want to know that it's X to pass and Y to shoot). There are health and safety instructions, installation procedures and even the address that people in Germany should contact about their extended warranties (see also 93: Extended Warranties). It's pointless.

Here's the instruction manual for my oven (*108* pages) edited down to what I actually need.

THE GRILL IS THE FIRST BUTTON ON THE LEFT, AND THE OVEN IS THE SECOND BUTTON.

WHEN YOU'RE USING THE OVEN, PRESS THE SECOND BUTTON ON THE RIGHT FOR OPTIMUM COOKING.

YOU SEE THAT TEMPERATURE DIAL? THAT SETS THE TEMPERATURE.

THE ONLY COMPLICATED THING YOU MIGHT NEED TO DO IS TO CHANGE THE TIME WHEN THE CLOCKS GO FORWARD OR BACK. DON'T BOTHER: YOU'LL ONLY HAVE TO DO IT AGAIN IN SIX MONTHS.

THANK YOU FOR PURCHASING THIS OVEN!

My hair-drier instruction manual (18 pages) edited down:

PLUG IT IN.

PUT IT ON MEDIUM AND PRESS 'ON'.

And, finally, my mobile-phone instruction manual (60 pages):

ASK JOHN AT WORK TO SHOW YOU.

So, there you have it: instruction manuals are an extraordinary waste of time and trees, which simply serve to hide the tiny amounts of information you genuinely need.

If you disagree, please write to:

Klaus Reinhardt
Punctloss Buch GmbH
741 Koeningsstrasse
Düsseldorf 47538
Deutschland

AMERICAN WORDS
FOR ENGLISH FOOD

What's that you say? Another quiz? Well, OK, seeing as you asked so nicely.

Going to an American restaurant can be daunting for a number of reasons:

**THE WAITRESS SEEMS GENUINELY PLEASED
TO SEE YOU**

YOU ARE THE THINNEST PERSON THERE

THAT GUY IN THE CORNER HAS A GUN

**YOU HAVE JUST BEEN GIVEN A STEAK THAT IS BIGGER
THAN YOUR HEAD**

THERE IS NO VINEGAR FOR YOUR CHIPS

YOU KNOW THAT AT SOME POINT YOU'RE GOING TO HAVE TO ASK FOR 'THE CHECK' INSTEAD OF 'THE BILL', WHICH IS ALREADY MAKING YOU FEEL SELF-CONSCIOUS

But added to these complications we have the fact that Americans have different words for food. Below are fifteen British foodstuffs: can you decipher the American name for each one? The winner gets a free popsicle.

 POINTLESS QUIZ

Do you know the American word for these foods?

1. Aubergine
2. Candyfloss
3. Porridge
4. Buck's fizz
5. Jam
6. Cornflour
7. Crisps
8. Rocket
9. Jelly
10. Courgette
11. Icing
12. Coriander
13. Biscuit
14. Scone
15. Chips

TELLING PEOPLE THAT THEY ARE TALL

I am very tall. It is the first thing you would notice about me. I am six foot seven inches, unless I'm trying to get an upgrade on a plane, in which case I'm six foot eight.

Over the years, believe me, it hasn't escaped my notice that I'm tall. I hit my head on things, I'm tutted at in cinemas, and I find it difficult to buy adequately lengthy trousers.

But even if these little reminders weren't there, I would still know that I'm tall, and this is why. I am told that I'm tall ten to fifteen times a day, every day, by total strangers.

Which means that, from the age of about seventeen, when I reached my full mighty height, I have been told that I'm tall roughly 87,600 times. (Is my maths right there? That seems like a *lot*.)

Mostly it's lovely. People are interested, amused or, more rarely, powerfully aroused by such height. After they have involuntarily blurted out, 'Goodness, aren't you tall?' you can have a nice chat and both leave smiling. This is the good thing about being told you're tall, and spreads happiness throughout the land. A friend of mine who is six foot five ('Titch', I call him) was once in a supermarket, when a very tiny grey-haired lady asked if he could get her a jar of pickles from the top shelf. He was glad to help, and as he handed them to her, she said, 'Thank you, love. Now, is there anything I can get you from down here?' What's not to love about that?

No, it's the *other way* of being told you're tall that's pointless. The daily stream of people who shout after you in the street, 'Oi, mate, you're tall!' before guffawing to their sidekicks. Occasionally people will even lean out of their van windows to let me know I'm tall. You have to admire that level of commitment sometimes.

I have given this phenomenon a bit of thought over the years, and I can only assume that the mindset of all these people is the following: you are wandering around minding your own business, when ahead of you, you spy a very tall man. A tall man who *maybe doesn't know* he's tall. Looking around quickly, it appears that no one else has noticed, so it's up to you, and you alone, to be the hero. So, what do you do? Clearly you need to let this person know that he's tall. That's your public duty. But how? A quiet word in the tall man's ear? No, no! That won't work: you're too short to reach his ear. Slip a note in his huge hand as he walks past? No, that won't work either: you don't know how to write.

There's only one thing for it. Look the giant straight in the eye and say, 'Oi, mate! You're tall.' Job done, no need for medals, just performing a public service.

To these people I would say, 'Honestly, your work is done. Rest, relax, kick back. No need to warn me about my tallness any more. Telling me I'm tall is as pointless as going up to a shop and shouting, "Oi, mate! You're a shop!" or going up to a mirror and shouting, "Oi, mate, you're a clueless, tiny-membered dunderhead!"'

To reiterate, though, if you see me in the street and inadvertently blurt out, 'Goodness, you're tall,' rather than 'Oi, mate, you're tall,' then I suspect you're probably one of the lovely ones.

And to all you lovely ones I give this quiz question, the answers to which are all people shorter than me.

POINTLESS QUIZ QUESTION

Who are the tallest people ever to

a) Become President of the USA?

b) Win an acting Oscar?

c) Sing on a UK number-one single?

KEEP CALM SPIN-OFFS

Sorry, but it's just irresistible – it's like something out of that *Dad's Army*. Absolutely marvellous. And completely genuine too. The original posters were designed by His Majesty's Stationery Office in the early 1940s but for use in the event of a German invasion. With no invasion being forthcoming, the whole lot was pulped apart from a few rogue ones that found their way into private possession. So, the public didn't actually see this design until a copy was found a few years ago in a second-hand bookshop in Northumberland. And the rest, as they say, is – ha ha ha ha, sorry. It's history.

As we all know, where baffling overnight success stories lead, dismaying cash-ins and a film starring Julie Walters surely follow. While the movie is still presumably in

KEEP GOING
TILL THE TRAFFIC LIGHTS
THEN IT'S ON YOUR RIGHT

GO PLACIDLY
AMIDST THE
NOISE AND HASTE

KEEMA NAAN
AND
CURRY SAUCE

```
┌─────────────────────────┐
│                         │
│      ADD FOUR           │
│        AND              │
│     CARRY ONE           │
│                         │
└─────────────────────────┘
```

```
┌─────────────────────────┐
│                         │
│   KEITH FLOYD           │
│      AND                │
│   KENNY HOM             │
│                         │
└─────────────────────────┘
```

development,* here are some of the less successful spin-offs of the poster itself.

....

* Set in rural Devon during the build-up to World War Two. Tom Hiddlestone is the man from the Ministry of Information. Spends two months in remote village community. After inauspicious start and much mutual suspicion, dates primary-school teacher (Carey Mulligan), takes lead role in local am-dram production, steps in to save farmer's prize herd from mud-slide, then comes to the village's aid by advising HM Govt not to bulldoze the area to build a chemical-weapons testing facility. Returns to London to make history as the very first fatality of the Blitz.

POINTLESS FACT

The poster was never actually used in wartime. The other two posters in the series read: 'Freedom is in Peril' and 'Your Courage, Your Cheerfulness, Your Resolution will bring us Victory.' Why is no one putting that on a tea towel?

6
ZOO 'FILLER'

We all love going to the zoo. It can be educational, thought-provoking and cute, and it usually has a café.*

But it's time we stopped kidding ourselves about why we're there. We are not there to 'look at ALL the animals'. Anyone who has ever been to the zoo with a child will know that you're actually only there to look at FOUR animals.

These are the only animals you're there to see:

LIONS, TIGERS, MONKEYS, PENGUINS

(In my opinion, the Big Four has recently become the Big Five

....

* Does anybody else feel guilty eating meat at a zoo? I do.

and we should now add meerkats to the list. However, Xander disagrees, and I will let him tell you why in a separate box.)

No one is going to the zoo to see:

Goats, giraffes, snakes, small things that look like deer, birds of any kind, insects, donkeys, otters (though they are quite cute), llamas, rabbits, fish, moths.

I mean, fish and moths! Come off it, zoos!

Yes, everything outside the Big Four/Five is zoo filler, yet we dutifully troop round, looking at small South American mammals, reading facts about lizards, and watching a man in a green polo-shirt throwing fish to a seal. But we know in our hearts that we're simply killing time, just pretending that all animals were created equal.

If zoos were really honest with us their timetables would look like this:

10 A.M.: ARRIVE!

10.02: LAUGH AT SOME PENGUINS

10.03: IGNORE A GOAT

10.05: WATCH A MONKEY DO A POO AND THROW IT AT ANOTHER MONKEY

10.06: TUT AT A STICK INSECT

10.07: POINT OUT A SLEEPING TIGER TO YOUR CHILD. COUGH INCREASINGLY LOUDLY TO SEE IF HE'LL WAKE UP. HE WON'T; THEY NEVER DO. TO BE HONEST, I'D BE SHOCKED IF THEY WERE REAL TIGERS. IT'S A SCAM

10.08: SHUN A BISON

10.10: FAIL TO SPOT WHERE THE LION IS HIDING. THEN TRY AND COMFORT YOUR DISAPPOINTED CHILD BY SAYING 'WELL AT LEAST WE GOT TO SEE SOME MOTHS.'

10.12: GO TO SHOP TO BUY CUDDLY LION/TIGER/ MONKEY/PENGUIN

10.15: GO TO CAFÉ. FEEL GUILTY ABOUT EATING MEAT

 MEERKATS

Listen, I have nothing against meerkats – I love 'em, the little rascals. But bless them they've gone through something of a downgrade haven't they? Haven't they, though? Meerkats? They used to be quite rare with their clever standing up and looking in the same direction. But now we see them all the time. All the bloody time. Possibly even too much. Some might say that I'm just bitter that at no stage was I involved with doing any of the voice-work for those 'funny' adverts that everyone seems to love so much. But that couldn't be further from the truth. Not bitter at all. No, no, no.

POINTLESS FACT

Berlin zoo houses 1500 different species, the most of any zoo in the world. 1496 of them are rubbish.

5
CENTRAL AFRICAN REPUBLIC

We couldn't have a list of pointless things without celebrating the achievements of Central African Republic, a country of 4.4 million inhabitants, nestled neatly between Chad, Sudan, South Sudan, the Democratic Republic of Congo and Cameroon. Its chief exports include diamonds and peanuts (an album title rejected by Prince).

Central African Republic holds a place close to all of our hearts because it has been the most consistently pointless answer in the history of *Pointless*.

Central African Republic has been a pointless answer in *every single one* of the following categories:

AFRICAN COUNTRIES

COUNTRIES BEGINNING WITH C

FRENCH-SPEAKING COUNTRIES

NATIONAL FLAGS WITH STARS

NATIONAL FLAGS WITH THE COLOUR GREEN

COUNTRIES THAT HAVE HAD A FEMALE LEADER

AFRICAN COUNTRIES IN THE NORTHERN HEMISPHERE

COUNTRIES WITH FIVE OR MORE BORDERS

COUNTRIES WHOSE CAPITAL BEGINS WITH B

And it doesn't end there. The capital of Central African Republic is Bangui. And Bangui itself has twice been a pointless answer:

CAPITAL CITIES BEGINNING WITH B

AFRICAN CAPITAL CITIES

Bangui also provided us with one of the most pointless *facts* in 'Pointless' history.

Bangui sits on the Ubangi River, making it the only capital city in the world to sit on a river which is an anagram of its own name.

I'm willing to bet money that you didn't know *that*. And if you *did* know that, then please come and join the 'Pointless' question writing team. You would fit right in.

And there's more. Central African Republic PM Faustin-Archange Touadéra was *also* a pointless answer in the category

POLITICAL LEADERS AND THEIR COUNTRIES

And *yet another* pointless answer was scored by the Central African franc in the category

COUNTRIES AND THEIR CURRENCIES

Interestingly, Central African Frank is also the name of the guy who sells diamonds and peanuts from the boot of his car outside my local pub.

So, all hail, Central African Republic. It has had its rivals over the years for the title of most pointless answer. The countries of Tuvalu and Nauru have run it close a couple of times, as has the element Yttrium. But nothing can topple the true master.

This, of course, has led to the one piece of advice we give to all new *Pointless* contestants:

'IF IN DOUBT, SAY, "CENTRAL AFRICAN REPUBLIC"'

Sometimes it doesn't work. It is not, for example, a great answer for 'The Films of Sean Connery', or 'Winners of the US Open Golf Championship', but it works for pretty much any other question.

4
MALE GROOMING

Oh, what would our grandfathers have made of it? Men who lived through a world war, men who forwent bananas, men who didn't even cry when the smoke from their Senior Service was licking their eyes. What would they make of the Male Grooming Market of the twenty-teens?

Well, they may have resisted Hitler but even they would've been powerless in the face of what's been unleashed on us in the last ten years. This is a market driven by people who know *exactly* what men's Achilles' heels are. They know the prides and jealousies of men, they know the tribes into which men divide themselves and they have targeted each group remorselessly.

For those who like to consider themselves sportsmen, they merely had to use the words 'Sport', 'Extreme' or 'Power' and they were in.

For office executive types products were called things like 'Skinexcell 7' or 'Multivitamin Problem Solver' and he, too, was in. Cerebral man was powerless to resist.

For the CEREBRAL man came products called things like 'Dr Nokoyama' or 'Kauschmann', products that clearly had philosophy behind them. Then he, too, caved in.

But the real genius was reserved for the man who felt he was above all this nonsense and for him 'Estd' was brought off the shelves, dusted down, and popped into contexts like 'Glossops of Mayfair, Estd 1848'.

Below I have listed some popular male grooming products. However, I have made one of them up. Can you spot the ringer?

LOGISTICS FOR MEN FACIAL CLEANSER

HYDRA ENERGETIC X-TREME TURBO BOOSTER MOISTURISER

HIGH RECHARGE ENERGY SPLASH INSTANT MOISTURISING LOTION

AQUAPOWER MOISTURISER

EXTREME CYCLE ESSENTIAL FACE BALM

HYDROSYSTEMS MOISTURE LOCK-IN

KYOKU EXFOLIATING FACIAL SCRUB

3
QUEUING IN CINEMAS

I hate queues. And I mean I *really* hate queues.

In the next thirty years I could win an Oscar, a Nobel Peace Prize and Miss World 2017, and the eulogy my kids read out at my funeral would still be titled 'My dad. Boy, did he hate queues'.

I would rather do ANYTHING than queue. If my dentist rang while I was in the queue at Sainsbury's I would greet him like an old friend and gladly suggest an immediate emergency tooth extraction.

This does mean, though, that I have become something of a bad queue connoisseur. There are some notorious bad queues: late-night taxi queues, lunchtime post-office queues, the queues for the toilets at Glastonbury while Paolo Nutini is playing. But over the years I have identified the three worst queues* in the world.

THIRD WORST QUEUE IN THE WORLD:
RAIL TICKET MACHINES

If *The Guinness Book of Records* want to witness the undisputed record for 'Number of People Simultaneously Tutting at Foreign Students While Looking Irritably at Their Watches, Then Looking Wistfully in the Direction of a Train They Turned Up in Plenty of Time to Get but Now They're Going to Miss', may I suggest they visit the queue for the self-service ticket machines at Cambridge station on any Saturday morning?

Why is it that all young people seem to be permanently attached to iPods, iPads, mobiles and laptops, yet when presented by the touch-screen technology of the self-service rail ticket machines it takes them twenty-five minutes to work out how to buy a day return to Peterborough? And then, with their oversized rucksack still swinging into your face, they try to pay using the Visa card of their Greek bank, which ran out of money the previous Tuesday?

Did I mention I hate queues?

....

* Try typing the word 'queues' over and over again. It's frustrating. So far I've managed 'queus', 'queueus' and 'ques'.

SECOND WORST QUEUE IN THE WORLD: FOREIGN PASSPORT CONTROL

Particularly in America. Made worse by the fact that you can't tut because you suspect if they spot it you'll be deported, or – in the case of a particularly big tut – shot.

WORST QUEUE IN THE WORLD: THE MULTIPLEX CINEMA QUEUE

All I want is popcorn for my daughter, some Maltesers for my son, and a bottle of water.

Quite apart from the fact that this will cost me £17.50 (How, Cineworld? *How?*), I am now faced with the worst queue in the world.

Multiplex queues are the perfect storm, thanks to:

1. Separate lines – psychologically devastating.
2. People buying tickets and refreshments in the same queue. Not acceptable.
3. People in front of you seemingly unfamiliar with the concept of ever having been to the cinema,
4. and seemingly not having chosen which film they want to see, thus requiring a review of each one,
5. and seemingly not knowing before they reach the front

of the queue – despite that having taken twenty minutes – that they are going to have to choose between salty and sweet popcorn.

6. An over-representation of teens. As we all know, teens insist on paying individually for everything, then changing their minds about their order, then paying separately again.

7. The cinema company deciding that, even though, say, *Avengers Assemble* is opening today, they will probably only need Darren and Jackie serving. And perhaps Josh can stand next to the ice-cream cabinet chatting to Jackie. I do empathise with the cinema chains a bit, though: after all, it is hard to afford staff when you're only charging £8 for some Fruit Pastilles and a Sprite.

8. The fact that – believe it or not – you actually have to *be somewhere* at a *specific time*, and hearing the teen in front of you ask, 'And how much is the Hot Dog Nacho Meal Combo?' for the seventh time isn't getting you there any quicker. And neither is the same teen furiously complaining about a violation of his human rights because he's not allowed to use his Orange Wednesdays voucher on a Saturday evening.

9. Boy, do I hate queues.

I wouldn't mind so much, but these queues are pointless. Your local art-house cinema can manage to sell you a ticket and a nice packet of dried mango, and have a conversation about whether the film you're about to see represents a genuine renaissance in Iranian cinema, without any trouble at all. And the price of their Hot Dog Nacho Meal Combo is clearly printed next to the till.

POINTLESS QUIZ QUESTION

The first multiplex in the UK was far from pointless. Why was that?

BEING NUMBER 2

'Second place is first loser.'

Such wise words, and who said them? That's right, it was Dale Earnhardt. And if you don't know who Dale Earnhardt is then you'll have to Google him, like I just had to. Done that? Good. Nice moustache, no?

Whether you're Tim Henman, Buzz Aldrin, Captain Scott or Ray Quinn,* coming second is absolutely pointless.

No one remembers the second man to climb Everest, and no one remembers the *first* man to climb K2 because it's the *second* highest mountain. No one knows the second man to

....

* Who's Ray Quinn? you ask. Well, exactly.

swim the Channel, or the second woman to fly the Atlantic. While you're on Google, why don't you ask it what the world's second biggest search engine is? History will not remember.

And while we *do* remember that Germany came second in two world wars, they've never exactly won any plaudits for it.

Being second means putting in the same hours of blood, sweat, effort and devotion as the person who comes first, without any of the glory. Admit that if someone in the pub showed you an Olympic silver medal you'd simply shrug your shoulders and go back to your pint. They might as well have come *seventh*.

So, our final quiz is a celebration of coming second. I'm going to give you the titles of twelve songs that only ever reached number two in the UK charts. Can you name the band or artist who performed each one? By all means play against your family. Just make sure that you finish first.

POINTLESS QUIZ

Your questions are:

1. 'Perfect 10'
2. 'Hound Dog'
3. 'Yesterday Once More'
4. 'Rule The World'
5. 'Agadoo'
6. 'Roll With It'
7. 'Love Shack'
8. 'Reach'
9. 'Brown Sugar'
10. 'Let It Be'
11. 'Paper Roses'
12. 'Save A Prayer'

1
SAYING EVERYTHING
IS POINTLESS

We hope you've enjoyed our list of the 100 most pointless things in the world. We hope there have been some nods of recognition, we hope there have been some titanic family quiz battles, and most of all we hope we've persuaded you to stamp out the evil of ready-salted crisps.

But here's our number one: 'Saying everything is pointless' is pointless. And that's because pointlessness could, and should, be a wonderful thing.

Whether you believe we all live on God's green earth, part of a greater and finer plan, or that we're just monkeys on a rock whizzing through space, come and gone in a blink, it stills adds up to a fabulously pointless world.

Just think of the magnificent pointlessness of art, sport, literature, fashion, TV soaps, theatre and jokes. We don't *need* to do any of these things, but we choose to.

Most of the things we love are pointless. Listening to *The Archers*, making a birthday card for Mum, sitting in the sun, watching our cat chase his tail, buying a new handbag, opening a bottle of wine with friends, gardening, reading about the Tudors, eating chocolate, telling anecdotes about our new boss, playing 'Call of Duty', walking on the beach, watching daytime TV. We don't need to do any of this (except watch daytime TV). It doesn't have a 'point' other than that it makes us happy. So our motto is this:

No one *needs* to bake, but we all like cupcakes.*

We have been presenting *Pointless* for nearly four years now, and the whole experience has been such a joy from start to finish (not that it's finished: surely someone at the BBC would have told us). It has given us endless hours of pleasure and laughter, working with a wonderful team, and meeting such varied and fascinating people every day. And the viewers have always been our favourite bit, so we hope it has entertained and amused you too. Let's finish with a little deal.

....

* But please don't forget our other motto 'If in doubt, say, "Central African Republic."' These two mottos will see you through anything.

If you continue to enjoy it, we'll continue to make it. But we'll all know secretly, from the bottom of our hearts, just how spectacularly, relentlessly and joyfully pointless it all is.

ANSWERS

100 INTRODUCTIONS TO BOOKS

Postman. Patrick Clifton is Postman Pat's full name.

97 JUKEBOX MUSICALS

1. *Mamma Mia!* – Abba (95)
2. *Good Vibrations* – The Beach Boys (66)
3. *Jersey Boys* – Frankie Valli and the Four Seasons (16)
4. *All Shook Up* – Elvis Presley (68)
5. *Ring of Fire* – Johnny Cash (38)
6. *All the Fun of the Fair* – David Essex (8)
7. *Tonight's the Night* – Rod Stewart (21)
8. *Never Forget* – Take That (11)
9. *We Will Rock You* – Queen (74)

10. *Movin' Out* – Billy Joel (2)

11. *Our House* – Madness (48)

12. *Saturday Night Fever* – The Bee Gees (57)

96 PANDAS

Pandas only use their opposable thumbs to hold bamboo while they eat it. The idiots.

95 4 A.M.

It was 4.07 a.m. when Richard woke up and wrote that entry.

91 TV SHOW SPIN-OFFS

1. *The Green, Green Grass – Only Fools and Horses* (46)

2. *George and Mildred – Man About the House* (46)

3. *The Colbys – Dynasty* (27)

4. *Lewis – Inspector Morse* (67)

5. *Tucker's Luck – Grange Hill* (38)

6. *Rhoda – The Mary Tyler Moore Show* (4)

7. *Torchwood – Doctor Who* (67)

8. *Mork and Mindy – Happy Days* (11)

9. *A Different World – The Cosby Show* (3)

10. *Frasier – Cheers* (43)

11. *Benson – Soap* (7)

12. *Knots Landing – Dallas* (38)

90 INAPPROPRIATE CARAVAN NAMES

The made-up caravan name is Regal Connoisseur.

89 ONE PENNY COIN

Since 1992, 1p coins have been magnetic. They now have a mild steel core electroplated with copper.

88 SHARING PACKS

1. So twist – Wotsits
2. Nut boy – Bounty
3. Kilt sets – Skittles
4. Ice churn – Crunchie
5. Bloke reduced – Double Decker
6. Trust bars – Starburst
7. Girls pen – Pringles
8. Barn oil – Lion Bar
9. Alter mess – Maltesers
10. Frailest tulips – Fruit Pastilles
11. Irk milady – Dairy Milk
12. Slim rents – Minstrels
13. Thriftily shrug desk – Frys Turkish Delight
14. Dole rewoken an achiness – Cheese and Onion Walkers
15. Earthlings worries – Werthers Originals

86 PALINDROMES

1. Classic 1952 Western 'High . . .' – Noon (64)
2. Martin Shaw's TV judge John – Deed (51)
3. Singer Shola – Ama (36)
4. Australian supermodel Macpherson – Elle (90)
5. Miley Cyrus character Montana – Hannah (81)
6. Two crotchets – Minim (23)
7. 1974 Eurovision Song Contest winners – Abba (86)
8. Object-detection system – Radar (30)
9. Bing Crosby's 'Road' partner, Hope – Bob (32)
10. Canoe used by Inuit – Kayak (32)
11. Surname of widow of John Lennon – Ono (75)
12. Modern county town of Meath – Navan (pointless!)

83 READY-SALTED CRISPS

1. Cheese and onion
2. Salt and vinegar
3. Steak and onion
4. Smoky bacon

Poor old prawn cocktail came seventh.

81 US STATES

1. Heavy laundry – Washington (Washing-ton)
2. Something's missing from my shed – Idaho (I had a hoe)

3. A feelm weeth James Caan – Missouri (Misery)
4. A Chiming Mess – Michigan (anagram)
5. Specialist Subject – 'Only Fools and Horses' – Delaware (Del-aware)
6. Honour among thieves – Connecticut (Con etiquette)
7. Horsehair – Maine
8. Sick badger – Illinois (Ill Annoy)
9. Sick badgers – Massachusetts (Mass 'atchoo' setts)
10. Derby County – Kentucky
11. Heaven with a heavy cold – Nevada (Nirvana)
12. Cole and Solskjaer both did – New York (Knew Dwight Yorke)
13. Two things you might need for a PhD – Alabama (A lab and an M.A.)
14. Exploding Osmannite! – Minnesota (anagram)
15. Tweed proprietor – Arizona (Harris Owner)
16. Nothing greeting nothing – Ohio (o Hi o)
17. Tiny snake in German/French mountain – Vermont (Verm/Mont)
18. Get prisoners to their cells quickly – Wisconsin (Whizz cons in)
19. Motorway Man – Rhode Island (Road/Isle of Man)
20. . . . And I'll fetch the gravel   Utah (You tar. . .)
21. Smilie's cruise ship – North Carolina (Carol liner)
22. Vorderman's cruise ship – South Carolina (Carol liner)
23. I can't understand why you can't be more merciful – Wyoming (Why, oh Ming?)
24. Breaks an' breaks – Nebraska (anagram)

25. Mum lent me £20 – Iowa (I owe her)

26. I wonder if Mum will lend me another £20 – Alaska (I'll ask her)

27. Smash a frail icon – California (anagram)

28. Switch off saw – Oregon (Horror gone)

29. Boo! your mandible is rubbish! – Georgia (Jaw jeer)

30. Walsh date Ford – Louisiana (Louis Walsh see Anna Ford)

31. Nicolas Sarkozy's sunbed – Montana (mon tanner)

32. Hneswlug – Pennsylvania (Pencil (weather) vane ear)

33. Virgin theme park – Maryland

34. Oxicemo – New Mexico (anagram)

35. Noah's Christmas list – Arkansas (ark and saw)

36. Revisit Wigan in disguise – West Virginia (anagram)

37. Bring back Bergerac! – New Jersey

38. Carreras – Tennessee (Tenor C)

39. What posh people don't like paying – Texas

40. Jack eats a pavlova – Indiana (Anna (Pavlova) in (Jack) Dee)

41. The bottom of a tin – Kansas (Can's ass)

42. Arrest our spending – Colorado (Collar our dough)

43. T

   A – South Dakota (Bottom of Dakota)

44. D

   A – North Dakota (Top of Dakota)

45. Fine French writer – Oklahoma (OK la Homer)

46. Andover and over – New Hampshire

47. Never heard a thing – Virginia (Virgin ear)

48. More ruddy – Florida (Florrider)
49. Pines for Neil Pye – Mississippi (Misses Hippy)
50. Aah! wii broken! – Hawaii (anagram)

78 RESTAURANTS ADVERTISING THEMSELVES WHEN YOU'RE ALREADY EATING THERE

The extraordinary place that Pizza Hut delivered a pizza to in 2001 was the International Space Station.

77 NOVELTY SONGS

1. 'The Chicken Song' – Spitting Image (1)
2. 'Combine Harvester' – The Wurzels (40)
3. 'The Elements' – Tom Lehrer (2)
4. 'The Birdie Song' – The Tweets (1)
5. 'Barbie Girl' – Aqua (37)
6. 'Ullo John, Got A New Motor?' – Alexei Sayle (11)
7. 'Do The Bartman' – The Simpsons (27)
8. 'Star Trekkin'' – The Firm (3)
9. 'Can We Fix It?' – Bob the Builder (68)
10. 'Doctorin' The Tardis' – Timelords (pointless!)
11. 'Snooker Loopy' – Matchroom Mob with Chas 'n' Dave (10)
12. 'Ernie (The Fastest Milkman In The West)' – Benny Hill (42)
13. 'The Laughing Gnome' – David Bowie (23)
14. 'Who Let The Dogs Out?' – Baha Men (9)

15. 'My Old Man's A Dustman' – Lonnie Donegan (58)
16. 'The Winner's Song' – Geraldine (5)
17. 'Funky Gibbon' – The Goodies (38)
18. 'Achy Breaky Heart' – Billy Ray Cyrus (21)
19. 'I Am A Cider Drinker' – The Wurzels (52)
20. 'Agadoo' – Black Lace (22)
21. 'Tie Me Kangaroo Down Sport' – Rolf Harris (86)
22. 'Whispering Grass' – Windsor Davies and Don Estelle (7)
23. 'Right Said Fred' – Bernard Cribbins (17)
24. 'What Are We Gonna Get 'Er Indoors?' – Dennis Waterman and George Cole (1)

72 ANIMAL HYBRIDS

1. Pumapard – puma and leopard (53)
2. Huarizo – alpaca and llama (1)
3. Hinny – horse and donkey (7)
4. Grolar – grizzly bear and polar bear (11)
5. Dogote – dog and coyote (35)
6. Beefalo – bison and cow (32)
7. Zedonk – zebra and donkey (45)
8. Liger – lion and tiger (69)
9. Cama – camel and llama (31)
10. Dzo – yak and cow (1)
11. Leopon – leopard and lion (18)
12. Yakalo – yak and buffalo (30)

68 TOASTER SETTINGS

The electric toaster was invented in 1893; the invention of factory sliced bread came 35 years later.

67 BAD FILMS

1. *Rambo 3* – Sylvester Stallone (41)
2. *Battlefield Earth* – John Travolta (6)
3. *G.I. Jane* – Demi Moore (29)
4. *Big Daddy* – Adam Sandler (11)
5. *Showgirls* – Elizabeth Berkley (3)
6. *Catwoman* – Halle Berry (15)
7. *Basic Instinct 2* – Sharon Stone (25)
8. *All About Steve* – Sandra Bullock (1)
9. *The Blair Witch Project* – Heather Donahue (pointless!)
10. *Armageddon* – Bruce Willis (15)
11. *Stop, or My Mom Will Shoot* – Sylvester Stallone (14)
12. *Under the Cherry Moon* – Prince (3)
13. *The Blue Lagoon* – Brooke Shields (8)
14. *Robin Hood, Prince of Thieves* – Kevin Costner (31)
15. *Glitter* – Mariah Carey (14)

63 UNADJUSTABLE SPANNERS

The Monkey wrench was reportedly named after its inventor Charles Moncky.

62 CELEBRITY BIOGRAPHIES

1. *Dear Fatty* – Dawn French (26)
2. *I Don't Mean to be Rude, But. . .* – Simon Cowell (1)
3. *A Long Walk to Freedom* – Nelson Mandela (27)
4. *Ooh What a Lovely Pair!* – Ant and Dec (10)
5. *Dreams from My Father* – Barack Obama (7)
6. *The Woman I was Born to Be* – Susan Boyle (1)
7. *It's Not What You Think* – Chris Evans (1)
8. *My Booky Wook* – Russell Brand (42)
9. *Look Who It Is!* – Alan Carr (3)
10. *The Sound of Laughter* – Peter Kay (13)
11. *Humble Pie* – Gordon Ramsay (5)
12. *Moonwalk* – Michael Jackson (34)
13. *My Side* – David Beckham (2)
14. *Learning to Fly* – Victoria Beckham (4)
15. *A Whole New World* – Katie Price (12)

61 EXPLAINING RULES ON EPISODE 400 OF A QUIZ SHOW

The TV shows you would find the following deliberately complicated TV quiz show spoofs are:

a) Numberwang – *That Mitchell & Webb Look*
b) Quizzlesticks – *The Adam & Joe Show*
c) Bamboozled – *Friends*

60 SIGNS

a) Araf – Slow

b) Ildiwch – Give way

c) Nid wyf yn y swyddfa ar hyn o bryd. Anfonwch unrhyw waith i'w gyfieithu – 'I am not in the office at the moment. Send any work to be translated.' (Mistakenly written on a road sign in 2008 which should have said 'No entry for heavy goods vehicles, residential site only'.)

59 INSTINCTIVELY CLUTCHING YOUR VALUABLES WHEN WALKING PAST SUSPICIOUS-LOOKING YOUTHS

The first mobile phone call was made on June 17th 1946 by Bell Labs scientists in St Louis Missouri. Let's assume the phone was stolen minutes later by a gang of suspicious-looking Missourian youths.

57 TRADITIONAL WEDDING ANNIVERSARIES

1. 3rd – leather (5)
2. 25th – silver (59)
3. 35th – coral (9)
4. 40th – ruby (35)
5. 50th – gold (69)
6. 55th – emerald (4)
7. 1st – paper (63)

8. 5th – wood (12)
9. 10th – tin (5)
10. 11th – steel (3)
11. 30th – pearl (14)
12. 60th – diamond (38)

55 KNICK-KNACKS ON CHAT-SHOW SETS

1. Angry tower – Terry Wogan
2. Lankier champions – Michael Parkinson
3. Lane joy – Jay Leno
4. Charlatan Smith – Alan Titchmarsh
5. Drug payola – Paul O'Grady
6. My jerky eel – Jeremy Kyle
7. Ash on Trojans – Jonathan Ross
8. Croon nodes – Des O'Connor
9. Hangman rotor – Graham Norton
10. Hard candid jury – Richard and Judy

51 CLASSICAL MUSIC

Which composers wrote the following pieces?

1. *The Four Seasons* – Vivaldi (41)
2. *The William Tell Overture* – Rossini (6)
3. *Eine Kleine Nachtmusik* – Mozart (17)
4. *4'33'* – Cage (1)

5. *Samstag aus Licht* – Stockhausen (pointless!)
6. *Ride of the Valkyries* – Wagner (16)
7. *Rhapsody in Blue* – Gershwin (17)
8. *The Blue Danube* – Strauss (26)
9. *Peter and the Wolf* – Prokofiev (6)
10. *Variations on a Theme of Frank Bridge* – Britten (pointless!)
11. *The Planets* – Holst (42)
12. *The Trout Quintet* – Schubert (4)

51 POEMS AND THEIR POETS

Which poets wrote the following pieces?

1. 'Jabberwocky' – Lewis Carroll (23)
2. *The Charge of the Light Brigade* – Alfred Lord Tennyson (8)
3. 'If . . .' – Rudyard Kipling (22)
4. *Paradise Lost* – John Milton (34)
5. *The Rime of the Ancient Mariner* – Samuel Taylor Coleridge (18)
6. 'The Raven' – Edgar Allan Poe (26)
7. *The Ballad of Reading Gaol* – Oscar Wilde (21)
8. 'The Owl and the Pussy Cat' – Edward Lear (26)
9. *The Wasteland* – T. S. Eliot (15)
10. 'To a Mouse' – Robert Burns (13)
11. 'Ode to a Nightingale' – John Keats (22)

12. 'I Wandered Lonely as a Cloud' – William Wordsworth (52)
13. 'Anthem for Doomed Youth' – Wilfred Owen (6)
14. 'The Soldier' – Rupert Brooke (4)
15. *The Divine Comedy* – Dante (18)

45 GAME-SHOW HOSTS

1. *3–2–1* – Ted Rogers (18)
2. *Only Connect* – Victoria Coren (1)
3. *The Crystal Maze* – Richard O'Brien (16)
4. *Fifteen to One* – William G. Stewart (9)
5. *The Weakest Link* – Anne Robinson (77)
6. *Bullseye* – Jim Bowen (40)
7. *Blockbusters* – Bob Holness (37)
8. *Turnabout* – Rob Curling (pointless!)
9. *The Cube* – Phillip Schofield (55)
10. *Going for Gold* – Henry Kelly (13)
11. *The Generation Game* – Bruce Forsyth (62)
12. *Every Second Counts* – Paul Daniels (11)

43 CVs

The CV belonged to Leonardo da Vinci.

42 TIES

According to James Bond, the Windsor Knot is the mark of a cad.

39 WEIRD HOBBIES

1. Vexillologist – flags
2. Philatelist – stamps
3. Arctophile – teddy bears
4. Horologist – timepieces
5. Lepidopterist – butterflies/moths
6. Oologist – birds' eggs
7. Numismatist – coins/medals
8. Conchologist – shells
9. Deltiologist – postcards
10. Discophile – records/CDs
11. Bibliophile – books
12. Oenophile – wine
13. Philographist – autographs
14. Porcelainist – porcelain
15. Notaphilist – banknotes

35 OVER-COMPLICATED HOTEL SHOWERS

The bathroom innovation that Sir Winston Churchill first used in the US in 1942 was the mixer tap.

1 Buon giorno – Italy (64)

2 Kalimera – Greek (25)

3 Selamat siang – Indonesian (pointless!)

4 Dzien dobry – Polish (20)

5 Guten Tag – German (97)

6 Dia duit – Gaelic/Irish (2)

7 Bore da – Welsh (28)

8 Xin chao – Vietnamese (1)

9 Hyvaa huomenta – Finnish (5)

10 Shalom – Hebrew (19)

11 Bonjour – French (98)

12 Hola – Spanish (64)

29 TWIX

Starburst and Snickers both had to have their name changed (from Opal Fruits and Marathon) to fit in with the rest of the world, while our two-fingered biscuity hero did the exact opposite, forcing the rest of the world to change from Raider to Twix.

28 MASCARA INNOVATIONS

Baton Noir Cryproof Nasa-tec Lash Treacle is the made-up mascara.

27 CHRISTMAS NUMBER-ONE SINGLES

1. Dr Owl – Mad World (anagram)
2. 'Mind the gap!' – Sound of the Underground
3. Are thongs twisted? – Earth Song (anagram)
4. 'I've watched it back, and it's taken a deflection off the defender, but it was going in anyway so I'm claiming it' – That's My Goal
5. Cheryl Cole is – Reet Petite
6. Consideration of family sleepiness – Mull of Kintyre
7. Lonely sheep – Only You
8. When do you go to the Early Learning Centre? – When a Child is Born
9. Hydrophobia means disaster – Bohemian Rhapsody (anagram)
10. Mrs Isla Yingstrom – Killing in the Name (iSLA YINGstrom)

25 UNNECESSARY BLOODY MARY INGREDIENTS

1. Co-pilot Osman! – Cosmopolitan
2. Rank vomit aid – Vodka Martini

3. Molls tonic – Tom Collins
4. Nostalgic deadline – Long Island Iced Tea
5. Inhaled foods – Old-fashioned
6. Why kiss Euro? – Whiskey Sour
7. Ailing spongers – Singapore Sling
8. Queasier insult – Tequila Sunrise
9. Backs urinals – Black Russian
10. Cheese 'n' hatbox – Sex on the Beach

21 THOSE LONG WORDS THAT DOCTORS USE

1. Daltonism – colour blindness (pointless!)
2. Hypertension – high blood pressure (38)
3. Varicella – chicken pox (6)
4. Tinea pedis – athlete's foot (1)
5. Myocardial infarction – heart attack (37)
6. Myopia – short-sightedness (51)
7. Infectious mononucleosis – glandular fever (3)
8. Rubella – German measles (38)
9. Allergic rhinitis – hay fever (36)
10. Otaglia – earache (10)
11. Halitosis – bad breath (66)
12. Lateral epicondylitis – tennis elbow (1)
13. Dentalgia – toothache (24)
14. Tetanus – lockjaw (30)
15. Epistaxis – nosebleed (8)

16 PHONE BOXES

The only building in Washington D.C. to have a red telephone box outside is the British Embassy.

15 TERRIBLE MOVIE TAG-LINES

1. 'Choose Life' – *Trainspotting* (35)
2. 'Enter the World' – *Avatar* (pointless!)
3. 'Who Ya Gonna Call?' – *Ghostbusters* (64)
4. 'I See Dead People' – *Sixth Sense* (38)
5. 'Be Afraid, Be Very Afraid' – *The Fly* (2)
6. 'His Scars Run Deep' – *Edward Scissorhands* (1)
7. 'The Mission Is a Man' – *Saving Private Ryan* (1)
8. 'Don't Go in the Water' – *Jaws* (48)
9. 'On the Air, Unaware' – *The Truman Show* (1)
10. 'A Romantic Comedy, with Zombies' – *Shaun of the Dead* (11)
11. 'Houston, We Have a Problem' – *Apollo 13* (36)
12. 'Collide with Destiny' – *Titanic* (pointless!)

9 AMERICAN WORDS FOR ENGLISH FOOD

1. Aubergine – eggplant (41)
2. Candyfloss – cotton candy (23)
3. Porridge – oatmeal (31)
4. Buck's fizz – Mimosa (6)
5. Jam – jelly (60)

6. Cornflour – cornstarch (10)
7. Crisps – (potato) chips (82)
8. Rocket – arugula (1)
9. Jelly – Jell-o (47)
10. Courgette – zucchini (33)
11. Icing – frosting (24)
12. Coriander – cilantro (6)
13. Biscuit – cookie (65)
14. Scone – biscuit (11)
15. Chips – (French) fries (89)

8 TALLEST PEOPLE TO:

a) Become President of the USA? – Abraham Lincoln 6'4"
   (people don't like sitting behind me in theatres either)
b) Win an acting Oscar? – Tim Robbins 6'5"
c) Sing on a UK number-one single? Long John Baldry 6'7"
   with 'Let the Heartaches Begin'.

4 MALE GROOMING

HydroSystems Moisture Lock-In is the made-up male
grooming product

3 QUEUING IN CINEMAS

It was 'The Point' in Milton Keynes.

2 BEING NUMBER 2

1. 'Perfect 10' – The Beautiful South (13)
2. 'Hound Dog' – Elvis Presley (81)
3. 'Yesterday Once More' – Carpenters (38)
4. 'Rule The World' – Take That (5)
5. 'Agadoo' – Black Lace (25)
6. 'Roll With It' – Oasis (30)
7. 'Love Shack' – B-52s (28)
8. 'Reach' – S Club 7 (9)
9. 'Brown Sugar' – Rolling Stones (50)
10. 'Let It Be' – The Beatles (75)
11. 'Paper Roses' – Marie Osmond (27)
12. 'Save A Prayer' – Duran Duran (17)

Robert Louis Stevenson
Teller of Tales

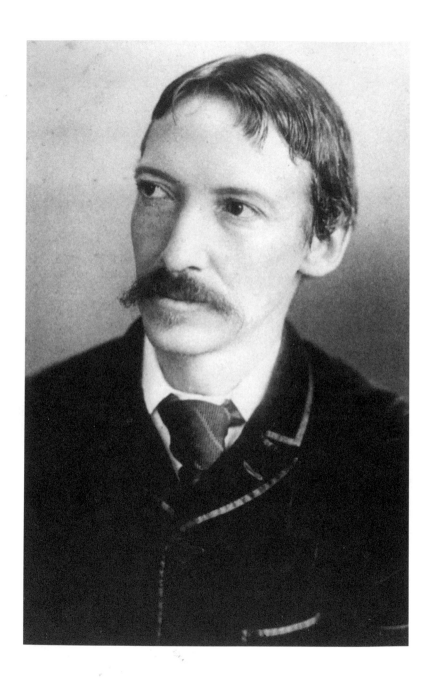

Robert Louis Stevenson
Teller of Tales

~

Beverly Gherman

Atheneum Books for Young Readers

Grateful acknowledgment to Edmond Reynolds, Director,
Silverado Museum, for his expert advice on the manuscript

ATHENEUM BOOKS FOR YOUNG READERS
AN IMPRINT OF SIMON & SCHUSTER CHILDREN'S PUBLISHING DIVISION
1230 AVENUE OF THE AMERICAS   NEW YORK, NEW YORK 10020
Copyright © 1996 by Beverly Gherman
Book design by Patti Ratchford
The text of this book is set in Adobe Garamond
First edition
Printed in the United States of America
10   9   8   7   6   5   4   3   2   1

Library of Congress Cataloging-in-Publication data:
Gherman, Beverly.
Robert Louis Stevenson, teller of tales / Beverly Gherman.—1st ed.
p.   cm.
Includes bibliographical references and index.
Summary: Narrates the life of the Scottish author who showed an early talent for writing
and produced adventure stories including *Treasure Island.*
ISBN 0-689-31985-1
1. Stevenson, Robert Louis, 1850-1894—Biography—Juvenile literature. 2. Authors,
Scottish—19th century—Biography—Juvenile literature. [1. Stevenson, Robert Louis,
1850-1894. 2. Authors, Scottish.] I. Title.
PR5493.G48   1996   828'.809—dc20   95-52448   CIP   AC

Photo credits for *Robert Louis Stevenson*
Courtesy of the California Department of Parks and Recreation: cover, frontispiece, viii, 4, 5,
7, 9, 27, 44, 74, 87, 97, 104, 107, 115. Courtesy of the Silverado Museum: cover, 29, 53,
57, 62, 66, 78, 92, 112. Courtesy of the Bancroft Library: 46. Courtesy of Lee Ann Slaton:
84. Reprinted with the permission of Atheneum Books for Young Readers, an imprint of
Simon & Schuster: On page 68, jacket from *Treasure Island* by Robert Louis Stevenson, illustrated by N. C. Wyeth. Copyright 1911 Charles Scribner's Sons: copyright renewed 1939 by
N. C. Wyeth. On page 71, jacket from *The Black Arrow* by Robert Louis Stevenson, illustrated by N. C. Wyeth. Copyright 1916 Charles Scribner's Sons: copyright renewed 1944 by
N. C. Wyeth. On page 81, illustration from *Kidnapped* (facing page 116) by Robert Louis
Stevenson, illustrated by N. C. Wyeth. Copyright 1913 Charles Scribner's Sons; copyright
renewed 1941 by N. C. Wyeth.

For the wee-bairn who have joined our family:
Zachariah Gherman Whiting
Matthew Michael Gherman

Important Dates

November 13, 1850 Robert Louis Stevenson is born in Edinburgh, Scotland

1867 Attends Edinburgh University to study engineering

1871 Abandons engineering for law

1875, July Becomes Scottish advocate

1876 Meets Fanny Osbourne
Travels canals of northern France

1878 Publishes *An Inland Voyage*
Travels with donkey in Cévennes

1879 Publishes *Travels with a Donkey*
Travels to America to join Fanny

1880, May 19 Fanny and Louis marry
Return to Scotland

1881 Publishes *Virginibus Puerisque*

1883 Publishes *Treasure Island* and *The Silverado Squatters*

1885 Publishes *A Child's Garden of Verses* and *Prince Otto*

1886 Publishes *The Strange Case of Dr. Jekyll and Mr. Hyde* and *Kidnapped*

1887 His father dies
Louis and Fanny return to the United States

1888 Sails on *Casco* to South Seas
Publishes *The Black Arrow*

1889 Builds Vailima in Samoa

1894, December 3 Dies in Samoa

∾ *Contents*

Louis, at about age 35, writing at his desk

CHAPTER 1

~

"If I Am Spared"

When I am grown to man's estate
I shall be very proud and great,
And tell the other girls and boys
Not to meddle with my toys.

I n August 1881, thirty-year-old Robert Louis Stevenson began to write an adventure story he called *The Sea-Cook*, which became *Treasure Island: A Story for Boys*. He described it as a story about a map and a treasure and a mutiny, and the ideas poured out of him.

In the evening his family gathered around him in the drawing room of their Braemar cottage in northern Scotland. Outside a storm howled, but inside a fire warmed the room, and gas lamps flickered against the walls. Wrapped in his maroon shawl, Louis read aloud from the chapter he had completed earlier that day. He switched voices from the boyish, excited tone of Jim Hawkins to the more dignified words of Doctor Livesey or the sinister shouts of Long John Silver, trying all the while to keep the

1

suspense high and his family on the edge of their chairs.

Thomas, his father, especially loved storytelling and had constant suggestions to offer: Hide Jim in a barrel. Fill the seaman's chest with maps, pistols, a bar of silver, seashells. Lloyd, his young stepson, wanted action. Get the *Hispaniola* out to sea. Into a storm. Bring on the pirates.

Louis could hardly wait to get to work each morning and found that he could produce at least a chapter a day. "You just indulge the pleasure of your heart," he said, "just drive along as the words come and the pen will scratch!" In great haste he wrote the first sixteen chapters and sold them to *Young Folks* magazine, which would issue them a chapter at a time beginning in October 1881.

It was one of the few times in his life when Louis was so absorbed in his writing he forgot about his illnesses. For the truth is that Robert Louis Stevenson lived his whole life expecting to die at any moment. Even as a child when asked what he would be when he grew up, he said perhaps a minister like Grandfather or an engineer like Father or an adventurer. Always adding, "If I am spared."

~

CHAPTER 2

All Night Long

Whenever the moon and stars are set,
Whenever the wind is high,
All night long in the dark and wet,
A man goes riding by.

Robert Louis Stevenson was born in the wet and windy month of November, 1850, in Edinburgh, Scotland, where winters are harsh and summers are not much better. "One of the vilest climates under heaven," he described his birthplace. Scotland is known for its harbors and lighthouses, many of them built by Louis's father and uncles. It is famous also for its picturesque scenery and its poets. Louis was nurtured by his country no matter how much he tried to escape it. And although Scotland's dampness made him ill, Scotland's writers inspired him throughout his short life.

Louis was the only child of Margaret and Thomas Stevenson, both of whom had grown up in large families of thirteen children each. They nicknamed him Smout, or

Louis wearing tartan dress, age four, with his mother, Margaret Stevenson small fry, and delighted in their chubby, cheerful son. When he was almost two, Smout began to have fevers and coughs that kept him in bed for days at a time. It seemed he had been born with the weak lungs of his mother and her father, his grandfather Balfour. In those days children often died from infectious diseases such as tuberculosis, diphtheria, and scarlet fever. If "the delicate die early," Louis had good cause to worry. Whether he ever had tuberculosis no one is certain. Certainly he had croup and bronchitis with such terrible coughing that he named it his "night hag." Because Margaret's own respiratory diseases prevented her from looking after Smout and Thomas Stevenson had to travel to

Thomas Stevenson, Louis's father

build and maintain his lighthouses, they hired Alison Cunningham to help with their son.

Cummy, as she was called, was twenty-nine when she came to care for young Smout. A determined, no-nonsense young woman, she believed strictly in her Bible and the teachings of Calvinism. She became Louis's nurse, his second mother, and his teacher. She set up a bed in the nursery at the top of the house and was there when he woke with fevers or vivid nightmares or was frightened by noisy Edinburgh storms. He clung to Cummy when imaginary horsemen produced thunder and lightning in the sky above his head.

On clear nights, before she tucked him in, the two of them stood and watched for Leerie the lamplighter to pass along the streets with his ladder and long pole to light the gas lamps. If Louis woke, she carried him to the nursery window and pointed to any lights she saw where "gas still burned behind the windows of other sick-rooms." Those lights were for small boys like himself who were ill and frightened by their dreams, she told him.

As he grew older Louis was afraid to close his eyes to sleep because his dreams were so troubled. Over and over he dreamed that he was being forced to swallow all the people in the world or that he was summoned before the "Great White Throne" to recite and he couldn't remember a single word.

In the light of day Cummy read Bible stories to Louis, warning him about "hellfire and eternal damnation." His parents were not concerned about her terrifying warnings but saw only the positive influence of Cummy's teaching when young Smout, pretending to be a minister, pushed a chair to the middle of the room to use as his pulpit and "preached" the stories and sang the songs he had memorized.

He remembered having to be especially good on Sundays, unable to play or do anything he liked. It was a day with a "hush . . . over everything." He even worried that his parents would be punished and go to hell because they had dinner parties and played cards with their friends.

Cummy, in her thirties, in 1865

Cummy thought his words important enough to record them in her journal. "I wrote down every word he spoke. It pleased the bairn and I read his havers to his mother at the nursery fire." What a shame she burned the journal when she was quite elderly and thought death was close.

His mother's diaries, too, were filled with details about Louis. When he was three years old she described how he brought her a "doiley off the table, unfolded it, and carefully spread it over her, saying 'That's a wee bittie, Mama,'" mimicking the way Cummy had covered her with a shawl. Margaret enjoyed watching him concentrate on his games or his chalks, but was often startled when he would stop abruptly and come to her, asking, "Do you think I'm looking very ill?"

Thomas assumed his son would outgrow his illnesses and become strong enough to join the family tradition. He, his father, and his brothers were all engineers who had created many of the country's harbors and lighthouses. Sometimes when Smout was recuperating from an illness, Thomas told him tales about building lighthouses or adventure stories about a brave mail-coach driver who rode long distances and fought off marauders and robbers.

Thomas was a terrible worrier, but he loved a good story. Margaret was more optimistic and fun-loving than her husband and was always quick to find the positive in any situation.

The adults in his life all doted on Louis, but still he was a lonely child. He remembered feeling left out of his parents' close relationship and insisted later that "children of lovers are orphans." Because he was not physically strong and had to miss many days of school, the other children teased him and made fun of his clothes, especially the yellow cape and straw hat he wore for walks with Cummy. "Hauf a laddie, hauf a lassie, hauf a yellow yite," they jeered.

Louis dictated stories he made up to Cummy or his mother. When his uncle David announced a contest for the best story about Moses, five-year-old Louis created and illustrated one in which Moses was hidden in the rushes by his mother so that he would be saved. Later the Israelites, wearing top hats and yellow trousers, crossed the Red Sea carrying bundles on their shoulders. Louis drew them "leading camels . . . and smoking huge cigars." He won the contest.

Margaret wrote in her journal, "From that time forward it was the desire of his heart to be an author." Louis might have added, "If I am spared."

Louis, age four, wearing yellow cape made by Cummy

CHAPTER 3

~

Cousin Bob and Colinton

Here is the mill with the humming of thunder,
Here is the weir with the wonder of foam,
Here is the sluice with the race running under—
Marvellous places, though handy to home!

Cousin Bob Stevenson, three years older than Louis, called him his "first and best friend" in the whole world. He said he only spoke to others so that he could report the conversation to Louis. Together they visited silver-haired Grandfather Balfour, who was minister at Colinton Manse and who wrote his sermons in the study. His daughter, Louis's aunt Jane, kept life running smoothly for Grandfather and the many family members who were always visiting; sometimes as many as ten cousins stayed there at one time. Their maiden aunt Jane was especially fond of Louis and gave him his first set of toy soldiers. For her birthday he sent her a picture of a ship with a dictated note, describing the ship: its mast "tumbling down with the wind because it is very stormy. It is raining too."

Only five, he already knew how to set a scene.

Bob and Louis invented kingdoms and drew intricate maps of them: "Encyclopaedia" for Louis and "Nosingtonia" for Bob. Their food was perfect for games, also. Bob's porridge sprinkled with sugar became a country "continually buried under snow" while Louis covered his porridge with milk and called it a country "suffering gradual inundation."

Only three miles southwest of Edinburgh, Colinton seemed a world away for Louis and his many cousins (he had at least fifty). He called the path near the church "the Witches Walk" and pretended the mill was the edge of friendly territory. He turned washbaskets into boats, hunted wild animals among the laurels, and led the others through the churchyard with its frightening rows of tombstones.

The cousins played hide-and-seek and although Louis could not run because of his weak lungs, he was skilled at every "shift and dodge" and became the best player. Then he rested on the swing hanging from a giant yew tree and planned their next adventure in the wild hedges.

One of his cousins, Minnie, had just returned from India, and Louis fell in love with her and with the exotic tales she told him about her life abroad. He was so taken with her, he proposed marriage to Minnie when she was eight or nine and he was not much older.

When Cousin Bob came to stay with Louis at 17 Heriot Row, they set up a miniature wooden theater Louis had been given for his sixth birthday. They performed dramas such as *Robin Hood, Aladdin,* and *The Old Oak Chest* on its tiny stage using cardboard characters they had bought from Mr.

Smith's the Stationers on Leith Way. The stage was open on both ends and had wooden grooves that held the cardboard actors. Bob and Louis took turns opening the real silk curtains and moving the cardboard actors across the stage.

Purchasing the characters was drama itself. Mr. Smith's shop was "dark and smelt of Bibles," Louis remembered. "The shopmen . . . frowned us down, snatched each play out of our hand ere we were trusted with another; Old Mr. Smith himself, worn out with my eternal vacillation once swept the treasures from before me, with the cry: 'I do not believe, child, that you are an intending purchaser at all!' "

Once a choice was made, Louis "was forth again, a little late for dinner, the lamps springing into light in the blue winter's even. On what gay feet he ran, and how he laughed aloud in exultation!"

As bright as he seemed, Louis was not yet reading at age seven. Perhaps he didn't need to learn for himself since Cummy continued to read to him from her favorite books, the Bible and *Pilgrim's Progress*. His parents worried that Louis was a slow learner. At last, when he was nearly eight, Louis began to read on his own. For the rest of his life he always referred to the "shock of that pleasure."

One day he found a comfortable chair in Grandfather's book-lined study at Colinton and was absorbed in reading stories from *The Arabian Nights*. Slowly he turned the pages and studied the exotic illustrations of evil jinns transforming themselves into animal and human forms. In his mind he was a million miles away when he heard a strange noise. Louis jumped. He was "blind with terror."

Then he saw Grandfather Balfour in the doorway smiling. "How I envy you," his grandfather said, happy to see his young grandson so lost in the world of books.

Grandfather Balfour died shortly after that and Louis's lovely years at Colinton came to an end. But still he had his "kingdom" at 17 Heriot Row with tin soldiers, picture books, paint boxes, colored chalks, and theater cutouts.

CHAPTER 4

~

Early Education

When I was sick and lay a-bed,
I had two pillows at my head,
And all my toys beside me lay
To keep me happy all the day.

T homas Stevenson never cared much for organized education, but he finally agreed to let Louis attend Cannonmills School when he was seven. Louis was eager to join in the activities with the other children just as he did with his cousins at Colinton. But most of the time he didn't feel strong enough. Instead he watched from the sidelines while they played ball or chased each other at tag. Often he was kept home because a minor cold led to severe bronchitis, or a stomachache became gastric fever, or swollen glands turned into whooping cough.

By the time he returned to school, his classmates had learned their sums, studied maps, and recited poetry that Louis had missed. After he caught up in school, he broke out in a rash and was home for weeks struggling to get over chicken pox. The pattern was the same month after month. No sooner was he back to school than he came down with some new disease. Back to bed he went for six more weeks.

Louis missed school for another reason. Whenever his parents wanted to get away from the dampness of Edinburgh's weather, they planned a trip to the south of France, where they would find sun and warmth, and they took Louis with them. Often they hired a tutor to teach him his lessons, but most of the time he was learning a great deal about people and nature and geography simply by traveling. He also learned to speak French and German so that he could talk with workers, townspeople, and children he met in other countries.

Until he was eleven, his parents enrolled him in one school after another near their home. Then when he was a bit older, they sent him to a boarding school near London. He was not happy there and came home after one term, saying the English boys were more interested in cricket and other sports than they were in literature. Fortunately he had a quick, curious mind and spent most of his time reading on his own. He wrote letters home filled with exercises in Latin and Greek and even wrote whole letters in French. By the time he was fourteen he was reading the plays of Shakespeare and the adventure novels of Sir Walter Scott and Alexandre Dumas.

He and a friend published two magazines, writing and illustrating most of the articles and stories for them. *Schoolboy* was full of wild adventure tales and *Sunbeam* was more realistic. And at one school he won a writing prize for an essay on William Wallace, the Scottish patriot who had stood against the English in 1296. But for the most part he took little interest in doing well in his studies.

When he was twelve his parents took Louis and his cousin Bessie on a trip to London, then through France, Italy, Switzerland, and Germany. Cummy was shocked by what she saw and reported in her diary that Europeans were heathens who did not honor the Sabbath or much of anything. She also complained that she could never find a tasty cup of tea in Europe. Louis liked the vitality of the French and Italian people he met. They didn't seem as concerned about proper behavior as did the Scottish people he knew. His father introduced him to grown-up settings. They joined other men in smoking rooms, and he was able to participate in political and financial discussions as if he were an adult.

One of Louis's favorite places in Scotland was the seaside resort of North Berwick, where the family spent a summer. There Louis gathered other boys together in the evenings. They fastened tin lanterns onto their belts and moved through the darkness. As lantern bearers, the trick was to keep the lantern lit without burning oneself and to keep it hidden under one's coat without letting it go out. In the dark of night they wandered under the trees, delivering messages and using special passwords to identify themselves. It was almost as good as being back at Colinton leading his cousins in adventures.

CHAPTER 5

~

University Life

At evening, when the lamp is lit,
Around the fire my parents sit;
They sit at home and talk and sing,
And do not play at anything.

B y the time seventeen-year-old Louis started college at
the University of Edinburgh, he thought of himself as
"lean, ugly, idle, unpopular." Others agreed that he was
skinny and looked odd, mainly because of the clothing he
chose. He always wore a dark velvet coat over an equally
dark shirt and soon people began calling him "Velvet Coat."
His hair was long and straggly while his trousers often
seemed too short.

Often he came late to classes or didn't attend at all. He
preferred to spend his time at The Green Elephant or The
Twinkling Eye, pubs in Old Town, a part of Edinburgh
where seamen, chimney sweeps, and other workmen lived.
He felt comfortable in these howfs, as the Scottish called
them, listening as the men shared local news and told tales

of work and play. They were honest, hard-working people with no airs about them. No matter which setting he chose, the University or the pub, Louis was an observer. He liked to watch the others, but chose to remain separate from them. In a way he was studying human nature so that he could describe it in his later novels.

Charles Baxter was a great friend who loved practical jokes. Together he and Louis invented characters and carried on one-sided conversations with them. They sent empty parcels to local citizens and caused no end of trouble. When he attended classes at all, Louis made no effort to fit in. He sat on one of the benches in the back of the hall and read a book or pretended to take notes when he was really writing "original nonsense." He was never without a book to write in, as well as the book he was reading at the time. Whether he was sitting in a pub or a classroom or by the side of the road on one of his long treks, Louis was able to pull open one book to read or the other to record his thoughts.

Scholarly work did not intrigue him. After a few months he stopped taking Greek and finally gave up Latin in his second year at the University. He was supposed to be preparing himself for a career as an engineer like his father and grandfather before him. But that same year he was asked to join the Speculative Society and found something else that delighted him. The group debated literary or philosophical questions, and Louis was a "dazzling performer" who always presented new ideas and had new ways of expressing himself. The evening meetings were held in a room lit only by a glowing fire and flickering candles that illuminated the members' faces as they dined and drank and then debated. Louis found he had a great talent to charm people with his words.

He had always loved to read—not necessarily what he was supposed to for class. Nor did he look up unfamiliar words in a dictionary. He preferred to figure them out for himself from the context. One of his favorite writers was the American poet Walt Whitman. He felt Whitman's work should be reserved for "those who have the gift of reading" as he did, readers who could appreciate books and ideas even though they might disagree with them.

Louis was asked to work on a college magazine. He wrote sketches about his past experiences, about the gardener at Swanston house where the family spent summers, about the lack of goals he found in most students at the University. He, along with his friend from the Speculative Society, Walter Ferrier, and several others, produced four issues of the magazine before it folded. The four had to ask their fathers to pay off the printer's bills.

Fleeming Jenkin was Louis's engineering professor. Because Jenkin had so many interests in addition to engineering, he also became a friend and mentor to young Louis. Jenkin and his wife produced amateur dramas and encouraged Louis and other students to get involved. Louis helped behind the scenes and even acted a role or two, but found he was not as comfortable reciting other people's words as he was creating his own.

In his first two years at the University, Louis studied physics, optics, algebra, and trigonometry in order to become an engineer and carry on the Stevenson tradition. But gradually his interest in engineering and lighthouses was disappearing, and he realized that all along he only had been trying to please his father. As a thirteen-year-old, he had gone with Thomas to inspect lighthouses on the coast of Fife and loved the "wildness, the gaunt beauty, the challenge of terrain and the elements." When he was older he toured harbor works and even wrote a paper on a lighthouse at Anstruther. During the day he worked right along with the other men who were repairing the damaged structure. But at night he came alive when he sat in his room and wrote dramatic monologues in verse.

Thomas took him to Wick, where the harbor he had designed was destroyed by storms. For the first time Louis went down in "diving-dress" and found it exhilarating. "My hand shook so that I could not draw for some time after with the excitement," he wrote. The following summer he and Thomas toured Orkney and Shetland. Then they went to the Isle of Erraid, which Louis would use many years later as a site for David Balfour's shipwreck in *Kidnapped*. In his later writing, he used all he had learned about the power of the sea on lighthouses. But after three-and-a-half years he was certain he didn't want to make this his life's work. He just wasn't sure how to tell his father.

Then one spring day in 1871 when Louis was twenty, he and Thomas left 17 Heriot Row and set off on a long walk. Without any warning Louis blurted out the truth: That he wanted to quit his engineering studies. That he got his greatest pleasures from writing and that he did not have the physical strength required to become a harbor engineer. He knew he was disappointing his father by breaking the family tradition, but he hoped Thomas would understand and try to accept his decision.

Thomas asked what he would do instead. Louis was vague. To himself he had vowed to learn to write, and already he was trying to imitate his favorite writers. Still he was not confident that he would succeed. Thomas suggested he study law. That way he could earn a living as an advocate if his writing did not succeed. Relieved to see that his father understood, Louis agreed to study law. His friends at the University, Charles Baxter and Walter Simpson, were both studying law. He would join them.

Before long Louis began having nightmares again, perhaps because he was still trying to follow dreams that were not his own. One night he dreamed that he was a surgeon trying to correct terrible distortions in his patients. Another night, he was lost and unable to find his place in a boardinghouse no matter how high he climbed.

Just two years later Louis was to shock his father even more. Throughout his university years he questioned everything he had accepted earlier. The more he read, the more he wondered about the world and about religion until at last he could not accept the strict Calvinist religious upbringing he had received from Cummy and his parents. First he had told his father he would not become an engineer. Now, in January 1873, he announced he no longer believed in God.

His father was devastated. "You have rendered my whole life a failure," he told Louis. In a letter to Charles Baxter,

Louis admitted, "the thunderbolt has fallen with a vengeance now." His father stalked the house, his face grim. He no longer whistled as he used to. He was angry, but he was also worried about Louis's future. Would his precious son be destined to go to hell? Thomas blamed his nephew, Louis's cousin Bob. It was all Bob's fault that Louis had turned away from religion. Bob was a bad influence. He had always been a freethinker, artistic, a troublemaker. Thomas told Louis he would have to stay away from his cousin, and he warned Bob not to get in touch with Louis.

Louis wrote a desperate letter to Baxter. "Now, what is to take place? What a curse I am to my parents! O Lord, what a pleasant thing it is to have just *damned* the happiness of (probably) the only two people who care a damn about you in the world!" He signed the letter, "Ever your affectionate and horrible atheist, R. L. Stevenson."

The first two years of college had been lonely and miserable for Louis. He spent hours in the graveyard, reading epitaphs and feeling miserable. The last two years he was happier and had made a few good friends. Also, Cousin Bob returned from France. The two men ignored Thomas's threats because they meant so much to each other. Louis could confide his feelings to Bob, and together they could laugh and enjoy life. His cousin lifted the weight of sadness from his shoulders.

CHAPTER 6

~

Another Disappointment

But as some lone, wood-wandering child
Brings home with him at evening mild
The thorns and flowers of all the wild,
From your whole life, O fair and true
Your flowers and thorns you bring with you!

Friends were very important to Louis. As an only child he worked hard to maintain his friendships with his cousins and with students he met at the University. He gave a great deal of himself to his friends and expected them to do the same for him.

During a visit to his cousin Maud in England in the summer of 1873, Louis met Frances Sitwell and her young son Bertie. At that time Mrs. Sitwell was separated from her husband and had just lost her other son. Louis was sad for her. He was also smitten by her.

Now twenty-two, he didn't care that she was an older woman of thirty-four. He spent every moment he could talking with her when they were together, and when he returned to Edinburgh he wrote her daily: long, detailed letters describing how he spent his days, how he worried his parents. He sent her the essay he had written about his walks along the Suffolk roads while he had visited there, and asked her opinion of it.

She liked it and introduced him to her friend Sidney Colvin. Colvin, a Cambridge professor, was six years older than Louis and had more experience within the literary world. He saw in the young Stevenson a "youngster, already to have lived and seen and felt . . . more than others in a lifetime." Both he and Mrs. Sitwell were quite charmed by Louis and recognized his great passion to write. Under their encouragement Louis worked at writing and rewriting his essays and travel pieces until he was satisfied with them. Then he sent them off to Colvin, who had contacts in the publishing world and would make sure they were published.

Louis had been so happy at Cousin Maud's, he was unprepared for the strained mood he found when he arrived at home. Thomas could hardly look at his difficult, wayward son. Margaret worried about both of them while trying to calm her husband. Whether the conflict was to blame or not, Louis grew ill again in the fall of 1873. The doctor found him suffering from "acute nerve exhaustion" and worried that his lungs were in danger. He recommended Louis leave blustery Edinburgh and go to a more favorable climate for the fall months. And the doctor insisted that he go alone. Louis chose to travel to Mentone in the south of France for rest and sunshine.

Settled at a small hotel, he was too weak to enjoy the lush

setting with its sturdy olive groves, fragrant lemon and orange trees, and a view of the sea. He could do nothing but lie in the sun and listen to the waves. "I lead the life of a vegetable," he complained in a letter to his mother. "I eat, I sleep, I sit in the sun." To Mrs. Sitwell he wrote, "If you knew how old I felt!" After several months the warmth and the companionship of friendly families at the hotel began to work their cure so that Louis was able to write again.

He sent long letters home and even longer letters to Mrs. Sitwell. He worked on essays about Victor Hugo and Walt Whitman. He took notes about his surroundings. He was supposed to be studying law, but he complained that "it seems to take away the power of writing from me."

He returned to Edinburgh in the spring, feeling strong even though everyone agreed he looked like a scarecrow walking around, with his clothes hanging from his lean body. His parents had missed him terribly. During his absence Thomas realized how much Louis meant to him and saw that he could lose him at any moment from one illness or another. It softened the way he treated his son. In May Louis and his parents traveled to their country home, Swanston Cottage, far above the sea. It was still wintry and cold there, but Louis felt well enough to hike the hills, where he came upon bleating sheep being shorn and saw partridges fluttering from their hiding places and baby rabbits in the brush.

Louis was a careful observer of the natural world. He studied the skies, the rivers, the woods. He listened to its creatures. He also studied people and tried to understand their behavior. Then he wrote exacting descriptions in his note-book or in letters to Mrs. Sitwell and other friends. If he saw an interesting woman or child along the roadside, he jotted down what they were wearing or how they walked. One evening he even found a small boy searching for his mother and rushed with him to the police station. Then he faith-fully described the whole episode in a letter. Another time he watched a man and woman saying farewell to each other at the train station. Both of them were unpleasant to look at, he with smallpox scars pitting his face, she with a blind, disfigured eye. Yet Louis saw how the woman's face changed "to a perfect heaven of love" when she looked at the man.

Louis reported to Mrs. Sitwell about his own situation: "We are all as jolly as can be together," and what a change that was from the previous months he was home. He was also pleased that his essay about the time spent in Mentone, "Ordered South," had been published and that readers were sending letters telling him how much it meant to them. His parents agreed to give him eighty-four pounds a year, and he felt that he "should soon make a good bit by [his] pen" as well.

While he was doing everything else (writing, traveling, acting in an amateur theatrical company, even attending church with his mother on Sundays), Louis was still reading law books and preparing to take the bar. It's hard to believe he expected to pass the exam when he preferred to work on his essays or to be outdoors wandering the hills and roads.

But pass he did. In July 1875 he was declared a Scottish Advocate. After the morning ceremony Louis, still dressed in formal wear, drove home in an open carriage shouting the news to passersby and waving his top hat. His parents celebrated. They were proud of his accomplishment and gave Louis one thousand pounds to mark his success. He purchased a white curled wig, which he would be expected to wear in appearances before the court, and his father had a brass plate attached to the house announcing "R. L. Stevenson, Advocate." For several months, dressed in wig and gown, Louis attended trials at Parliament House. But he could not keep it up. The law interfered too much with his other interests, he complained. To Mrs. Sitwell, he wrote: "You know, I lose all my forenoons at Court!" He sounded happy and active—reading, writing, speaking, or walking, and he was getting very good at wheel-skating.

And as soon as he could, he went off on another trip with his friend from the University, Walter Simpson, to Fontainebleau in France.

Louis wearing his advocate's robes, July 1875

CHAPTER 7

~

True Love

Mine eyes were swift to know thee, and my heart
As swift to love. I did become at once
Thine, wholly thine, unalterably thine
In honorable service, pure intent
Steadfast excess of love and laughing care.

A year after he became a Scottish Advocate, Louis, now twenty-five, traveled back to the south of France and the artists' colony at Grez where his cousin Bob was waiting for him. In the past only male artists and writers came together to work and socialize in this setting. Now it was rumored that women had invaded the place, and Bob had gone on ahead to discover the truth. On a lovely summer evening Louis hurried toward happy voices coming from Madame Chevillon's Inn. It was dinnertime. Looking in through the top of a double door, he saw an animated group of young people sitting around the table. Indeed, a woman had invaded the artists' colony! There she sat, her warm smile and black penetrating eyes turned toward

Fanny Osbourne when she first met Louis

him. She was dark, mysterious, intriguing. Louis vaulted over the bottom of the door. After his grand entrance the young men in the dining room jumped up to greet him. But Louis could not take his eyes off the exotic-looking woman. At last Bob introduced him to Fanny and he knew he was in love. He had fallen in love the moment he first saw her.

Louis was a romantic and a storyteller. It's natural that he would tell stories about his own life, embellishing them when it suited him. Still, this time it seemed he was telling the truth about his feelings. Fanny remembered their meeting differently. She wrote to friends describing her interest in his cousin Bob, whom she met before Louis. She was attracted by Bob's liveliness and his reputation as a painter, a musician, and an athlete. Next to his cousin, Louis was a scarecrow. He had a thin face, thin body; even his mustache was thin and drooping. Not only that—he was moody and often withdrawn. But given time, she would discover that no one could match his persuasive verbal charm.

Earlier that year Fanny had run away from home in the United States with her three children. Belle was seventeen, Lloyd seven, and Hervey four. She had told her husband, Sam, she could no longer live with a man who continued to see other women. Off she went to Paris, where she and Belle enrolled in art classes. But when young Hervey became ill, Fanny dropped out of her classes to care for him. Her golden boy seemed to get better for a time. But before long, he fell ill again. Then no matter what Fanny or the physician tried, Hervey died of scrofulous tuberculosis. Fanny in her grief took Belle and Lloyd to the quiet countryside of Grez and settled at Madame Chevillon's Inn. After their initial surprise at having women in their midst, the young artists there took a liking to the family, and their attention was especially healing for Fanny.

Louis had deadlines to meet. He stayed at the inn for only a few days before returning to his family's country house in Scotland at Swanston. He needed to complete two stories he was working on by the end of July so that he could be off again on new travels. He and his friend Walter Simpson had taken a canoe trip from Antwerp to Brussels in Belgium and then to France. From his experiences on that trip Louis wrote *An Inland Voyage,* which two years later in May 1878 became his first published book.

When he returned to Grez he proudly showed Fanny and her children the canoes he and Simpson had used, called *Cigarette* and *Arethusa,* and regaled them with their experiences. Already he was making an impact on the Osbourne children. Belle called him "such a nice looking ugly man." Young Lloyd called him "gay and buoyant" and said that he made them all laugh. He liked Louis very much. In fact, he said he quickly grew to love the man he called Luly.

While staying at Grez, Louis wrote a story, "Providence and the Guitar," inspired by some strolling players with a crippled child who came through the area. When the story was published he gave the money to the musicians for their child. Louis always was quick to lend money to his friends or help the needy, even when he should have been concerned about taking care of himself.

The following year Fanny and Louis were together at Grez again for most of the summer. Cousin Bob played Cupid, telling Fanny about Louis and what a fascinating man he was. By then Louis hardly needed his cousin's help. He was enchanted by Fanny and she seemed to be quite interested in him. He carried her art supplies to the location she selected. He read to her while she painted. He played his penny whistle for her. They went walking through the nearby forest and boating on the river. In the evenings Fanny rested in a hammock while Louis told her about his work and, soon, his dreams. Louis followed Fanny and the children back to Paris in the fall. It did not concern him that Fanny was ten years older than he. After all, Mrs. Sitwell was a dear friend to him and she was also an older woman. He continued to write to her even after he met Fanny.

He wrote about his feelings for Fanny in "On Falling in Love," which was published in *Cornhill Magazine* for all the world to see. His parents, Margaret and Thomas, were beside themselves with worry. Fanny was a married woman! She had two children! Louis was only twenty-seven and not earning enough money to take care of himself, let alone a family! Thomas was still paying all his bills!

Louis and Fanny tried to ignore his parents' concerns. They were in love. Fanny became his nurse for the first time when Louis developed an eye infection that threatened to blind him. Unable to cure it, Fanny took him to London, where a doctor saved his eyesight with the correct medications. While there, Fanny was forced to have foot surgery and was taken to recuperate at Mrs. Sitwell's home, where she met William

Henley and some of Louis's other friends. They were all cautious with Fanny, perhaps out of jealousy at not wanting to share their friend with anyone else. Or perhaps because they felt that an older woman with two children, and an American at that, was not the right person for him.

The close relationship between Louis and Fanny changed abruptly. She was still married to Sam Osbourne, who had been paying her bills while she was in France. Now he was going to stop doing so. Fanny and the children had to return to America. With a heavy heart, Louis saw them off on the London boat train in August of 1878.

His parents were very relieved to hear that Fanny was gone and would no longer be a part of their son's life. No matter how Louis tried to explain that Fanny and Sam had no real marriage any longer and that he and Fanny were in love and considered themselves married to each other, Margaret and Thomas would not hear him. They considered divorce scandalous and Fanny an evil woman. But Louis knew that in spirit Fanny was married to him, not to the American she had left in the United States. In her mind her marriage to Sam Osbourne was over when she left for France. Now she and Louis had to be apart for a time, but both of them looked at it as only a temporary separation.

He explained to his friend Sidney Colvin that he was not writing letters to Fanny because they had said all there was to say to each other; they already knew everything there was to know and before long they would be together. He was preparing for his next excursion through the southeastern mountains of France, which he would describe in the book *Travels with a Donkey in the Cévennes.*

In September Louis bought a small mouse-colored donkey from Father Adam, a local priest, for sixty five francs and a glass of brandy. He named her Modestine. He and the donkey "jogged along with our six legs by many a rocky" road, Louis said, describing the twelve days and 120 miles they traveled. Modestine carried his supplies: a sleeping sack he had designed that unfolded to six feet square, a change of clothes, books, cakes of chocolate, tins of sausage, bread, wine, a leg of mutton, and, of course, a lined notebook. At night when they came to a resting place, Louis wrapped himself in his sack, put a fur cap on his head to keep warm, and read near the firelight or made notes on what he had seen of the French highlands they had passed through during the day. He wrote down stories about the people he met or described how similar the mountainous areas were to his familiar Scottish landscape. He started out with little affection for the donkey who carried his goods. After many days together, however, she became more than a beast of burden. She became a friend and a confidant.

The book was dedicated to Sidney Colvin, but he "put a thousand messages of love for Fanny in it," Louis told his cousin Bob. After describing a pleasant meeting with a Protestant pastor, he wrote: "And if we find but one to whom we can speak out of our hearts freely, with whom we can walk in love and simplicity . . . we have no ground or quarrel with the world or God." He was probably thinking of Fanny as that special one.

Later, passing under chestnut trees, Louis described how

he heard the voice of a woman singing a sad ballad as evening was approaching. It made him lonely, and he wrote: "How the world gives and takes away, and brings sweethearts near, only to separate them again into distant and strange lands; but to love is the great amulet which makes the world a garden." Certainly he was thinking of Fanny here.

On the last evening Louis and Modestine reached the top of St. Pierre, where they shared their final meal together, "I on a heap of stones, she standing by me in the moonlight and decorously eating bread out of my hand." The next morning he sold the donkey for thirty-five francs and took a stagecoach to the next village to collect his mail. He remembered that Father Adam had wept when he sold Modestine to him; now Louis, too, felt like weeping.

CHAPTER 8

~

Across the World

Of where or how, I nothing know;
  And why, I do not care;
  Enough if, even so,
My travelling eyes, my travelling mind can go
By flood and field and hill, by wood and meadow fair,
Beside the Susquehanna and along the Delaware.

After Louis said farewell to his donkey and to France, he visited his friends Sidney Colvin at Cambridge and William Henley in London. He complained to them, "I can do no work. It all lies aside . . . I want to be happy; I want the moon or the sun or something. I want the object of my affections badly anyway." Fanny had been gone for months. He wanted to follow her. His friends advised him to forget her. She had her own life in the United States. He needed to get on with his work.

Then suddenly Fanny cabled Louis in early August of 1879. There is no record of what she said in the cable, but it must have been urgent because Louis made an abrupt decision to go to her immediately. He sailed from Glasgow, Scotland, on August 7 without even telling his parents. From the ship that first day he wrote to Cousin Bob telling him how ill Fanny was and that he was rushing to be with her. He hoped to return in a month or two. He also sent a letter to his parents and to other friends telling them he was on his way to his beloved Fanny. He must have known how upset everyone would be to hear his news but now Fanny came first in his thoughts.

He could not be stopped. Not even if his parents threatened to leave Scotland because they couldn't face the gossip about their son running off to be with a married woman. Not even if they threatened to disinherit him. He would not change his mind. "No man is of any use until he has dared everything," he wrote Colvin. "I feel just now as if I had, and so might become a man."

Louis borrowed thirty pounds from Charles Baxter to pay for his tickets. Instead of staying in steerage—the lowest class on the ship—he spent an extra two pounds to travel second class because it would allow him the use of a writing table. He planned to do more than just write letters. He wanted to finish a complicated short story, "The Story of a Lie," about the difficult relationship between a father and his son.

He was also recording his impressions of his shipboard companions in preparation for a future work he hoped to write about the voyage. He questioned everyone—the stowaways, the gentlemen, the laborers—and found them all good talkers willing to share their stories with him.

"As I walked the deck and looked round upon my fellow-passengers, thus curiously assorted from all northern Europe, I began for the first time to understand the nature of emigration," he wrote. "Emigration, from a word of the most cheerful import, came to sound most dismally in my ear. There is nothing more agreeable to picture and nothing more pathetic to behold."

He was fascinated by the children on board. "The children found each other out like dogs and ran about the decks . . . 'What do you call your mither?' I heard one ask. 'Mawmaw,' was the reply." There was "one little fellow . . . [a] child of three . . . crowing with laughter and beating an accompaniment to his own mirth with a tin spoon upon a tin cup" even when "his family lay sick and prostrate around him."

The officers aboard ship "referred to my absurd occupation with familiarity and breadth of humorous intention . . . 'Well!' they would say: 'Still writing?' And the smile would widen into a laugh."

Yes, he was still writing, even when the seas were rough and he had to watch his ink bottle slide back and forth across the table, which he described as "the table playing bob-cherry with the ink-bottle." He loved traveling by sea. No matter how high the waves, he felt better than he had ever felt on land. Sometimes he slept on deck because there was not enough air for him below. He tried to encourage others to join him there, but when they didn't he went alone. He wrote of the "clear note of the clapper on the brass and the beautiful sea-cry, 'All's well!' I know nothing, whether for poetry or music, that can surpass the effect of these two syllables in the darkness of a night at sea."

Early in the evening he often joined the other passengers in song and dance. There might be a fiddle or an accordion leading jigs or reels and sometimes even a formal quadrille. Just for those few moments, everyone forgot their worries as they twirled together in a tiny space on deck.

One day he visited the steerage passengers living in the lowest level of the ship and saw firsthand how difficult it was to be poor. While he was there three passengers from first class also came down to steerage. Louis saw how they mocked the less fortunate passengers and put on superior airs as they picked their way through the family groups. "It was astonishing what insults these people managed to convey by their presence. They seemed to throw their clothes in our faces." In his journal he noted every gesture the arrogant visitors made.

After ten long days aboard the *Devonia,* Louis arrived in New York on a Sunday evening in the midst of a pouring rain. He was able to find a boardinghouse near the docks, where he spent his first night in the United States. Awakening early the next morning, he had much to accomplish on his first day in New York. "I went to banks, post-offices, railway-offices, restaurants, publishers, book-sellers, money changers," leaving a puddle everywhere from the drenching rains.

The publishers were not impressed by his bedraggled appearance or his mention of the travel books he had already written and those he intended to write. In a bookstore he bought a six-volume edition of Bancroft's *History of the United States,* which he packed in his valise. But best of all he found his own book in the shop and described the experience in a letter: "Bought a copy of my own work. The man said, 'by Stevenson.' 'Indeed,' says I. 'Yes, sir,' says he. Scene closes."

At the post office he found a letter from Fanny awaiting him. Afterward he wrote Henley that "Fanny has inflammation of the brain," and he was going to her immediately. He rushed to buy his train ticket for California and to exchange his Scottish money for dollars.

That evening, traveling by ferry to Jersey City, he found the first of several trains that would take him west to his Fanny. There were hundreds of people waiting to board, sitting on their bundles or their valises while the train cars were being cleaned and supplied with coal. His quick action prevented a child from being harmed by the pushing crowds, and he proudly wrote, "With my own hand . . . I saved the life of a child as it sat upon its mother's knee." Once the cars were ready, the passengers pushed forward in a mass to find seats. Louis sat up that first night damp and dozing. In the morning the train stopped in Philadelphia. Louis got out. He was delighted with the green, open country before him. "The sun rises with a different splendour in America," he wrote home.

He transferred to another train in Chicago that was even more crowded than the first one had been. Passengers were so tightly squeezed together that smells from food and bodies became intolerable as the days passed. At one stop he bought a board and straw cushions for $2.50 so that he could put them across the seats and use them for his bed.

During the day he sat on the roof of the train watching golden cornfields and tall sunflowers whiz by. Taking notes on the passing scenery, he recorded the names of each new town and river—Delaware, Dubuque, Susquehanna—and used some of them in a poem that he sent to Colvin.

"In America . . . the food is heavenly," he raved. But a few days later he complained that he was not eating and was losing weight quickly, only drinking tea. Passing through the middle of the country, he became more uncomfortable with diarrhea and fever. Now he saw "ghostly deserts . . . without form or colour, a sad corner of the world." By the time the train passed over the Rocky Mountains, Louis was so sick he couldn't appreciate the sight.

By Saturday, August 30, Louis finally reached San Francisco. He had been traveling for twenty-three long days and had not yet reached Fanny. He still had to cross the bay to Oakland, take the Southern Pacific Railroad to the town of Salinas, then a narrow-gauge train from there to Monterey, where she and her sister Nellie and the children were staying.

He arrived in Monterey wearing a "seedy blue serge suit and bowler hat," coughing, his hands covered with rash, and his purse flat. He had lost weight on the trip—a stone, he said, which is about fourteen pounds. Looking more like a scarecrow than ever, Louis stood at Fanny's door and called out "Folly!" his nickname for her. How relieved he was to see that Fanny looked well and had recovered from whatever illness she might have had. It was a joyous reunion. Not until later when he discovered that she was

41

still married to Sam Osbourne and had no definite plans to ask him for a divorce did he feel discouraged.

Depressed and physically weak after his long journey, Louis set off to explore the new area and to think about what he should do next. He hired a horse and traveled about eighteen miles up into the Santa Lucia hills. Unable to go farther, he dismounted and collapsed under a tree. Local goat ranchers found him two days later and took him home with them. With their good care, total rest, and nutritious food Louis was soon better. To thank the men he began teaching the ranch children how to read. But he was frightened. He realized how close he had come to dying. Fanny also was scared into action. It was time to ask Sam for a divorce.

Once Louis was stronger he found Monterey to be a perfect setting. He enjoyed walking along the white sand of its beaches, watching the sandpipers race the waves, listening to the ocean break against the coast. "Monterey is a place where there is no summer or winter, and pines and sand and distant hills, and a bay all filled with real water from the Pacific," he wrote Colvin in September 1879.

And to Henley the following month he wrote, "This is a lovely place, which I am growing to love. The Pacific licks all other oceans out of hand; there is no place but the Pacific coast to hear eternal roaring surf." Here in Monterey the houses were built of adobe brick, the sidewalks were boards, the streets were paved with sand, and there were no streetlights. What a contrast to the Edinburgh Louis had left. But he found the people very friendly and was able to ride horseback everywhere now that he was feeling better. The rash on his hands was finally cured by an ancient Indian woman who used a poultice of balsamea.

By then Louis was staying at the home of a local doctor "in great airy rooms with five windows opening on a balcony" and eating his meals at Jules Simoneau's, "a most pleasant old boy with whom I discuss the universe and play chess daily." He never forgot the kindness of Jules and his wife, Doña Martina, and continued to write them, later sending leather-bound copies of his books.

He worked as a reporter for the local paper, *Monterey Californian*, which paid him two dollars a week. Louis had no idea that his friends at Jules's restaurant were paying his salary by secretly passing a gravy bowl. They had sworn not to tell him because they knew he would not accept their money no matter how desperately he needed it. But they also knew the paper couldn't afford to pay him.

Fanny's sister Nellie remembered how Louis often read his stories to them in a "full sonorous voice—a voice that always seemed remarkable in so frail a man—his face flushed and his manner embarrassed, for, far from being overconfident about his work, he always seemed to feel a sort of shy anxiety lest it should not be up to the mark."

Almost daily Louis walked along the sandy beach planning his articles or working out his stories. Sometimes he walked with Fanny's son Lloyd, and together they made up adventure tales. Eleven-year-old Lloyd might act out the role of a pirate or an Indian or a naval officer with secret messages from a spy.

Lloyd remembered one particular day when they took an unusually dull walk without creating a single make-believe character. Lost in thought they watched the waves chase tiny birds along the sand. Against the roar of the ocean Louis at last spoke to Lloyd, saying: "I want to tell you something. You may not like it, but I hope you will. I am going to marry your mother." Lloyd was silent. After they had gone a short distance, Louis felt Lloyd's small hand grasp his own and squeeze it.

Lloyd Osbourne, Fanny's son, when he was a boy

Chapter 9

~

Marriage

From where the dogs of Scotland call the sheep around the fold.
To where the flags are flying beside the gates of gold.
It's there I was sick and sad, alone and poor and cold,
In yon distressful city beside the gates of gold.

Fanny left Monterey at the end of October with Lloyd and her sister Nellie to return to their home in Oakland. A few months earlier Belle, her daughter, had eloped with an artist, and she and her new husband, Joe Strong, had gone to San Francisco. Louis was left alone in Monterey. He had made a home for himself there and seemed happy to stay on without the others. He had been well and productive for several months and was surrounded by caring friends.

But suddenly in early December he came down with pleurisy and was so sick he was forced to stay in bed. For days he thought he was dying. In November he had turned twenty-nine. He was certain this birthday was the last one he would celebrate. "But death is no bad friend; a few aches

San Francisco with horse-drawn carriages and cable cars, 1880s

and gasps, and we are done," he told a friend. This time Jules and his wife nursed him back to health. Louis was grateful to them, but his feelings for Monterey had changed. "To live alone in such a hole, the one object of scandal, gossip and imaginative history—well it was not good," he wrote William Henley, completely reversing what he had said earlier about life in the beautiful town.

He had to get away. In December he said farewell to Jules Simoneau and his other companions, telling them he had decided to live in San Francisco, where he would be closer to Fanny, who was just across the bay in Oakland. There he found a boardinghouse run by the Carsons on Bush Street. His money was almost gone, so he tried to spend as little as

46

possible on meals. For ten cents he had coffee, a roll and butter for breakfast; he bought a fifty-cent lunch that included wine and then spent another ten cents for soup and a roll at suppertime.

By mid-January Louis had to cut his spending even more so he ate a twenty-five-cent dinner. When Fanny was able to come across the bay and meet him for a meal, they were both careful not to spend much money on food. Louis was so desperate he wrote Charles Baxter to sell off his last few books and other belongings and to send him the few pounds they would bring.

At last Fanny's divorce from Sam was final. This cheered them both, even though they realized they would have to wait some months before getting married to keep people from gossiping and saying more rude things about them.

Louis was fascinated with San Francisco and began exploring his new city. He walked up and down the hills, some so steep horses couldn't make it to the top. Bush Street reminded him of home with its tall Victorian buildings so close to each other. He might have been back at 17 Heriot Row. He still carried two books and recorded all the details of his new surroundings in one: the creaking of coaches along the streets, the calls of newsboys on the corners, the cries of seagulls near the ocean, the rattle of cable cars along metal tracks. While the damp, foggy days didn't please him, they certainly were familiar. He delighted in the streets of Chinatown with their delicacies and musical language. He sat in Portsmouth Square and soaked up the sunshine before climbing to the top of Nob Hill to see where the millionaires lived.

Louis still looked "scrawny and threadbare," but he was working hard and sent off to Sidney Colvin the beginning sections of *The Amateur Emigrant* describing his travels on ship and trains from Scotland to America, and he began a first draft of the novel *Prince Otto*. He was proud to be a writer and told everyone, "My name is Robert Louis Stevenson—I sling ink." Often he would wrap up in his jacket and stay under the covers in bed so that he could keep warm while he wrote. That way he didn't need as much coal or kindling for his fireplace.

Most days he rushed back from his meager breakfast and greeted Mrs. Carson and her young son, Robbie, before going upstairs to his room to write. "Dere's de author," the child said every time he saw Louis. One day Louis found Mrs. Carson in tears when he returned. Robbie was terribly sick with pneumonia, she told him. She was afraid he might die and was rushing to his room to care for him. Louis offered to help her. Between them they sat up with Robbie night and day, giving him broth and cooling his burning forehead whenever the fever grew worse. Louis suffered as if Robbie were his own child. Or as if he were still the sick child who had spent so many of his days in bed, soothed by his nurse Cummy and his parents.

He wrote Colvin, "My landlord and landlady's little four-year-old child is dying in the house; and O, what he has suffered! . . . O, never, never any family for me!"

After many weeks Robbie's fever broke and they began to hope he might recover. But within days Louis himself was sick. Now he had fever, a terrible cough, and for the first time he was coughing up blood. "Bluidy Jack" he called the hemorrhages. The exhausted Mrs. Carson took over Louis's care. This time there was no question. Louis knew he was going to die. With his last bit of strength he sent Colvin a drawing of the tomb and the words he wanted on it at his gravesite in Scotland:

> *Robert Louis Stevenson*
> *Born 1850 of a Family of Engineers*
> *[Blank for date of death]*
> *Home is the sailor, home from the sea,*
> *And the hunter home from the hill.*

Later he wrote that Fanny had been divorced in January and "yours truly will be a married man as soon thereafter as the law and decency permit. The only question is whether I shall be alive for the ceremony."

Fanny was so frightened by his condition she moved him over to Oakland so she could care for him. She was sure he had tuberculosis and that he would die from it. "For about six weeks . . . it was a toss-up for life or death . . . but I won the toss," Louis wrote afterward. He was grateful to his devoted nurse Fanny and his doctor for his recovery. He gave the doctor a copy of *Travels with a Donkey*. "But for your kindness and skill, this would have been my last book, and now I am in hopes that it will be neither my last nor my best."

Whether Louis really had tuberculosis at this time has never been determined, but he certainly suffered from a weakness of his lungs, and today's experts think he might have suffered from a disease called bronchiectasis.

In April when his parents heard how ill Louis was, they immediately wired that they wanted him to have 250 pounds a year so that he would no longer have to worry about his future earnings. "I always light on my feet, and the best part of my legs is my father," he exulted to Fanny. To Charles Baxter, he confided, "Since I have gone away I have found out for the first time how much I love that man; he is dearer to me than all except Fanny." The best of all news was that his parents sent regards to Fanny and no longer seemed to be against her becoming his wife.

All of this helped Louis recuperate. Fanny read to him for hours until he was able to sit up for a short time each day. Then he felt good enough to tell stories to Lloyd and to work with him on his lessons. Soon he had enough energy to write again. Nellie served as his secretary, or as it was then called, his amanuensis, when he dictated revisions for *The Amateur Emigrant* and began a new novel. Fanny listened to what he had written, offering criticism and editorial assistance. Soon he was back to his normal routine of writing most of the morning. With the money his parents had sent, he was able to have his decaying teeth repaired, which made him feel even better.

When he saw that he was going to live, he persuaded Fanny that they should set a wedding date at last. On May 19, 1880, they were married in San Francisco by Dr. William Scott of St. John's Presbyterian Church on Post Street, with Fanny's close friend Dora Williams as their witness, along with the minister's wife. It hardly mattered to either of them that Fanny was already forty and Louis not yet thirty. His only regret was that he did not have enough money to buy Fanny a wedding gift. Instead he gave her a collection of love poems he had written just for her.

After touring the area, they decided to find a place where they could live in Silverado, several hours north of San Francisco. To get there they took a train and then transferred to a wagon, that hauled them up the slopes of Mount St. Helena. As they wandered through the deserted mining town, they came upon a dilapidated wooden shack that had been a bunkhouse for mine workers. "Not a window-sash remained. . . . We . . . found a fair amount of rubbish . . . and through a chink in the floor, a spray of poison oak had shot up and was handsomely prospering in the interior. It was my first care to cut away that poison oak. . . . That was our first improvement by which we took possession." The air was clear and dry. Louis was sure he would feel healthy in this climate and that they could make a home here.

Used to hard physical work, Fanny cleaned out the cabin, covered the bare windows with fabric, and stuffed mattresses with hay. Louis rose early each morning, drew water from the spring, chopped kindling, and then sat in the shade under madrona trees to write for four or five hours. The only interruption came when Fanny brought him rum punch at eleven and three.

He took careful notes of the setting for the book he would write later that became *The Silverado Squatters*. He described their days and nights, the sounds and the people, the plants and trees, the insects, and the rattlesnakes. There were noisy crickets and noisier branches rustling in the trees and an out-of-tune bird. They befriended the owners of the Silverado

Hotel and the Jewish shopkeeper who gave credit to all but then was disliked because everyone owed him money. Some readers called Louis anti-Semitic in the way he portrayed the man. Louis was shocked. "What a strange idea, to think me a Jew-hater! . . . We are all nobly born. . . ." He pointed out that "Jews and Scotch [are] the most clannish [people] in the world," and even suggested that were he Jewish, "I do not think I could ever forgive the Christians; the ghettos would get in my nostrils like mustard or lit gunpowder."

Louis was determined to continue writing and to earn a living doing it. Having the money from his parents was a safeguard in case he did not sell an essay or story as quickly as he hoped to, but there was no longer any question about his dedication to writing. "I always feel as if I must write a work of genius some time or other," he told Sidney Colvin just after his last close call with death. His letters and conversations with friends were filled with details about the technical aspects of writing. "It's not the first writing that troubles me, and I don't mind the second; it's the third version of my work that kills me." But he knew that sometimes it took many more than three attempts to get a sentence right. To his cousin Bob he complained, "I have been working like Hell at stories and have, up to the present, failed. I have never hitherto given enough attention to the buggers speaking—my dialogue is as weak as soda water."

After their marriage, Fanny wrote frequently to her new mother-in-law, hoping to build a positive relationship. "Taking care of Louis is as you must know," she confided to Margaret, "very like angling for shy trout; one must

A sketch by Joe Strong of Fanny and Louis in their honeymoon cabin at Silverado understand when to pay out the line and exercise the greatest caution in drawing it in." Louis could be shy and sensitive, but he could also be exuberant and animated. Fanny too had changing moods. Their marriage would require a constant adjustment to these qualities in each other.

Fanny wanted Louis's parents to do more than accept her. She wrote to Margaret, "I do so earnestly hope that you will like me, but that can only be for what I am to you after you know me." She assured them that Louis was recovering from his recent illness and their time together at Silverado was giving him physical and mental health. Lloyd had joined them for the summer and was learning to use a printing press. With his new skills as a printer, he created small books from Louis's poetry. They were also together for "two hours daily nightmare known as 'Lloyd's lessons.' "

Margaret and Thomas kept urging Louis to bring Fanny to meet them. On August 7, 1880, exactly a year after Louis first had arrived in the United States, the three of them departed from New York for Scotland. Louis was healthy and happy and was bringing his new family to meet his parents. He had written to prepare the way: "If you can love my wife, it will, I believe, make me love both her and you the better."

CHAPTER 10

~

Home Again

We travelled in the print of olden wars,
Yet all the land was green,
And love we found, and peace,
Where fire and war had been.

S idney Colvin met Louis and Fanny on board the ship when it docked at Liverpool. He was shocked by Louis's appearance: "so small . . . you could put your thumb and finger round his thigh," he exaggerated in his report to Henley. Meanwhile Louis's parents were waiting nervously on shore. They had worried about their son every single day of the year he was gone, fearing they might never see him again. At last he was returning, with a wife and a stepson they had never met.

When they finally came ashore, Margaret was so relieved to have her son back, she didn't even comment on how thin he looked. She thought he looked "better than we dared to hope."

Along with her letters to Margaret and Thomas, Fanny had sent a photograph of herself, cautioning them that the picture was not accurate—it made her seem prettier than she really was. She didn't want them to be disappointed when they met her. And it seems they were not.

Margaret welcomed her new daughter-in-law to 17 Heriot Row with open arms. From trunks and cupboards she brought out gifts of clothing and linens for Fanny. This woman had brought her son back to them, and Margaret could not do enough to show her gratitude. She also found brand-new outfits for Louis that he had never been willing to wear as a student, when he was trying to look like a Bohemian artist in his velvet coat. Now the young couple dressed up in their fine outfits to please his parents.

Margaret wrote in her diary, "Fanny fitted into our household from the first." And she also noted how "entirely she agreed with my husband on all subjects." Margaret realized how wise Fanny was in getting along with Thomas. But she was startled to see her stand up to him as well.

One night at dinner Thomas repeatedly scolded a young servant girl who nervously continued to make more mistakes. Fanny could stand it no longer. She rose and firmly told Thomas she would leave the house if he could not show respect to the servants. At first Thomas was taken aback. After that, she and Thomas became the best of friends. Fanny was so eager to please Thomas she started wearing more conservative dark stockings when he was shocked by her white ones. He admired her spunk and called her "Cassandra" because sometimes it seemed she could read the future and "the Vandegrifter" for her maiden name. She called him "Master Tommy."

Before he knew her, Thomas had thought of her as the

Fanny in 1880 after she and Louis arrived in Scotland

divorced woman who was stealing his son away. Now he realized she was not only charming, she was intelligent and clever and would make the perfect wife for Louis.

Louis was eager to see as much as possible and to introduce Fanny to his dear "Auld Reekie," an affectionate nickname for Edinburgh. He led her through the streets of Old Town, showing her his favorite taverns. He brought her back to New Town and showed her the streetlights he had loved as a child. They visited Sir Walter Scott's home and the college quadrangle with its handsome archway. They walked the Lothian Road and strolled along Leith Walk.

After a time the whole family traveled together to the Highlands, along with Woggs, the black Skye terrier Walter Simpson had given them for a wedding present, and a family cat. They stayed at a lovely hotel in the rolling hills, but the constant rains and mists soon caused Louis to feel ill. His physician uncle, George Balfour, suggested Louis not remain in Edinburgh for the winter. Physicians then believed it was healthier for patients with lung problems or tuberculosis to live in high, cold, dry climates. He recommended the mountains of Davos, Switzerland. But he did not tell his nephew to stop smoking. Few of his physicians did, though Louis was a chain-smoker who was never seen without a cigarette. In those days no one realized that smoking might have made his lung problems worse.

Louis, Fanny, and Lloyd packed their belongings again, put Woggs in one basket, the cat in another, and set off for the high mountains of Switzerland. They found the hotel filled with tuberculosis patients, but Louis was determined to avoid spending time with sick people. Instead he was out every morning on the slopes tobogganing until he was exhausted. Later in the day he played billiards or gave readings for the other guests and was delighted to befriend another writer, John Addington Symonds. Symonds was also a patient, but Louis made an exception for him and the two of them had much to share about writing.

While they were staying there, Mrs. Sitwell brought her young son to Davos, hoping the climate would cure his tuberculosis. But the child was already far too ill to recover. When the boy died, Louis wrote a moving poem for him, "In Memoriam F. A. S." Here is the second stanza:

> *Doomed to know not Winter, only Spring, a being*
> *Trod the flowery April blithely for a while,*
> *Took his fill of music, joy of thought and seeing,*
> *Came and stayed and went, nor ever ceased to smile.*

He also wrote several essays that winter but found little energy to do more. He thought of himself as a violin not being played: "I begin to lose what music there was in me." Lloyd said it was the "only time I remember his having . . . mental inertia." He felt he was in a prison. Fanny couldn't tolerate the high altitude so she was often sick also. By April neither of them could stand Davos any longer. Lloyd was off at school, and they slowly headed to France before returning to Edinburgh.

In June they moved again to a rented house, Kinnaird Cottage, near Pitlochrie. Water of the River Garry flowed nearby and on dry days it was lovely, but that summer it rained constantly and Louis was kept indoors instead of being able to tramp about as he wanted to. At least he was working. He completed a short story written mainly in Scottish brogue, "Thrawn Janet," which was so dark and terrifying it even frightened Louis himself.

The story tells what happened to turn the Reverend Murdoch Soulis, minister of a small moorland parish, into a raving madman who frightened everyone in the village. It begins with a paragraph in English describing how the villagers were afraid to go near the minister's house because he might be found there "often after dark, sometimes groaning aloud. . . ."

It continues in what Louis called "broad Scotch" with a villager recounting how Mr. Soulis came as a young man to be the parish minister, how he studied day and night using his huge number of books:

> He had a feck o' books wi' him—mair than had ever
> been seen before in a' that presbytery; . . . he wad sit
> half the day and half the nicht forbye, which was
> scant decent-writin', nae less; . . .

The old man tells how Reverend Soulis searches for a servant to keep the manse and see to his meals. He hires Janet, who turns out to have been dead for years and her body taken over by the devil. That explains why she is called a twisted, "thrawn" creature.

There's little doubt but it was him that dwalled sae
lang in Janet's body; but he was awa' at last; and
sinsyne the deil has never fashed us in Ba'weary.

The supernatural tale ends with the minister's shock as he
scares the devil away. But he is left "ravin' in his bed; and
frae that hour to this, he was the man ye ken the day."

The night Louis finished it, there was a terrible storm
with crackling thunder and sharp flashes of lightning. He
and Fanny crept down the stairs, holding hands, "frightened
to death" as the candle flickered and the wind and rain beat
upon the house.

Louis was extremely proud of "Thrawn Janet," but he
assumed no English editor would publish a story written in
Scottish. You had to grow up speaking the language to
understand it, he thought. The editor of *Cornhill Magazine*
surprised him. He liked the story and was eager to publish
it. English readers also liked this eerie work and seemed to
have no difficulty with the dialect. Best of all, one can imagine Louis reading the story aloud on a dark and stormy
night, his deep voice penetrating every corner of the room
with frightening images of the devil.

Still searching for a more healthful setting, Louis and
Fanny settled at Braemer in northern Scotland. Nearby
was Balmoral Castle, where Queen Victoria spent a good
deal of time. Daily they saw her carriage pass their small
rented house. She was never to visit them, but many of their
friends did come to call. Soon Margaret and Thomas joined
them and Lloyd was also home from school.

Braemar Cottage, Scotland, where Louis began *Treasure Island*

Again the weather was awful, and while Fanny spent her days painting, writing, and homemaking, Louis and Lloyd had to find things to keep themselves occupied. Lloyd brought out his paints and they both began painting.

After doodling on several sheets, Louis found himself drawing the map of an island. He added trees and caves. He put in rivers and hills. One he called Spyglass Hill. He put in North Inlet. He added a smaller island, which he called Skeleton Island. Louis grew more and more excited. Faces appeared to him. Ideas for chapters came next.

Spurred on by Lloyd, who begged him for an adventure story, not another "horribly dull" essay or travel book, he began to write with great speed, almost a chapter a day. In the beginning he called it *The Sea-Cook* by Captain George

North. Sitting by the fire while it stormed outside he worked on the pirate story—"The *best* book about the Buccaneers that can be had."

After a few evenings he gathered everyone together and began to read the first chapters he had written. His father was delighted. So was Lloyd. They insisted on one "exciting episode after another," and Louis was able to comply, although he admitted it was difficult to write about buccaneers without curses or oaths. "Buccaneers without oaths—bricks without straw," he told his friend William Henley.

He wrote in the mornings and then read the pages to Lloyd and the others every evening. All of them were pleased with the story. All but Fanny. She thought he was wasting his energy writing a "boys' book."

From the time Louis was small, Thomas had told him adventure stories. Now Thomas was full of ideas for Louis's story. He suggested young Jim should hide in an apple barrel to overhear Long John Silver's plotting. He made a list of items for Billy Bones's chest: tools and tobacco, a bar of silver, pistols. Lloyd also had suggestions for the plot and insisted no women be allowed. "I had counted on one boy. I found I had two in my audience," Louis confided to a friend.

Louis used his friend William Henley, with his tangled hair, thick red beard, and crutch, as a model for the one-legged Long John Silver.

The story was published one chapter per week in a boys' paper, *Young Folks*, beginning on October 1, 1881. Instead of *The Sea-Cook*, the editor suggested it be called *Treasure Island* and Louis agreed. No one wrote to say they liked the weekly stories. Instead there were letters with comments like, "This stuff isn't good enough; chuck it." Tell the writer to "get a move on," to "cut the cackle" and come to the "osses" as a writer of adventure stories should. They were bored with the slow start and felt there was too much description and not enough suspense. How could it take ten chapters before young Jim was ready for action, they wondered.

In the 1890s one reviewer said that fathers objected to the book because there was too much "blood splashed up and down the story" and perhaps too many gruesome murders, but "for pure invention *Treasure Island* is as fine a piece of work as Stevenson ever did." Louis thought the best tribute of all to the book came when questions about it were included in school exams in England and Scotland.

Louis was paid the lowest possible rate for the chapters, ten shillings per thousand words, which was equal to only $1.20. The money would keep him in cigarettes but not much more. Still, he was having a delightful time writing the first nineteen chapters. It was a story of a ship, the *Hispaniola,* bound for the South Seas, with pirates and buried treasure and a parrot squawking "Pieces of Eight." And he was in no hurry to sail out of that world.

But the real world he lived in was not so favorable. "I love my native air, but it does not love me," Louis complained while they were staying at Braemar. His uncle Balfour suggested a respirator, which would help him breathe, but he also recommended that Louis return to Davos for the winter. Again Louis, Fanny, and Lloyd took an eight-hour drive up to the top of the mountain and moved into a small chalet rather than stay at the hotel where Louis would be surrounded by patients. Once settled Louis tried to finish the remaining chapters of *Treasure Island*, but now the ideas would not come to him. Moving had interrupted his momentum with the sea story.

Instead he found his notes from their honeymoon at Silverado and began to shape them into a story about those few happy months when he and Fanny had camped in an old miner's cabin and enjoyed life in a healthy climate. He was able to complete that book, *The Silverado Squatters*, describing their stay in the golden California mountains while he was living in the freezing Swiss mountains.

Back he went to the adventure story. But still he could not finish it. He did everything else. Late into the night he and Lloyd devised war games with hundreds of miniature tin soldiers and tiny cannon. General Stevenson against General Osbourne, they got down on their knees, drew maps all along the attic floor, and wrote detailed battle plans. It didn't seem to matter that Louis was in his thirties and Lloyd was a boy of twelve; they shared the same plea-sure in boyhood games.

When they tired of war games, they turned to publishing. On his small printing press, Lloyd ran off the poems and woodcuts that Louis created. The tiny books were crude, but they printed ninety copies of *Moral Emblems*, which later became collector's items.

Finally one morning Louis found a way to go on, "and behold! it flowed like small talk" after that. Louis finished the last chapters of *Treasure Island* so that the magazine

A woodcut from *Moral Emblems* created by Louis and Lloyd

could continue printing them each week. Several years later Louis was asked to revise them so they could be made into a book. This time he was paid a hundred-pound advance. "A hundred pounds, all alive O! A hundred jingling, tingling, golden minted quid," he wrote his parents, mimicking the "Yo, ho, ho" of the book's buccaneer song. "Is not this wonderful?"

The book came out in London in November 1883 and shortly after that in America. Fanny finally had to admit that his "boys' story" was going to be a popular success. And Louis was at last able to say, "It does look as if I should support myself without trouble in the future. . . . It is dreadful to be a great, big man, and not be able to buy bread."

CHAPTER 11

~

"A Pair of Walking-Shoes"

When at home alone I sit
And am very tired of it,
I just have to shut my eyes
To go sailing through the skies—

Louis had spent a most productive winter at Davos.
While there he finished *Treasure Island,* and wrote *The
Silverado Squatters* and more than ninety pages of articles
for *Cornhill Magazine.* "No man can say I have been idle,"
he wrote his mother in April 1882 just as he was preparing
to leave the Swiss mountains.

The doctor at Davos told Louis his lungs seemed healthy
and that he could leave there and try living in the south of
France. He quickly wrote the good news to Henley after the
doctor gave him a "cruel examination, an *exanimation* I may
call it." They moved from place to place until in March
1883 they found a house called Chalet la Solitude in
Hyères, France. It was situated inland above the old town
and beneath a ruined castle. "The loveliest house you ever
saw with a garden like a fairy story," he wrote Mrs. Sitwell.

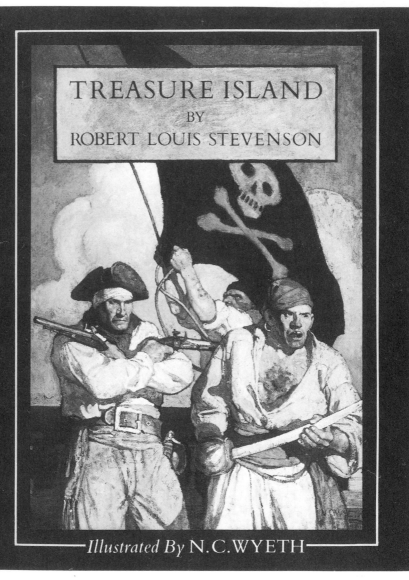

Cover illustration of *Treasure Island* by N. C. Wyeth

There were olive trees, orange trees, palms and cactus, fragrant roses and marigolds. Nightingales nested in the trees, and for the first time Louis heard their haunting song. He especially loved the garden at night in the moonlight. "Angels I know frequent it; and it thrills all night with the thrills of silence . . . and by day it is gone."

Fanny planted vegetables and tiger lilies, which she loved so much that Louis often called her his "Tiger Lily." Louis was not a gardener. He helped by collecting the many snails hiding among the plants. "I have gathered about a bushel, which, not having the heart to slay, I steal forth withal and deposit near my neighbour's garden wall." He knew they would find ample food in the plantings next door.

Afterward he said this was the happiest time in his life. He wrote every morning. At lunchtime he and Fanny went over what he had written. They took walks around the garden or hiked to the ruins above the house, with Woggs at their heels. Both of them spent the late afternoon hours answering letters or writing to family and friends. Louis seemed almost well. He had his long hair cut and grew a small pointed beard, which made him look more like a Frenchman.

Since their marriage Fanny had tried to protect him from germs. No one who had a cold could come anywhere near Louis; she inspected every visitor and every handkerchief. Somehow Louis caught a cold anyway and was ill for weeks with terrible coughing spells and the frightening hemorrhages he called "Bluidy Jack." Fanny's wonderful sense of humor helped both of them get through Louis's constant illnesses, although she sometimes grew weary of being his nurse and came down with ailments of her own.

Money was always a problem for them. Traveling cost a great deal of money. Houses required repairs. Staying in hotels was costly. So was entertaining. Louis realized that he could earn some much needed money and also enjoy doing it if he wrote another serial for *Young Folks*. This time he decided to write a story of medieval warfare that took place during the English War of the Roses in the 1400s. It's a "tushery," he told Henley, a romantic adventure story similar to *Ivanhoe*. He called it *The Black Arrow*.

In summer they traveled to Royat, a resort in the high mountains of France with healing waters. Louis was disrupted again and could not remember how he had intended to get his energetic character Richard Crookback out of the predicament he was caught up in. He finally worked it out and sent off the installments to the paper. His young readers were much more excited by this story than they had been with *Treasure Island*. The book was full of action and once again showed how a character might be likable even though he was not to be trusted.

In September Louis and Fanny went back to Hyères and Lloyd back to school at Bournemouth. While Louis wrote, Fanny painted. She did portraits of the local French people she met as well as landscapes inspired by her surroundings.

In January Charles Baxter and William Henley visited la Solitude and persuaded Louis to go off to Nice with them. Louis caught another cold and was so sick that this time the doctors did not expect him to make it. Fanny was frightened. She wired his parents that Louis might die before they could reach him. The next day Louis seemed to be

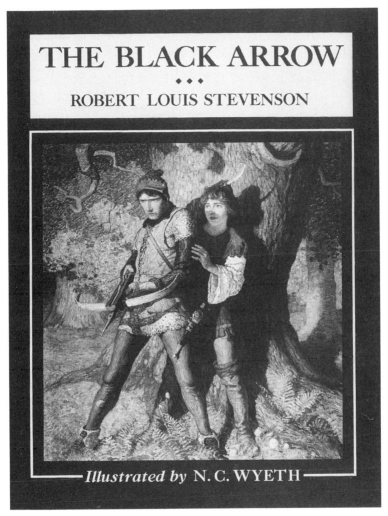

THE BLACK ARROW
• • •
ROBERT LOUIS STEVENSON

Illustrated by N. C. WYETH

Cover illustration of *The Black Arrow* by N. C. Wyeth

improving a bit. Again she wired them, this time with the good news. When he was stronger he sat up in bed and began answering all his mail. To Cousin Bob he wrote, "I survived, where a stronger man would not. . . ." But the scare was over for now, and he did not intend to follow the doctor's orders to sit by the fire like an invalid.

"If I could but heal me of my bellowses, I could have a jolly life—have it, even now, when I can work and stroll a little, as I have been doing till this cold," he wrote Sidney Colvin. "I have so many things to make life sweet to me, it seems a pity I cannot have that other one thing—health."

Just when he thought he was on the mend, he developed an eye infection. He also began hemorrhaging from the lungs again. The doctor gave him drops for his eyes and told him to stay in a darkened room, day and night until they healed. To prevent any new hemorrhages he put Louis's right arm in a sling so that he could not move it about. Even worse, he told Louis not to talk because that too might bring on the bleeding. Wrapped in his maroon shawl, Louis sat up in bed in the darkened room and used his left hand to scribble more verses for his Penny Whistle book.

Earlier, while they were staying in Braemar, he had found Kate Greenaway's *Birthday Book for Children* and was enchanted by her verses. Why couldn't he write verses about his own childhood? Beginning with great speed he wrote twelve poems in no time. "By jove, I believe I could make a little book of those things if I wrote a few more; they are trifling enough, but not without a certain charm." The poems give no hint that Louis wrote them from his bed, in a darkened room, using his left hand, while he was fearful of hemorrhages or of blindness. Instead they tell of joyful moments in a healthy child's life.

My Shadow
I have a little shadow that goes in and out with me,
And what can be the use of him is more than I can see.
He is very, very like me from the heels up to the head;
And I see him jump before me, when I jump into my bed.

In February 1883 he wrote to Cummy about the verses:

> I have just seen that the book in question must be
> dedicated to
>   Allison Cunningham,
> the only person who will readily understand it. . . .
> This little book, which is all about my childhood,
> should indeed go to no other person but you, who
> did so much to make that childhood happy.

He teased Cummy by telling her he would not let her
see the dedication until the book came out. "Keep the jelly
for the last, you know, as you would often recommend in
former days, so now you can take your own medicine."
There would be no book for two years. She would have
to wait while Louis revised the first verses until he was satisfied with their sound and rhythm. Then he had to write
another four dozen verses. It was finally published as *A
Child's Garden of Verses* in 1885 and is still remembered as
one of his most popular works.

He worried that the verses might "look ghastly in the cold
light of print; but there is something nice in the little ragged
regiment for all; the blackguards seem to me to smile, to

Cummy when elderly

have a kind of childish treble note that sounds in my ears freshly; not song, if you will, but a child's voice." To a reviewer who had liked the book very much, he wrote, "Thank you for THE BEST CRITICISM I EVER HAD." In a post-script he went on, "My childhood was in reality a very mixed experience, full of fever, nightmare, insomnia, painful days and interminable nights; and I can speak with less authority of gardens than of that other 'land of counterpane.' " Who would guess that "Land of Counterpane" and many of the other verses were about their author's illnesses?

By fall 1884 Louis and Fanny had left Hyères for Bournemouth, a fishing village on the English coast where Lloyd was studying with a clergyman. They were surprised to find that Lloyd, who was now sixteen, had turned into a "little English gentleman" in the year he was away and was no longer the playful young boy they had sent off. Bournemouth was thought to be a good climate for lung patients, with its sea air and mild temperature. Again they moved from house to house until April when Thomas bought them a two-story brick cottage of their own as a belated wedding present and gave them money to furnish it. They both loved the cottage with its garden and small studio for Fanny's painting, and she happily set out to find furniture for it. Louis named the house Skerryvore after the lighthouse his family had built, and Fanny planted fruit trees, roses, and her beloved tiger lilies.

Fanny often had premonitions about future events. For days she walked around telling Louis how worried she was that something had happened to Virgil Williams far away in San Francisco. Just as she feared, Fanny received a letter from Dora Williams telling her that Virgil had died. The couple had been dear friends and very supportive when they knew Fanny and Louis were to be married. At their wedding Dora had served as their "best man," matron of honor, and witness, all in one.

In June 1885 Louis also lost one of his close friends,

Professor Jenkin, who had been his mentor at the University of Edinburgh. He wrote of his great sadness to Mrs. Jenkin, telling her he had never known "a better man, nor one to me more lovable." He agreed to write a memoir of her husband, who had been his friend and guide ever since his student days. It had been two years since his good friend Walter Ferrier died and Louis still mourned for him. It was depressing to lose people who had been important in his life. Death and illness always seemed to surround him.

It also made Louis uneasy that he had not written as much or as well as he hoped to. He told his old friend Will Low, "The great work is not yet done—not yet even conceived." The more he wrote the more he realized how difficult it was to write well. "Eight years ago, if I could have slung ink as I can now, I should have thought myself well on the road after Shakespeare; and now—I find I have only got a pair of walking-shoes and have not yet begun to travel. And art is still away there on the mountain summit."

CHAPTER 12

Good and Evil

From breakfast on through all the day
At home among my friends I stay,
But every night I go abroad
Afar into the Land of Nod.

One night Louis cried out in his sleep until Fanny woke him. "Why did you waken me?" he scolded. "I was dreaming a fine bogy-tale." When he came down to breakfast in the morning, he rushed through his meal and could hardly wait to get back upstairs. He warned Fanny and Lloyd not to bother him, not even if the house caught on fire. He was concentrating on an important story. For the next three days everyone tiptoed around while Louis, wrapped in his shawl, sat in bed writing without a pause.

Finally, he was ready to share the story with them. In his deep, dramatic voice Louis read about the tall, elegant Dr. Jekyll, who drank a potion and turned into the small, evil Mr. Hyde, with hairy hands and an ugly, distorted face. A his shoulder, spying at the door. And all the time the door remained inexorably closed; none entered in, none came forth; the particles of the town swarmed close by, but did not touch it. Yet the ~~was~~ not to be beaten. He had made a ~~solemn agreement with him~~ ~~to penetrate this mystery of Mr Hyde.~~ "If he be Mr Hyde," he thought, "I shall be Mr Seek." ~~Let him but set eyes upon the man~~ he could judge him.

And at last his patience was rewarded. It was a fine dry ~~night~~ frost in the air; the streets as clean as a ballroom floor; the lamps unshaken by any wind, drawing a regular pattern of light and sh~~ade~~. By ten o'clock, when the shops were closed, the bystreet was very ~~lonely~~ and, in spite of the low growl of London from all round, very s~~ilent~~ ~~to the ear.~~ Small sounds carried far; domestic sounds out of the ~~houses~~ were clearly audible on either side of the roadway; and the rumour of the approach of any passenger preceded him by a long ^time^ ~~way~~. Utterson had been some minutes at his post, when he was aware of an odd, light footstep drawing ~~rapidly~~ near. In the course of his nightly patrols, he had long grown accustomed to the quaint e~~ffect~~ with which the footfalls of a single person, while he is still a gr~~eat way~~ off, ^suddenly^ ~~spring~~ spring out distinct from the vast hum and clatter of the city. Yet his attention had never before been so sharply and de~~cisively~~ arrested; and it was with a strong, superstitious prevision of ~~success~~ that he withdrew into the entry of the court.

The steps drew swiftly nearer, and swelled out suddenly l~~ouder~~

man who was capable of killing. As soon as he finished reading Fanny took a deep breath and began to criticize what Louis had written. Yes, it was a powerful story. But he had written a mere horror story when he might have written a masterpiece. Don't just try to scare people, she cautioned. Both men are so evil they don't seem real. Louis listened to everything she had to say. He was furious. Rising from his chair he stalked out of the room.

Later he returned, telling Fanny he had burned the whole manuscript. "You are right!" Louis admitted. "I have absolutely missed the allegory, which after all, is the whole point of it." He began all over again. For another three days he wrote in a frenzy. Now when he read it to Fanny, she smiled and shook her head with pleasure. He *had* created a masterpiece. He had made Jekyll a believable man with real feelings, not a one-dimensional character on paper. When he could no longer keep himself from turning into the evil Hyde, readers would sympathize with his plight. They would be moved by his tale about the good and evil that can exist in the same man.

He spent a few more weeks revising the story and sent it to an English publisher, who planned to bring it out as a "shilling shocker" right after the holidays in January 1886.

In the story Dr. Jekyll mixes a potion and as soon as he swallows it he becomes Mr. Hyde, "younger, lighter, happier in body," but also "more wicked, tenfold more wicked." He "had in his hand a heavy cane . . . with ape-like fury, he was trampling his victim under foot, and hailing down a storm of blows, under which the bones were audibly shattered." Dr.

Jekyll changed back and forth from respectable gentleman to vicious creature until he ran out of one of the ingredients that made up his magical potion. When he purchased a new supply of that powder, the potion no longer controlled the changes. At any moment he might turn from himself into Hyde, shrinking in size, hairs covering his hands.

The small book, called *The Strange Case of Dr. Jekyll and Mr. Hyde,* soon received a positive review in a newspaper and caught on with the reading public. It sold fifty thousand copies in just a few months. Readers were fascinated with the idea that a man could be transformed from good into evil. It was discussed by people on every level of society. Ministers used its moral tale in their sermons. Society people at dinner parties debated its meanings. Journalists and literary critics added their viewpoints. One reviewer was so taken with the book he said, "The reader scarcely breathes while the story proceeds." Today the term "Jekyll and Hyde" has become part of the language. We use it when we speak of an individual who is unpredictable, capable of changing moods from one moment to another.

In those years Louis was almost an invalid from hemorrhages, terrible coughing, and fevers. But his mind was full of ideas for new books. He began another thriller for young people called *Kidnapped.* He said that this was the first time in which his characters took matters into their own hands. "In one of my books and in one only, the characters took the bit in their teeth. . . . [I]t was they who spoke, it was they who wrote the remainder of the story." His young hero, David Balfour, sets out in Scotland to find an uncle who is

N. C. Wyeth illustration from *Kidnapped*

his only living relative. But the uncle is a scoundrel who has him taken aboard a ship against his will. There he befriends the young gentleman Alan Breck, and immediately the two of them battle the fifteen men who make up the crew.

The story was first serialized in *Young Folks* in the summer of 1886 and published as a book very soon afterward. One reviewer said that there was not a "single dull page between the two covers." Louis was paid twice as much for *Kidnapped* as he had been for *Treasure Island* and that made him feel that his reputation was growing and he would soon be able to stand on his own two feet without always having to ask his father for financial help.

There was no question Thomas appreciated Louis's writing even though he had been opposed to it in the beginning. But he didn't live long enough to see how his son's reputation would grow. For some time he had been ailing and he had become too weak to travel. His mind often wandered to the past, and he would pat Louis on the head and treat him like a little boy. Fortunately the two of them had become close friends before this. They had worked together on *Treasure Island* and had traveled together across Scotland and England.

But Louis was not prepared for Thomas to die. It was a terrible shock when Margaret sent for Louis on a May day in 1887. He rushed to 17 Heriot Row to be at his father's side. "Lou arrived this afternoon and his father does not know him," Margaret wrote in her diary. All night Louis sat beside his father's bed hoping Thomas would speak to him. Thomas died the next day without saying a word.

When Uncle Balfour saw how ill Louis looked, he cautioned his nephew not to attend his father's funeral. It would only make him sicker. Even the minister agreed. He said Louis was a "pathetic figure . . . thin, spare with pale cheeks." Sad and sick, Louis stayed at the house mourning his father while family and friends attended the burial.

A few days later the doctor told Louis he had to leave Edinburgh; the climate was going to kill him. While his father was still alive, Louis would not think about leaving. That's why they had stayed nearby for the past seven years. Now he could leave for the United States with a free mind and with added security from the three thousand pounds Thomas had willed him. He and Fanny invited Margaret to come with them. At first she said no. They kept insisting. She kept resisting until Fanny put her foot down. Louis needed to leave, Fanny insisted. But he would not go without her. That did it. Margaret agreed to join them.

Fanny and Louis left to get things in order at Skerryvore. They drove in an open cab along Princes Street, Louis calling "Good-bye, Good-bye," to all the sights of "Auld Reekie," including the castle on the hill. This was one of his favorite places because as a boy he had heard bugles blow morning and evening from that castle.

Both he and Fanny found it difficult to close up their Skerryvore home. Thomas had given it to them. It was filled with memories of happy moments spent with friends and with all the creative work Louis had produced there. Sadly, he covered all the furniture, including the chair in which the American writer Henry James had sat nightly.

The castle on the hill in Edinburgh

When they met, neither of them had liked the other. James thought Louis an affected young man, a fop; Louis thought James a pompous, snooty American who looked down on his own country when he came to live in England. But when James wrote a positive review of *Treasure Island,* Louis wrote to thank him and they began a stimulating correspondence. Through letters they discussed literature and whether art could be as realistic as life. Louis invited James to visit, and when James went to Bournemouth he dropped in on Fanny and Louis. He returned the next night and the next until Louis named a chair in their parlor "Henry James's Chair."

84

He and James would have to continue their friendship through letters, he told himself. He no longer had a choice. He had spent too many hours sick in bed here. Now it was time to go. By August they had packed up their books and settled financial matters. They were ready to leave.

This crossing was totally different from Louis's first trip to the United States. Then he'd run off without preparing his family and friends. He'd been in a weakened physical state and was desperate over Fanny's health. Now the four of them, Fanny, Louis, Lloyd, and Margaret were together. They had booked passage on a freighter, which was smaller and less expensive than other ships. What they hadn't known ahead of time was that the *Ludgate Hill* would be filled with animals being shipped to the New York Zoo. All day long they heard cattle lowing, monkeys chattering, and horses neighing, and they were surrounded by their pungent odors.

Louis didn't mind any of it. He loved being on the small ship, with its friendly crew and its menagerie of creatures. He was not even bothered by the rough seas, although the others were sick most of the time. He was having a jolly time and wrote Sidney Colvin, "I (at least) made a friend of a baboon . . . whose embraces have pretty near cost me a coat."

CHAPTER 13

~

Popularity

The world is so full of a number of things,
I'm sure we should all be as happy as kings.

After eleven days the *Ludgate Hill* reached New York harbor. How different this arrival was. When Louis traveled to the United States the previous time he was an unknown emigrant, a struggling writer. This time he was famous. Reporters mobbed his ship, notebooks in hand, shouting questions at him. "Where do you get your ideas?" one asked. Louis told them about the "Brownies" who supplied his mind during the night—little creatures who danced through his dreams. He told them that his writing came from a small amount of inspiration and a large amount of hard work.

With their trunks and other baggage, the four of them were bundled off to a downtown hotel. Waiting in the room were sacks of fan mail and more reporters. Louis received the reporters from his bed, his maroon shawl wrapped around his shoulders, the blanket littered with pillows,

Louis, in 1887, wearing a mourning band on his arm in memory of his father

papers, and books. They filled long newspaper columns with details about his life and wrote descriptions of him, such as "Mr. Stevenson has a classical head from which issues a hacking cough."

"My reception here was idiotic to the last degree and I confess the poor interviewer lads pleased me," he wrote Henry James immediately. "What a silly thing is popularity!" *Dr. Jekyll and Mr. Hyde* was just as popular in the United States as it had been in England, and a play called *Jekyll* was about to open in New York. *Kidnapped* and *Treasure Island* were selling well, too. He was a celebrity at last. "You have no idea how much is made of me here," he wrote Sidney Colvin after he had been in the States for a month. And to Charles Baxter, he quipped: "But I'm awfu' grand noo and long may it last!"

Artists painted him. Saint-Gaudens, the sculptor, made a bronze medallion showing him holding a cigarette in his hand as he always did. Sometimes when later copies of the medallion were cast, the cigarette was changed into a pen.

Publishers asked him to write monthly articles for them and offered to pay him a great deal of money. Scribner's said they would give Louis three thousand five hundred dollars for twelve articles during the year. He thought that was too much money, that it would spoil him because he had been getting paid so little in the past. "I do not want wealth, and I feel these big sums demoralize me," he told them. Many letters were sent back and forth until Louis finally agreed to write the articles and to accept payment for them.

After a short stay in New York City, the family found a place at Saranac Lake in upstate New York, close to Canada. Its high altitude was supposed to be healthy for lung patients. To get there the family traveled by train and then by horse buggy the last twenty-five miles. They were told to expect freezing cold winters so Fanny bought heavy buffalo coats, thick boots, and fur caps to keep them all warm. They moved into a rented cottage. A doctor reassured Louis that he did not have tuberculosis.

In Saranac Louis took long walks by himself and enjoyed skating with Lloyd. He also kept busy writing the essays for Scribner's and working on an adult novel, *The Master of Ballantrae,* which he had begun in Scotland when he was inspired by the country's lonely moors.

Warnings about the winters were correct. It was often so cold that his ink froze and so did his milk and water and even the handkerchief that he kept under his pillow. Snow reached to the top of their cottage and Louis was forced to write while bundled in heavy clothing and with a fire nearby, but he never let the cold prevent him from writing. While he wrote in the tiny sitting room, using pen and ink, he could hear Lloyd in the next room, typing furiously on his own novel. Lloyd often discussed it with his stepfather and Louis agreed to look it over. "Why, I could take up that book and in one quick, easy rewriting could make it *sing!*" Before he knew it, he was helping Lloyd revise the story. It became known as *The Wrong Box,* an amusing tale of dead bodies, family inheritance, and mystery.

In the spring Fanny went to California to visit her sister Nellie and her daughter, Belle. She was also on another mission. She was searching for a sailing ship. The editor Sam McClure had agreed to support Louis on a trip around the Pacific Islands if Louis would write travel letters for publication. The thought of being on a ship in a warm, healthy climate became very appealing to all of them, especially after the cold wintry weather of Saranac.

In April Louis, Margaret, and Lloyd returned to New York to await word from Fanny. At last Fanny wired Louis that she had found the perfect ship, the *Casco*, a ninety-five-foot yacht with broad sails and shiny brass trimming. "Blessed girl, take the yacht and expect us in a few days," he wired back. Quickly the three of them packed up and left on a train to California, where Fanny met them, and within about three weeks they managed to arrange everything. Fanny ordered loose dresses called *holakus* or *mumus* that hung straight from the shoulders and would keep her cool in the warm, humid climate she expected. No more tight-fitting corsets for her.

In San Francisco they visited with old friends, including Dora Williams, and Mrs. Carson, the landlady who had taken such good care of Louis when he lived there years before. They bought enough supplies to last for seven months, gifts for the islanders, and a camera for Lloyd. Louis packed books he expected to use, and soon they were prepared to leave. On the 28th of June the ship passed out to sea through the Golden Gate while they stood waving farewell to the hilly city.

CHAPTER 14

~

At Sea

If I could find a higher tree
Farther and farther I should see,
To where the grown-up river slips
Into the sea among the ships.

This is the life for a man like me, this is the life for ever!" Louis rejoiced. He was thrilled to be back on a ship. He was thirty-eight years old but felt as giddy as a boy again.

At first the captain of the ship was not pleased to have them aboard. He didn't care at all that Louis was a famous author. In fact he told Margaret that he had read *Treasure Island* and was not impressed. Your son may be a great author, but he sure doesn't know anything about ships, Captain Otis muttered. And he was not about to read anything else Louis wrote.

Captain Otis especially disliked having women aboard his ship. Don't talk to the men while they're trying to run the

The *Casco,* which took the family around the South Seas

ship, he ordered Margaret and Fanny. They finally learned
to get along with each other, and by the end of the voyage
Louis and Captain Otis were great friends and the captain
even had nice things to say about the women, especially
Margaret, who always managed to beat him at cards.

Fanny and Margaret shared one cabin. Louis and Lloyd,
who was now twenty, had their own separate cabins. Louis
wrote below or on deck, still making detailed notes about

the people around him. Later he used Captain Otis as a model for the villain in *The Wrecker*. Life aboard ship was thrilling for Louis. He took off his shoes, stripped down to a thin shirt and trousers, and climbed the riggings just as the other hands did. "The proudest moments of my life have been passed in the stern-sheets of a boat," he wrote Henley. After this trip no one would be able to accuse him of not understanding ships.

Many years earlier Louis had been intrigued by the South Seas and had read whatever he could find, including Herman Melville's novel *Typee*. "It seems too good to be true," he wrote Henry James about going there. He and Margaret were the best sailors aboard. They could tolerate the constant motion of the ship while Fanny was often sick and desperately searched the horizon for land. Day after day she prayed for a sighting.

At last, after thirty days on the *Casco*, land was spotted. They had reached the Marquesas, beautiful islands with tall mountains and dense green jungle. Louis said there was nothing to compare with one's first love, the first sunrise, and now the first South Sea island. They couldn't wait to go ashore, but the islanders swarmed aboard the ship, exclaiming over its rich furnishings, its velvet cushions, and framed mirrors. The women lifted their dresses and rubbed their skin against the velvet. The men, almost six feet tall, were covered with tattoos over most of their bodies. They all admired themselves in the glass and were thrilled when Lloyd typed their names on his typewriter. They even examined his gold-framed spectacles and called him "the young man with glass in his eyes." The Marquesans' name for Louis was "Ona," or owner, because they believed he was the wealthy owner of the ship.

After a few weeks the ship left for the coral atoll of Fakarava, a dangerous trip because of the hidden rocks and coral reefs beneath the water. They all watched with concern as Captain Otis maneuvered carefully to avoid damaging the ship. On deck one night Louis had a vision that took him back to Edinburgh, to Rutherford's Pub on Drummond Street, when he was a young man worrying that he would never be able to write a single book, find a single friend, and certainly never get married. Now, lying under the stars, rocked by ocean waves, Louis could see how full his life had become. He had a number of published books, many friends, and a wife who was dear to him.

Once they reached Fakarava they found the native people eager to have them stay in a small guest house they provided for the visitors. All day they sat around with the islanders sharing stories of supernatural lore. Louis recited parts of "Thrawn Janet" in his wonderful Scottish brogue, and they told him their favorite tales, which he noted and would use in later books. When it was time to depart, Louis caught cold and lost his appetite. They were aboard ship heading to Tahiti when he felt so sick he told Captain Otis that he might not make it and that he wanted to be buried at sea should he die. Fanny insisted they get off the ship and move inland by wagon across the island of Tautira. There Princess Moë came to greet them and when she saw how weak Louis was, she prepared him a special dish of raw fish that had been marinated in lime juice and coconut milk. It revived him and even put a little weight on his skinny bones. He was sure the dish saved his life.

When Captain Otis discovered that some of the ship's masts were rotted, he went back to Tahiti for repairs and left his travelers on Tautira. There Louis worked on *The Master* and studied the history of the islands for the book he planned to write. Louis was determined to write an accurate, serious study of the South Seas. "He has taken into his Scotch Stevenson head," Fanny complained to Bob Stevenson, "that his book must be a sort of scientific and historical impersonal thing." She wanted him to tell colorful tales about the exotic people they were meeting because that's what he did so well. Something similar, she told him, to the earlier travel books he had written. But Louis had changed since he wrote *Travels with a Donkey*. He understood more about people now and wanted to emphasize the history of the cultures he was observing rather than concentrate only on his impressions and experiences with the people.

He tried to explain this to Fanny as they continued to watch for the *Casco*. Weeks passed without a sign. Finally in December when they had almost given up hope, the ship was sighted. Captain Otis told them how hard it had been to get the repairs made, but the ship was at last in good shape. They packed up their few belongings and sailed on Christmas Day, 1888, heading north to Honolulu.

Suddenly a storm surrounded the small yacht. The rougher the voyage became, the happier Louis seemed. It gave him material. Afterward he wrote Cousin Bob describing the hurricane weather with its terrible squalls. How it buffeted the ship. How they were lost for days and ran out of their last morsels of food. He was thrilled by the danger of the storm, especially after it was over and land was near.

When at last they reached the harbor Fanny's daughter, Belle, her husband, Joe, and their young son, Austin, were waiting to meet them and help them find a house at Waikiki Beach. Louis was working on *The Master* and on ballads about the South Seas. He and Lloyd were continuing to collaborate on *The Wrong Box*. They had a wonderful time writing and laughing over the plot as they went along. "If it is not funny, I'm sure I don't know what is," Louis wrote to a friend. Louis worked in a small hut behind the beach house. He thought it wonderful because there were no walls and he could see in all directions. Simple as it was, the hut had electric lights. Since he knew electricity had not yet come to Edinburgh, he bragged about it in his letters to his friends.

He visited often with King Kalakaua and wrote his friend Henry James that he was having "more fun and pleasure of my life these past months than ever before, and more health than anytime in ten long years." He concluded that "I am never well but at sea."

In June 1889 he joined a group of nuns who were going to the island of Molokai, where people with leprosy were sent to live. While there he refused to wear gloves or to take precautions against contact with the people. Unlike others of that time, he did not think lepers should be shunned, and he didn't want them to think he was afraid of being with them or of contracting leprosy from them. They had a

Louis on the bowsprit of the *Equator*

disfiguring skin disease but they were still human beings. He played with the children and talked with their parents. They told him about Father Damien, the priest who had lived with the lepers for a long time before he became sick and died. Louis thought of him as a great hero and even defended him when others talked about his imperfections. "No stranger time have I ever had, nor any so moving," he said when he returned.

After a few more months Louis was ready to be on the move again. Even though it was much warmer than the weather he had found in the United States, he complained

that he had "withered in the cold" and found the civiliza-
tion of Waikiki stifling. He wanted to explore new islands.
When Captain Otis had to return to the States, they hired
the *Equator* with a young Scottish captain and sailed by the
end of June 1889. They were still living on the ship when
Louis turned thirty-nine in November. To celebrate they
cooked shark steaks and toasted him with iced champagne.

They spent twenty-six more days at sea before reaching
Samoa. From the ship they could just make out mysterious
Mount Vaea rising from the island of Upolu. They had no
intention of staying more than a few days in Upolu, but as
they toured the island, its brilliant colors, lush flowers, and
graceful people began weaving a spell on them. The climate
was warmer than Hawaii and communications with
England and America could be made easily from the port
city of Apia. Maybe they had found the perfect place to stay.

CHAPTER 15

~

Home at Last

I have trod the upward and the downward slope;
I have endured and done in days before;
I have longed for all, and bid farewell to hope;
And I have lived and loved, and closed the door.

After exploring Upolu for six weeks, Louis impulsively decided to buy three hundred acres of land on this Samoan island. They would build a house and plant crops for food and for profit. With great excitement he wrote his friends of the plan, saying their future letters should be addressed to him in care of the "ancestral acres." He named the site Vailima, or "Five Waters," because many rivers joined there. They would use only a small part of the land and leave the rest untouched with its thick forests and magnificent waterfalls.

Louis and Fanny pored over plans for the house and ordered redwood, glass, and other materials from Australia and the United States. They also decided to remodel the present cottage on the property. After the work was started, they left for a visit to England, first stopping at Sydney, Australia. Hardly had they settled in Sydney when Louis came down with fever and began hemorrhaging. Fanny found a ship to take them back to Samoa. Louis was terribly depressed about canceling their trip. He missed his friends and family in England and had looked forward to being with them. But soon life aboard the *Janet Nicholl* revived him. Once again he was on the sea surrounded by a colorful crew of men whom he could use in his writing. As usual, life at sea was the best medicine he could find.

He and Fanny made a return trip to Sydney in August, but Louis immediately got sick again. Now there was no choice. He could not think about traveling. England was out of the question. He was well in Samoa and that was where he needed to stay. His friends would have to come to him.

When they returned in October, they moved into the cottage while the large house was being finished. Louis felt well enough to work outdoors cutting undergrowth and helping Fanny plant. One day Henry Adams, an American historian, came to visit and was shocked to find how dirty and disheveled Louis and Fanny looked. "Imagine a man so thin and emaciated that he looked like a bundle of sticks in a bag," Adams wrote. "With him was a woman . . . her clothing no cleaner than her husband's."

They *were* dirty and messy. It was hard work planting crops. They had put in melons, tomatoes, and lima beans. They added artichokes, eggplants, peas, onions, lettuces, and radishes. Then they planted banana trees and mango trees. Finally they planted vanilla, cocoa, coffee, peanuts, and pineapples. The best part was that Louis was healthy. Not only was he writing, but he was able to do heavy physical labor. Henry Adams had not seen the whole picture.

Fanny was serious about her planting. "When I plant a seed or a root, I plant a bit of my heart with it. . . . I know that in a manner I am a creator," she said. "My heart melts over a bed of young peas, and a blossom on my rose tree is like a poem written by my son." She was also known to be a healer. She cured lumbago and treated puncture wounds by wrapping them with bacon fat. She made a flavorful drink called *kava* from the roots of the pepper tree, which they all found refreshing and slightly intoxicating.

Lloyd volunteered to go to Skerryvore and sell the house for them. He shipped the piano, the mahogany furniture, silver, china, books, family portraits, mirrors, and a sculpture by Auguste Rodin that Rodin had given them called *Le Printemps*. Margaret traveled to Edinburgh and shipped some of her furniture back to Samoa after she sold 17 Heriot Row.

By 1891 the Vailima house was finished. It was quite a sight, set beneath enormous ironwood trees with a broad lawn and a low stone wall enclosing it. Brilliant hibiscus plants and jasmine blossoms grew nearby. Painted a bright blue green, it had a red iron roof and a wide veranda all around the front. Someone said the inside reminded them of a big barn, but once the family's furniture and pictures were placed around the rooms, they were more inviting.

Fanny had no qualms about climbing up high ladders and swaying scaffoldings to direct the laborers for the next

101

projects. She showed them how to measure and lay out the tennis court and croquet ground and where to pipe in water from the mountain spring above the house. And of course all of them went barefoot during the day.

Every morning by five-thirty Louis was up to write. From his study window he had a view of the sea only two miles away. Listening to breaking surf and trilling dawn creepers, he drank his cup of chocolate or coffee. He worked until breakfast and went back to work until lunch. Sometimes he took a break and played music on his flageolet, which sounds like a cross between a flute and piccolo. He wrote again in the afternoon. After dinner the family came together to hear what Louis had written or to play cards or charades or to make music together. Lloyd played the banjo, Belle the piano, Fanny the guitar, Joe the accordion, Louis the flageolet. Louis loved to play even though he was terrible at it.

Louis said grace at meals and led prayers once a week in the great hall for the family and all the household servants. Sometimes he wrote his own prayers, emphasizing values like truthfulness, honesty, and hard work. Watching him lead the large group, Margaret must have remembered how Louis, pretending to be a preacher, had stood on a chair to recite prayers when he was small. She might also have remembered when Louis, the college student, told his father that he did not believe in God.

Louis was happy in Samoa. The climate agreed with him. The monthly mail service was good. He wrote Mrs. Sitwell, "In the South Seas, I have health, strength. I can walk and ride and be out of doors and do my work without distress."

Fanny was also happy, but her health was not always good. Earlier she had gallbladder disease. Now she suffered from depression and from a kidney disease that required treatment. She traveled to Sydney by herself for medical care that she couldn't receive in Samoa.

When Belle and Joe Strong talked about leaving Vailima, Louis urged them to stay. "You and Lloyd are all the family I have. I want a home and a family, *my* family, round me." Belle agreed they would stay if Louis would let her help as his secretary.

The only time any of them put on shoes and fancy clothing was for dinner and for special parties. Then Fanny came down in her gray silk or black velvet dress while Louis wore a pleated silk shirt, white jacket, and black dress trousers with shiny patent leather shoes on his feet. They sat at the mahogany dining table that had come from Skerryvore and used the family crystal and silver. Their household staff also dressed casually in simple *lavalavas,* a kind of wraparound skirt—unless it was a special occasion, and then they put on *lavalavas* that Louis had made in a Scottish tartan pattern, Royal Stewart, and with them the men wore striped blazers. The women always wore flowers in their hair.

Vailima became a setting for grand dinners and balls. They invited everyone from diplomats to naval officers, to barkeepers, clerks, and mechanics. To the background of Samoan and American music, couples danced all evening. Louis was one of the most enthusiastic dancers, especially when it was "a most fearful and wonderful quadrille" or a lively square dance.

The family and household on the veranda at Vailima

Margaret paid for the bathhouse and much of the plumbing in the new house. She also tried to help with the chores. When they discovered their books were being damaged by the humidity, she cleaned and varnished each volume to keep it from rotting or being eaten by insects.

After the first house was complete, they began planning a second building. Both would have wide verandas all around the front, and Louis insisted on including fireplaces even though the weather never got cold enough to need them.

He said they would be useful to warm his sheets.

The politics in Samoa were complicated because Germany, Britain, and America all wanted to control the island. Each country wanted to put in their own local leader, not understanding that Polynesian chiefs were born to royalty, not chosen. Louis wrote worried letters to the English papers saying that Germany was trying to swallow up Samoa. Louis had never fought in a real war. He had been a general only with miniature tin soldiers on the nursery floor. But his passion for justice was great, and he wanted to be sure his friends in Samoa would not be hurt by political battles.

Germany backed Chief Malietoa while Chief Mataafa was preferred by Britain and America and had become a special friend of Fanny and Louis. War broke out between the factions in July 1893. Many Samoan men were wounded or killed; Louis and Fanny tried to help where they could. Mataafa's forces lost the battle, and he and his men were put in jail. While they were locked up, Louis took them food and gifts of tobacco and Fanny's famous drink, *kava*. To show their gratitude when they were freed, the men built a road to Vailima for Louis, which they called Road of the Loving Heart.

CHAPTER 16

Tusitala, Teller of Tales

Where hath fleeting beauty led?
To the doorway of the dead.
Life is over, life was gay:
We have come the primrose way.

Louis was never satisfied with his writing. He always felt it could be better. He wrote Colvin in October 1894, "I am read by journalists, by my fellow-novelists, and by boys. . . . I cannot take myself seriously, as an artist the limitations are so obvious."

He also told Lloyd "that he himself was not a man of 'any unusual talent,'" that he had started off "with very moderate abilities," and that his success was due to his own "really remarkable industry!" He added, "What genius I had was for *work!*" And work he did, never stopping for illness, for travel, or for pleasure. First he wrote, then he played.

The Samoans gave Louis a new name—*Tusitala*, Teller of

Louis standing on the balcony of Vailima, 1893

Tales. In their culture there was no written history. They had a long tradition of telling stories aloud and passing them down from one generation to the next. They realized that Louis was doing the same thing with his stories. Only one of his stories, "The Bottle Imp," was translated into Samoan. Many of his Samoan friends thought it to be a true story, and they came to the house asking to see that magic bottle.

In the fable a man buys a milky-white bottle containing an imp, or genie, who will grant its owner any wish. The man wishes for a beautiful home filled with treasures. (As Louis describes the house, he could almost be describing Vailima.) But the man doesn't find happiness in his lovely home. Instead he is alone and miserable. He knows the imp is actually the devil and he must find a clever way to outsmart the evil spirit.

Next Louis wrote a novel *The Ebb-Tide* about the islands, and told Colvin, "Now I have got the smell, and the look of things a good deal. You will know more about the South Seas after you have read my little tale than if you had read a library." After that he wrote a short story, "The Beach of Falesá," which Louis thought was one of his best. It was written in the first person and told about a European man who decided to stay with his island woman and children rather than return to his former life.

Then Louis was ready to turn back to writing a novel about Scotland and the language he remembered from Cummy's Bible stories. He called it *Weir of Hermiston* and dedicated it to Fanny.

> *Take thou the writing: thine it is. For who*
> *Burnished the sword, blew on the drowsy coal,*
> *Held the target higher, chary of praise*
> *And prodigal of censure—who but you?*

Again Louis was writing about one setting while he lived in another. Early in his writing life he had mentioned this in a letter to Cousin Bob:

> I wrote about the sea whilst at Swanston, and about
> hills, wood etc. while at Anstruther and Wick [the
> lighthouses]. I suppose the real truth is that the
> objects themselves are far too complex for our
> comprehension, how much more for our description:
> five square feet of Scotch hillside would take a man a

lifetime to describe, and even then how lame, how
empty: after he had chronicled heather, whin, bracken,
juniper, grass, these little yellow flowers and the rest,
it would only be to find that each of these objects
taken separately are indescribable, and that their
combination is as much above human powers as flying.

Perhaps it was not possible to describe his memories adequately, but they were growing stronger the longer he was
away from Scotland and he had to try. In the mornings
Louis dictated letters to Belle and answered those he had
received. Then he turned to his book. He walked around,
acting out each of the characters as he recited their words to
Belle. The lines flowed from him without any hesitation, "as
clearly and as steadily as though he were reading from an
unseen book," Belle remembered.

Louis was convinced it would be the best of all his
books. He felt his women characters were strong as they
had not been in his earlier work. One evening he read the
first chapters aloud to the family. After he finished, Louis
looked to Lloyd for some kind of response. His stepson
was silent. And he had not written a word in his open
notebook. Louis waited a few more minutes, almost
pleading for some response. Still no word from Lloyd.
Louis finally took his pages and sadly left the room. Later
Louis came to Lloyd and they sat together in the dark,
both of them tearful. At last Lloyd was able to explain
that he had been so moved he couldn't speak. The story
had touched him deeply, he said, and he agreed with

Louis that it was going to be the best he had ever written.

Charles Baxter had convinced Louis to put together his early writings in an Edinburgh Edition that would bring in much needed money for all the building and living expenses they now had. He knew Louis was responsible for a large family and a large staff at Vailima. Now best of all, Charles himself was going to bring the first two volumes to Louis in Samoa. He knew Louis would be thrilled with the way they looked, printed on rich vellum and bound in crimson morocco. He hoped to get there in time for Louis's birthday or shortly afterward. Louis could hardly wait to see his dear friend. They had been separated for over six years.

Birthday celebrations were always important to Louis. In Samoa Fanny invited all their Samoan and American friends for a gigantic party, and everyone toasted Louis's good health. When Louis heard that Annie Ide, the teenage daughter of the United States' consul, was unhappy with her December 25th birthday, he gave her his November 13th birthday. To make it official he drew up a legal document, had it witnessed, and sent it to her home in Vermont in June of 1891. After that, he and Annie corresponded with each other. She told him about her life in Vermont and how grateful she was to Louis for his gift, but she worried about growing old too quickly now that she had two birthdays. Louis assured her that was not the case. Legally she now had only one birthday. "The very moment that the gentle deed was properly registered November 13th became her very own birthday," he wrote. She would then "cease to have been born on Christmas Day."

In November 1894, Annie moved to Samoa, and she and Louis celebrated their birthdays together at Vailima with a huge feast to which eighty guests were invited. It had been raining steadily for days, but on the morning of the thirteenth the weather cleared. At noon Louis and Annie made their entrance wearing wreaths of white jasmine and red hibiscus. They sat at the head table, ate and sang, watched dancers, and heard speeches. The party went on until dark. Chiefs brought them presents of turtles, woven fans and baskets, live pigs, and fresh pineapples. They also brought delicacies of cooked eels, prawns, and long, thin green worms that had been fried and looked a bit like spinach. These were found only a few days a year in the coral rocks and were presented with great pride to Louis and Annie.

On Thanksgiving a few weeks later they had another huge feast, with roast turkey and a red sauce Fanny made from berries she found in the woods that were similar to cranberries. Because there were no pumpkins she made sweet potato pies. Louis stood and offered a toast of thanks to Fanny, his mother, his stepchildren, and the "child in the house—Austin." It was wonderful for Louis to have Belle's son growing up under his roof. It meant that he and Lloyd could continue to play war games, that he could challenge Austin to swimming races and croquet games, and that he once again could be a French tutor for a young boy.

After the celebrations Louis went back to work on his book. His spirits were high because the writing on *Weir* was going so well and his friend Charles Baxter was on his way to Vailima. Fanny did not share his good mood. For three days

Louis dressed to ride his horse into Apia

she had a premonition that something terrible was going to happen. Louis tried to tease her out of it. On Sunday they gathered for family prayers as they usually did. After dinner they played charades until late in the evening. On Monday Louis dictated more pages of *Weir of Hermiston* to Belle.

On Tuesday, December 3, Louis rode into Apia on his horse and came back in the early afternoon. Before swimming he visited with the others. At about six o'clock he joined Fanny, who was still troubled. Again he tried to talk her out of it, insisting that nothing bad was going to happen to any of them. She could look around her and see that everyone was fine, that their life was going smoothly. This time she was worrying for nothing. He told her he would get a special bottle of wine for dinner. When he returned he began mixing a salad dressing.

Suddenly he touched his head and cried, "What's that? Oh, what a pain! Do I look strange?" Then he collapsed. Fanny rushed to him, calling for help. Sosimo, his servant, ran out to help her lift Louis into his grandfather's chair. By then Louis was unconscious. Lloyd jumped on a horse and galloped into Apia for the doctor. As soon as the Samoans heard Louis was ill, they began bringing gifts of flowers and fine woven mats. They sat in the large hall at Vailima, chanting prayers for his recovery.

Lloyd returned with the doctor, who rushed to Louis's side.

Fanny and Margaret watched helplessly as the doctor examined Louis and said there was nothing to be done. He had suffered a blood clot on the brain and was close to death. Almost to himself, the doctor mumbled as he held

Louis's gaunt arm, "How can anybody write books with arms like these?"

"He has written *all* his books with arms like these!" Margaret snapped.

Louis stopped breathing at 8:10 P.M. Fanny and Margaret dressed him in a white linen shirt, black trousers, and dark blue silk sash, his usual evening dress. His Samoan friends rose to kiss his hand and tell him to sleep: *"Tofa Tusitala!"*

Before dawn the next morning the chiefs began cutting a path to the top of Mount Vaea, where Louis had told the family he wanted to be buried. With axes and knives the men cleared the thick growth up to the small flat plateau seven hundred feet above Vailima.

That afternoon Samoan pallbearers wearing new black *lavalavas* carried Louis's coffin to the top of the mountain, with family and friends following behind. Unfortunately Charles Baxter did not arrive in time to see his old friend alive nor to attend his funeral.

Sometime later a tomb was built on Mount Vaea with a bronze plaque identifying it as "The Tomb of Tusitala." On one side is the poem Louis had written years before:

1850   Robert Louis Stevenson   1894

> Under the wide and starry sky,
> Dig the grave and let me lie.
> Glad did I live and gladly die,
>   And I laid me down with a will.

This be the verse you grave for me;
Here he lies where he longed to be;
Home is the sailor, home from sea,
    And the hunter home from the hill.

On the other side is a plaque for Fanny, who died in 1914, also from a cerebral hemorrhage, and is buried next to Louis. The two of them are together in death as they had been in life. Along with pictures of a tiger lily and hibiscus are the words: "Teacher, tender comrade, wife . . ." There is also a Biblical passage from the story of Ruth: " . . . thy people shall be my people, and thy God my God; where thou diest, will I die. . . ."

Louis's tomb on Vaea

EPILOGUE

~

Louis was already dead when his friend Charles Baxter reached Vailima bearing the first two volumes of Louis's collected works in the Edinburgh Edition. Baxter was devastated by the loss of his friend, but he stayed with Fanny and tried to advise her about the future.

In England, when Henry James heard about Louis's death, he was so upset he refused to believe it and kept waiting to be told it was all a mistake. At last he accepted the sad news and wrote Fanny a moving letter, saying, "You are nearest to the pain, because you were nearest the joy and the pride. . . . He lighted up one whole side of the globe." In their long correspondence the two men had shared ideas about their own writing as well as what they found valuable or lacking in other writers' works. James was left with a great hole in his life.

Fanny and Belle decided to remain at Vailima for a time even though they found the days empty without Louis. Earlier Belle had divorced Joe Strong, and she now sent her son, Austin, off to school in New Zealand. Lloyd, grief-stricken by Louis's death, soon came down with a serious illness. He took a sea voyage to convalesce. The following year

Fanny, Lloyd, and Belle returned to San Francisco.

Louis's mother, Margaret, returned to Edinburgh, where she died of pneumonia in 1897. That same year Fanny sold Vailima, but reserved an acre of ground on Mount Vaea, where Louis was buried, and the access road that led up to it.

Fanny and Lloyd both wrote about their life with Louis and worked hard to keep his reputation alive. They also benefited from the royalties of his many books. Fanny traveled back to England, and then returned to live in California until her death in 1914 at age seventy-four.

Many believe the novel Louis was working on when he died, *Weir of Hermiston,* would have been his finest. He certainly sensed that he had reached a new depth of emotion. He told Lloyd, "My work is profounder than it was; I can touch emotions that I then scarcely knew existed." He knew that the young man who wrote those early essays and stories no longer existed, but he was also wise enough to know that without his early writings he would never have grown to maturity in his later work. Life experiences taught him to observe more carefully those around him, to see beyond the surface, to value his Scottish heritage, and move from a child of Victorian Edinburgh to a man of the world.

Despite his poor health he produced an enormous amount of work—four hundred pages a year for twenty years.

The year before he died he wrote a friend:

> For fourteen years I have not had a day's real health; I have wakened sick and gone to bed weary; and I have done my work unflinchingly. I have written in bed,

and written out of it, written in hemorrhages, written in sickness, written torn by coughing, written when my head swam for weakness. . . . I am better now, have been, rightly speaking, since first I came to the Pacific; and still, few are the days when I am not in some physical distress. . . . I was made for a contest, and the Powers have so willed that my battlefield should be this dingy, inglorious one of the bed and the physic bottle.

Now, one hundred years after his death, we continue to recognize the value of his work. The complete volumes of his letters are being issued. New biographies are being written. We still recite his poems from *A Child's Garden of Verses* because they remind us of our own childhood. We read *Treasure Island* and *Kidnapped* because they are strong adventure stories. We read *The Strange Case of Dr. Jekyll and Mr. Hyde* because it frightens us and forces us to ask questions about our inner core of good and evil.

Robert Louis Stevenson once confessed regret that he had not been able to build lighthouses as well as write books, but for readers his books have been as lasting as lighthouses.

NOTES

~

PAGE   **CHAPTER 1 "IF I AM SPARED"**

1   "When I . . . toys." "Looking Forward" from Robert Louis
      Stevenson, *The Works of Robert Louis Stevenson in One Volume*
      (New York: Walter J. Black Co., 1926), 121.

1   Christened Robert Lewis Balfour Stevenson, he sometimes signed
      his letters using all those names. Soon he changed Lewis to Louis,
      shortened his signature to R. Stevenson and then to R. L. S.

2   "You just . . . scratch!" Robert Louis Stevenson, *The Letters of
      Robert Louis Stevenson,* edited by Sidney Colvin (New York:
      Charles Scribner's Sons, 1905, 1911), vol. I, 259.

2   "If I . . . spared." Robert Louis Stevenson, *Memoirs of Himself,*
      (Philadelphia: Original ms. in possession of Harry Elkins
      Wedener, 1912).

~   **CHAPTER 2 ALL NIGHT LONG**

3   "Whenever the . . . by." From "Windy Nights" Stevenson, *The
      Works,* 971.

3   "One of . . . heaven." Robert Louis Stevenson, "Notes on
      Edinburgh," *Portfolio: An Artistic Periodical* (London: Seeley,
      Jackson & Holliday, 1878), 82.

5   "the delicate . . . early." Ibid.

5   "night hag," James Pope Hennessy, *Robert Louis Stevenson* (New
      York: Simon & Schuster, 1974), 20.

6   "gas still . . . sick-rooms." Ian Bell, *Dreams of Exile* (New York:
      Henry Holt & Co., Inc., 1993), 30.

6   "Great White Throne." Laura C. Hinkley, *The Stevensons: Louis*

and Fanny (New York: Hastings House, 1950), 3.

6 "hellfire and eternal damnation." Anne Roller Issler, *Happier for His Presence: San Francisco and Robert Louis Stevenson* (Stanford: Stanford University Press, 1949), 21.

7 "hush . . . over everything." Hennessy, *Robert Louis Stevenson,* 60.

8 "I wrote . . . fire." Sidney Colvin, et al. *Robert Louis Stevenson and His Personality* (London: Hodder & Stoughton, 1924), 20.

8 Havers: the Scottish word for "stuff and nonsense."

8 "doiley off . . . Mama." Mrs. Thomas Stevenson, Pocket diaries, 2/11/29.

8 "Do you . . . ill?" J. C. Furnas, *Voyage to Windward: the Life of Robert Louis Stevenson* (New York: William Sloane Assocs., 1951), 6.

8 "children of . . . orphans." Jenni Calder, *Robert Louis Stevenson: A Life Study* (New York: Oxford University Press, 1980), 21.

9 "Hauf a . . . yite." Janet Adam Smith, *Robert Louis Stevenson* (Folcroft: Folcroft Library Editions, 1977), 50.

9 Yellow yite: a European bird called a yellowhammer.

9 "leading camels . . . cigars." Amy Cruse, *Robert Louis Stevenson* (New York: Frederick A. Stokes Co., 1915), 28.

9 "From that . . . author." Ibid.

~ CHAPTER 3 COUSIN BOB AND COLINTON

10 "Here is . . . home." "Keepsake Mill" from Stevenson, *Works,* 975.

10 "first and . . . friend." Hennessy, *Robert Louis Stevenson,* 51.

10 "tumbling down . . . too." Robert Louis Stevenson, *The Letters of Robert Louis Stevenson,* edited by Bradford Booth and Ernest Mehew (New Haven & London: Yale Univ. Press, 1994), vol. I, 86.

11 "continually buried . . . snow" and "suffering . . . inundation." Robert Louis Stevenson, "Child's Play," *Cornhill Magazine,* 923.

11 "shift and dodge." Smith, *Robert Louis Stevenson,* 15.

12 "dark and . . . exultation!" Robert Louis Stevenson, "A Penny Plain and Twopence Coloured," *The Magazine of Art* (London:

Cassell & Co, Ltd., April 1884, part 42), 227.

12 "shock of . . . pleasure." Hennessy, *Robert Louis Stevenson,* 55.

12 "blind with terror." Cruse, *Robert Louis Stevenson,* 36.

13 "How I . . . you." Ibid., 7.

13 "kingdom." Hennessy, *Robert Louis Stevenson,* 39.

~ CHAPTER 4 EARLY EDUCATION

14 "When I . . . day." "The Land of Counterpane" from Stevenson, *Works,* 972.

16 Lanterns were sold by shopkeepers to fishermen who took them to sea or to neighbors who used them in town.

~ CHAPTER 5 UNIVERSITY LIFE

17 "At evening . . . anything." "The Land of Story-Books" from Stevenson, *Works,* 983.

17 "lean, ugly, . . . unpopular." Hennessy, *Robert Louis Stevenson,* 63.

18 "original nonsense." David Daiches, *Edinburgh* (London: Hamish Hamilton Limited, 1978), 45.

18 "dazzling performer." Jean Marie Carre, *The Frail Warrior: A Life of Robert Louis Stevenson* (New York: Coward McCann, 1930), 33.

19 "those who . . . reading." Hinkley, *The Stevensons,* 36.

20 "wildness, the . . . elements." Jenni Calder, *The Robert Louis Stevenson Companion* (Edinburgh: Paul Harris Publishers, 1980), 10.

20 "my hand . . . excitement." Bell, *Dreams of Exile,* 45.

21 "You have . . . failure." Hennessy, *Robert Louis Stevenson,* 71.

22 "the thunderbolt . . . now." Carre, *The Frail Warrior,* 49.

22 "Now, what . . . Stevenson." *Letters,* Colvin, vol. I, 46.

~ CHAPTER 6 ANOTHER DISAPPOINTMENT

23 "But as . . . you!" *Underwoods XX,* from Stevenson, *Works,* 26.

24 "youngster, already . . . lifetime." Hennessy, *Robert Louis Stevenson,* 92.

24 "acute nerve exhaustion." *Letters,* Colvin, vol. I, 50.

25 "I lead . . . sun." *Letters,* Booth, vol. I, 382.

25   "If you . . . felt!" Ibid., 374.

25   "it seems . . . me." *Letters,* Colvin, vol. I, 104.

26   "to a . . . love." Ibid., 59.

26   "We are . . . together." Ibid., 85.

26   "should soon . . . pen." Ibid.

27   "You know, . . . Court!" Ibid., 127.

27   wheel-skating was an early term for roller skating.

〜   CHAPTER 7 TRUE LOVE

28   "Mine eyes . . . care." Stevenson, unpublished poem, Hinkley, *The Stevensons,* 151.

31   "such a . . . man." Hinkley, *The Stevensons: Louis and Fanny,* 155.

31   "gay and buoyant." Lloyd Osbourne, *An Intimate Portrait of RLS* (New York: Charles Scribner's Sons, 1924), 2.

34   "jogged along . . . rocky." *Letters,* Colvin, vol. I, 154.

34   "put a . . . it." Carre, *The Frail Warrior: A Life of Robert Louis Stevenson,* 88.

34   "And if . . . God." Robert Louis Stevenson, *Travels with a Donkey in the Cévennes* (New York: The Heritage Press, 1957), 128.

35   "How the . . . garden." Ibid., 142.

35   "I on . . . hand." Ibid., 151.

〜   CHAPTER 8 ACROSS THE WORLD

36   "Of where . . . Delaware." *Letters,* Colvin, vol. I, 167.

36   "I can . . . anyway." Furnas, *Voyage to Windward: The Life of Robert Louis Stevenson* (New York: William Sloane Assocs., 1951), 146.

37   "No man . . . man." Margaret MacKay, *The Violent Friend: The Story of Mrs. Robert Louis Stevenson* (Garden City: Doubleday & Co., 1968), 90.

37–8   "As I . . . behold." Henry Seidel Canby and Frederick Erastus Pierce, *Selections from Robert Louis Stevenson* (New York: Charles Scribner's Sons, 1912), 57.

38   "The children . . . him." Ibid., 60, 61.

38   "referred to . . . laugh." Ibid., ill.

38   "the table . . . .ink-bottle." Ibid., 196.

38   "clear note . . . sea." Ibid., 62.

39   "It was . . . faces." Ibid., 72.

39   "I went . . . changers." Ibid., 127.

40   "Bought a . . . closes." *Letters*, Colvin, vol. I, 167.

40   "Fanny has . . . brain." Hennessy, *Robert Louis Stevenson*, 143.

40   "With my . . . knee." Robert Louis Stevenson, *Across the Plains with Other Memories and Essays* (London: Chatto & Windus, 1910), 4.

40   "the sun . . . America." Ibid., 8.

41   "In America . . . heavenly." *Letters*, Colvin, vol. I, 168.

41   "ghostly deserts . . . world." Ibid., 169.

41   "seedy blue . . . hat." MacKay, *The Violent Friend*, 93.

42   "Monterey is . . . Pacific." *Letters*, Colvin, vol. I, 173.

42   "This is . . . surf." Ibid., 177.

43   "in great . . . balcony." Ibid., 178.

43   "a most . . . daily." Ibid., 176.

43   "full sonorous . . . mark." Nellie Van De Grift Sanchez, *Life of Mrs. Robert Louis Stevenson* (New York: Charles Scribner's Sons, 1923), 60.

44   "I want . . . mother." Hinkley, *The Stevensons*, 183–4.

~   CHAPTER 9 MARRIAGE

45   "From where . . . gold." Stevenson, "It's Forth Across the Roaring Foam," in *New Poems*, Bibliophile Society of Boston.

45–6 "But death . . . done." *Letters*, Colvin, vol. I, 186.

46   "To live . . . good." Furnas, *Voyage to Windward*, 167.

48   "scrawny and threadbare." MacKay, *The Violent Friend*, 104.

48   "My name . . . ink." Anne B. Fisher, *No More a Stranger* (Stanford Univ. Press, 1946), 30.

48   "Dere's de . . . author." *Letters*, Colvin, vol. I, 189.

48   "My landlord . . . me!" Ibid., 196.

49   "Bluidy Jack." Bell, *Dreams of Exile*, 132.

49   "Robert Louis . . . hill." Issler, *Happier for His Presence*, 101.

49   "yours truly . . . ceremony." Furnas, *Voyage to Windward*, 163.

49   "For about . . . toss." *Letters*, Colvin, vol. I, 197.

49   "But for . . . best." Ibid., 199.

50   "I always . . . father." John A. Steuart, *Robert Louis Stevenson: A Critical Biography* (Boston: Little, Brown & Company, 1924), vol. 1, 317.

50   "Since I . . . Fanny." Furnas, *Voyage to Windward*, 154.

51   "Not a . . . possession." Robert Louis Stevenson, *The Silverado Squatters,* (Ashland, Oregon: The Silverado Museum, 1974), 43–44.

52   "What a . . . born." *Letters*, Colvin, vol. III, 315.

52   "Jews and . . . world." Stevenson, *The Silverado Squatters*, 34.

52   "I do . . . gunpowder." *Letters*, Colvin, vol. III, 315.

52   "I always . . . other," *Letters*, Colvin, vol. I, 201.

52   "It's not . . . me." Issler, *Happier for His Presence*, 85.

52   "I have . . . water." Calder, *Robert Louis Stevenson*, 116.

52   "Taking care . . . in." MacKay, *The Violent Friend*, 119.

54   "I do . . . me." Hinkley, *The Stevensons*, 196–7.

54   "two hours . . . lessons." G. B. Stern, *He Wrote* Treasure Island: *The Story of Robert Louis Stevenson* (Melbourne, London, Toronto: Wm. Heinemann, Ltd., 1954), 77.

54   "If you . . . better." Furnas, *Voyage to Windward*, 181.

〜   CHAPTER 10 HOME AGAIN

55   "We travelled . . . been." Stevenson, "The Country of the Camisards XXXIII," from *Works*, 32.

55   "so small . . . thigh." Furnas, *Voyage to Windward*, 179–80.

55   "better than we dared to hope." Steuart, *Robert Louis Stevenson*, vol. I, 339.

56   "Fanny fitted . . . first." Bell, *Dreams of Exile*, 144.

56   "entirely she . . . subjects." Steuart, *Robert Louis Stevenson*, vol. I, 340.

58   Louis called his birthplace, Edinburgh, "Auld Reekie," a name that originally had been given to the town because of its buildings' dirty exteriors caused by smoke.

59   "Doomed to . . . smile." Stevenson, "In Memoriam F. A. S. XXVII," from *Works*, 30.

59   "I begin . . . me." *Letters*, Colvin, vol. I, 230.

59   "only time . . . inertia." Osbourne, *An Intimate Portrait*, 22.

60   "often after . . . aloud." Robert Louis Stevenson, *Works*, 787.

60   "He had . . . day." Ibid., 788, 794.

61   "frightened to death." *Letters*, Colvin, vol. II, 37.

62   "horribly dull." Stern, *He Wrote* Treasure Island, 84.

63   "The *best* . . . had." *Letters*, Colvin, vol. I, 258.

63   "exciting episode after another." Ibid.

63   "Buccaneers without . . . straw." Ibid.

63   "boys' book." Ibid., 261.

63   "I had . . . audience." Hinkley, *The Stevensons*, 208.

64   "This stuff . . . 'osses." Steuart, *Robert Louis Stevenson*, vol. I, 404.

64   "blood splashed . . . story." "For pure . . . did." Colvin, *Robert Louis Stevenson*, 104.

64   "I love . . . me." Steuart, *Robert Louis Stevenson*, vol. I, 392.

65–6   "and behold! . . . talk." MacKay, *The Violent Friend*, 155.

66   "A hundred . . . wonderful?" *Letters*, Colvin, vol. I, 311.

66   "it does . . . bread." Ibid.

~   CHAPTER 11 "A PAIR OF WALKING-SHOES"

68   "When at . . . skies—" "The Little Land," Stevenson, from *Works*, 984.

68   "No man . . . idle." *Letters*, Colvin, vol. I, 283.

68   "cruel examination . . . it." Ibid., 281.

68   "The loveliest . . . story." Ibid., 309.

69   "Angels I . . . gone." Ibid., 337.

69   "I have . . . wall." Ibid.

69   "Bluidy Jack." Calder, *Robert Louis Stevenson*, 176.

70   "tushery." *Letters*, Colvin, vol. I, 315.

71–2   "I survived . . . not." MacKay, *The Violent Friend*, 182.

72   "if I . . . health." *Letters*, Colvin, vol. I, 250, 251.

72 "By jove . . . charm." Osbourne, *An Intimate Portrait*, 45.

73 "I have . . . bed." "My Shadow," *A Child's Garden of Verses*, from *Works*, 973.

73 "I have . . . happy." *Letters*, Colvin, vol. I, 299–300.

73 "keep the . . . medicine." Ibid., 323.

73–4 "look ghastly . . . voice." *Letters*, Colvin, vol. I, 417.

74 "Thank you . . . counterpane.' " Ibid., 424.

75 "little English gentleman." Hennessy, *Robert Louis Stevenson*, 188.

76 "a better . . . lovable." *Letters*, Colvin, vol. I, 424.

76 "The great . . . conceived." Ibid., 344.

76 "Eight years . . . summit." Ibid., 345.

~ Chapter 12 Good and Evil

77 "From breakfast . . . Nod." Stevenson, *A Child's Garden of Verses*, from *Works*, 973.

77 "Why did . . . bogy-tale." Steuart, *Robert Louis Stevenson*, vol. II, 76.

79 "You are . . . it." Osbourne, *An Intimate Portrait*, 65.

79 "shilling shocker." Steuart, *Robert Louis Stevenson*, vol. II, 79.

79 "younger, lighter . . . wicked." Stevenson, *Works*, 166.

79 "had in . . . shattered." Ibid., 170.

80 "the reader . . . proceeds." Steuart, *Robert Louis Stevenson*, vol. II, 80.

80 "In one . . . story." Cruse, *Robert Louis Stevenson*, 111.

82 "single dull . . . covers." Steuart, *Robert Louis Stevenson*, vol. II, 86.

82 "Lou arrived . . . him." Calder, *Robert Louis Stevenson*, 224.

83 "pathetic figure . . . cheeks." Steuart, *Robert Louis Stevenson*, vol. II, 103.

83 "Good-bye, Good-bye." MacKay, *The Violent Friend*, 224.

84 "Henry James's chair." Ibid., 203.

85 "I (at least) . . . coat." Ibid., 229.

~ Chapter 13 Popularity

86 "The world . . . kings." Stevenson, *A Child's Garden of Verses*, from *Works*, 975.

86   "Brownies." Calder, *Robert Louis Stevenson,* 290.

87   "Mr. Stevenson . . . cough." Steuart, *Robert Louis Stevenson,* vol. II, 112.

88   "My reception . . . me." *Letters,* Colvin, vol. III, 5.

88   "What a popularity!" Ibid.

88   "You have . . . here." Ibid., 9.

88   "But I'm . . . last!" Ibid., 24.

88   "I do . . . me." Hennessy, *Robert Louis Stevenson,* 216, 217.

89   "Why, I . . . *sing!*" Osbourne, *An Intimate Portrait,* 65.

90   "Blessed girl, . . . days." MacKay, *The Violent Friend,* 254.

~   CHAPTER 14 AT SEA

91   "If I . . . ships." Stevenson, *A Child's Garden of Verses,* from *Works,* 970.

91   "This is . . . ever!" Stein, *He Wrote* Treasure Island, 113.

93   "The proudest . . . boat." *Letters,* Colvin, vol. I, 249.

93   "It seems . . . true." *Letters,* Colvin, vol. III, 59.

93–4 "the young . . . eyes." MacKay, *The Violent Friend,* 258.

95   "He has . . . thing." Robert Louis Stevenson, *Travels in Hawaii,* (Honolulu: The University Press of Hawaii, 1973), xxxiv.

96   "If it . . . is." Ibid., 102.

96   "more fun . . . years." *Letters,* Colvin, vol. III, 108.

96   "I am . . . sea." Furnas, *Voyage to Windward,* 312.

97   "No stranger . . . moving." Calder, *Robert Louis Stevenson,* 272.

98   "withered in . . . cold." *Letters,* Colvin, vol. III, 108.

~CHAPTER 15 HOME AT LAST

99   "I have . . . door." Stevenson, *Songs of Travel,* in Hinkley, *The Stevensons,* 335.

99   "ancestral acres." Hinkley, *The Stevensons,* 273.

100   "Imagine a . . . husband's." Calder, *Robert Louis Stevenson,* 291, 292.

101   "When I . . . son." MacKay, *The Violent Friend,* 339.

102   "In the . . . distress." Furnas, *Voyage to Windward,* 367.

103   "You and . . . me." MacKay, *The Violent Friend,* 355.

103　"a most . . . quadrille." Graham Balfour, *The Life of Robert Louis Stevenson* (New York: Charles Scribner's Sons, 1901), vol. II, 153.

∼　CHAPTER 16 *TUSITALA*, TELLER OF TALES

106　"Where hath . . . way." Stevenson, *Underwoods,* from *Works,* 21.

106　"I am . . . obvious." Hennessy, *Robert Louis Stevenson,* 301.

106　"that he . . . *work!*" MacKay, *The Violent Friend,* 451.

108　"Now I . . . library." *Letters,* Colvin, vol. III, 292.

108　"Take thou . . . you?" From "To My Wife" in *Collected Poems,* 236, as noted in Calder, *Robert Louis Stevenson,* 327.

108–9　"I wrote . . . flying." *Letters,* Booth, vol. I, 168.

109　"as clearly . . . book." MacKay, *The Violent Friend,* 451.

110　"the very . . . Day." *The Mentor,* May 1928, 64.

111　"child in . . . Austin." MacKay, *The Violent Friend,* 454.

113　"What's that? . . . strange?" Bell, *Dreams of Exile,* 263.

114　"How can . . . these!" Mrs. Margaret Stevenson, *Letters from Samoa 1891–1895* (New York: Charles Scribner's Sons, 1906), 327.

114　*"Tofa Tusitala!":* Sleep, *Tusitala.* Bell, *Dreams of Exile,* 263.

114–5　"Under the . . . hill." Stevenson, "Requiem," in MacKay, *The Violent Friend,* 95.

115　"Teacher, tender . . . die." Frank McLynn, *Robert Louis Stevenson: A Biography* (New York: Random House, 1993), 505.

∼　EPILOGUE

116　"you are . . . globe." Ibid., 507.

117　"My work . . . existed." Hinkley, *The Stevensons,* 339.

117　"For fourteen . . . bottle." Balfour, *The Life,* vol. II, 201.

BIBLIOGRAPHY

~

BALFOUR, GRAHAM. *The Life of Robert Louis Stevenson.* Vols. 1 and 2. New York: Charles Scribner's Sons, 1901.

BELL, IAN. *Dreams of Exile. Robert Louis Stevenson: A Biography.* New York: Henry Holt and Co., 1993.

BOOTH, BRADFORD, AND ERNEST MEHEW. *The Letters of Robert Louis Stevenson.* Vols. 1 and 2. New Haven and London: Yale University Press, 1994.

CALDER, JENNI. *Robert Louis Stevenson: A Life Study.* New York: Oxford University Press, 1980.

———. *The Robert Louis Stevenson Companion.* Edinburgh: Paul Harris Publ., 1980.

CANBY, HENRY SEIDEL, AND FREDERICK ERASTUS PIERCE. *Selections from Robert Louis Stevenson.* New York: Charles Scribner's Sons, 1912.

CARRE, JEAN MARIE. *The Frail Warrior: A Life of Robert Louis Stevenson.* Translated from French by Eleanor Hard. New York: Coward McCann, 1930. Reprint, Westport, Conn.: Greenwood Press, 1973.

COLVIN, SIDNEY, ED. *The Letters of Robert Louis Stevenson: To His Family and Friends.* Vols. I, II, III, and IV. New York: Charles Scribner's Sons, 1905.

COLVIN, SIDNEY, ET AL. *Robert Louis Stevenson: His Work and His Personality.* London: Hodder & Stoughton, 1924. Reprint, Philadelphia: Richard West, 1977.

CRUSE, AMY. *Robert Louis Stevenson.* New York: Frederick A. Stokes Co., 1915.

DAICHES, DAVID. *Edinburgh.* London: Hamish Hamilton Limited, 1978.

EDELSTEIN, JACK. *"A Child's Garden of Verses* and Robert Louis Stevenson." Unpublished Paper, 1989.

ELWIN, MALCOLM. *The Strange Case of Robert Louis Stevenson.* 1950. Reprint, New York: Russell & Russell, 1950.

FISHER, ANNE B. *No More A Stranger.* Stanford: Stanford University Press, 1946.

FURNAS, J. C. *Voyage to Windward: The Life of Robert Louis Stevenson.* New York: William Sloane Assocs., 1951.

HELLMAN, GEORGE S. *The True Stevenson: A Study in Clarification.* New York: Haskell House Publishers, Ltd., 1972.

HENNESSY, JAMES POPE. *Robert Louis Stevenson.* New York: Simon & Schuster, 1974.

HINKLEY, LAURA C. *The Stevensons: Louis and Fanny.* New York: Hastings House, 1950.

ISSLER, ANNE ROLLER. *Happier for His Presence: San Francisco and Robert Louis Stevenson.* Stanford: Stanford University Press, 1949.

LOW, WILL H. *Stevenson and Margarita.* New Rochelle: The Mayflower Press, 1922.

MACKAY, MARGARET. *The Violent Friend: The Story of Mrs. Robert Louis Stevenson.* Garden City: Doubleday & Co., 1968.

McLYNN, FRANK. *Robert Louis Stevenson: A Biography.* New York: Random House, 1993.

MURPHY, JIM. *Across America on an Emigrant Train.* New York: Clarion Books, 1993.

NICKERSON, ROY. *Robert Louis Stevenson in California: A Remarkable Courtship.* San Francisco: Chronicle Books, 1982.

OSBOURNE, LLOYD. *An Intimate Portrait of R L S.* New York: Charles Scribner's Sons, 1924.

SANCHEZ, NELLIE VAN DE GRIFT. *Life of Mrs. Robert Louis Stevenson.* New York: Charles Scribner's Sons, 1923.

SMITH, JANET ADAM. *Robert Louis Stevenson.* Folcroft: Folcroft Library Editions, 1977.

STERN, G.B. *He Wrote Treasure Island: The Story of Robert Louis Stevenson.* Melbourne, London, Toronto: Wm. Heinemann, Ltd., 1954.

STEUART, JOHN A. *Robert Louis Stevenson: A Critical Biography.* Vols. I and II. Boston: Little, Brown & Company, 1924.

———. *Robert Louis Stevenson: Man and Writer.* London: Sampson Low, Marston & Co., 1924.

STEVENSON, FANNY VAN DE GRIFT OSBOURNE. *The Cruise of the "Janet Nichol" Among the South Sea Islands. A Diary by . . .* New York: Charles Scribner's Sons, 1914.

STEVENSON, MRS. MARGARET. *Letters from Samoa, 1891–95.* New York: Charles Scribner's Sons, 1906.

———. Pocket diaries, 1851–97, dated 2/11/1829. File. Silverado Museum, St. Helena, California.

STEVENSON, ROBERT LOUIS. *Across the Plains with Other Memories and Essays.* 1892. London: Chatto & Windus, 1910.

———. *The Black Arrow.* 1888. New York: Charles Scribner's Sons, 1955.

———. "Child's Play." *Cornhill Magazine,* 1878.

———. *Memoirs of Himself.* Philadelphia: 1912. (Original Ms. in possession of Harry Elkins Wedener).

———. "Notes on Edinburgh," in *Portfolio: An Artistic Periodical.* Edited by Philip Gilbert Hamerton. London: Seeley, Jackson and Holliday, 1878.

———. "A Penny Plain and Twopence Coloured." *The Magazine of Art,* April 1884, part 42.

———. *The Silverado Squatters.* 1883. Ashland, Oregon: The Silverado Museum, 1974.

———. *The Strange Case of Dr. Jekyll and Mr. Hyde.* 1886. New York: Dover Publications, Inc., 1991.

———. *Travels in Hawaii.* Honolulu: The University Press of Hawaii, 1973.

———. *Travels with a Donkey in the Cévennes.* 1879. New York: The Heritage Press, 1957.

———. *Virginibus Puerisque and Other Papers.* 1881. Vol. 6. New York and London: The Co-operative Publication Society, 1904.

———. *The Works of Robert Louis Stevenson in One Volume.* New York: Walter J. Black Co., 1926.

"Stevenson Gives Away His Birthday." *The Mentor,* vol. 16, no. 4 (May 1928).

WILKIE, KATHARINE. *Robert Louis Stevenson: Storyteller and Adventurer.* Boston: Houghton Mifflin, 1961.

INDEX

~